Childhood and Growing Up

Childhood and Growing Up

(As per IP and other Universities Curriculum)

Prof. S.K. Mangal
M.A., M.Sc., M.Ed., Ph.D. (Education)

Prof. (Mrs.) Shubhra Mangal
M.Sc., M.Ed., M.Phil, Ph.D. (Education)

SHIPRA

Price: Rs. 900; US$ 45

ISBN: 978-93-86262-51-6

First Published in India in 2018

Childhood and Growing Up

Published by:
SHIPRA PUBLICATIONS
LG 18-19, Pankaj Central Market, I.P. Ext.
Patparganj, Delhi-110092, India
Tel: 91-11-2223 5152, 2223 6152
E-mail: info@shiprapublication.com
www.shiprapublication.com

Preface

Developmental years covering childhood and adolescence carry a wide significance in one's life. It is why utmost care is needed for helping the growing children in realizing their potential in a proper way. In this concern the teachers serving in the schools have to play a big role. They must be properly acquainted with the mechanism of growth and development going on in the developing children in all the dimensions of their personality. The environmental factors influencing their growth and development in the form of social agencies, poverty, globalization and adult culture etc. should also be a thing of great consideration for the teachers. They must also be equipped with the skills of handling social, health, and equity issues concerning them such as separation and loss of parents, child abuse and obesity as well as inclusion of differently abled children including marginalized groups. The question may here arise now from where a school teacher should get equipped him on this account. Surely the first and best opportunity for doing this to him lies in his pre service teacher education program such as B.Ed for the secondary school teachers. National Council of Teacher Education (NCTE) has asked the universities and teacher education institutes to have needed provision in their B.Ed course for the introduction of a compulsory paper named "Childhood and Growing up". Guru Govind Singh Indraprastha University, New Delhi has also introduced this paper in its efforts of bringing modification in the existing B.Ed. syllabus. This text is primarily meant for meeting the requirements of the Indraprastha University. However, on account of its wide coverage and depth, it is quite capable of meeting the requirement of similar courses entitled as "Childhood and Growing up" of the other Indian Universities.

The subject matter of this text has been organized into twelve chapters with a number of credit points such as below:

- It has been written according to the needs of the contents and topics included in the prescribed syllabus for the paper "Childhood and Growing up".
- The style as well as language adopted for the presentation of the subject matter is simple and easy to grasp by the average readers.
- Up to date references and suggestions for further study in the matter related to each and every chapter of the text have been given for the benefits of the students and teacher educators in the end of the text.

- For proper comprehension, revision and aid to evaluation, the study questions have been provided at the end strictly on the pattern of the present syllabus covering essay type and short answer type questions in the student edition.

For making all this, the authors have to take help from the works of many authors and information sources. These have been duly mentioned in the text. Authors feel a sense of gratitude for incorporating their ideas in the text.

Now the rest lies with you as a reader of this text. The authors and publisher would certainly appreciate your feelings and views for the further improvement of the present work.

It is earnestly hoped that the text will surely prove useful to those for whom it is intended.

With good wishes to its readers.

October, 2017

S.K. Mangal
Shubhra Mangal

Contents

1

Growth and Development: Concept and Principles

Introduction

The sole aim of education is to bring an all round development in the personality of educand. Educational Psychology, being a science and technology of education, should help in the realization of this aim. As we have seen earlier, human life starts from a single fertilized cell. The constant interaction with the environment results in the growth and development of the innate capacities, abilities and potentialities of the child. The task of formal as well as informal education is to help the child in his path of growth and development. Therefore, it is imperative that the individuals, supposed to be connected with the task of helping the child to grow and develop satisfactorily, must be acquainted with the nature of growth and development.

It is only with a knowledge of growth and development of the learner at each stage of his life that it is possible for the teachers to render proper guidance, arrange the learning situations and plan the instructional programmes for bringing desirable harmonious development in their personalities. In the following pages we would try to understand the concept and general principles governing human growth and development.

The Concept of Growth and Development

For understanding the concept of growth and development, we would like to throw light on the following aspects:

A. Growth and Development — Meanings and Distinction.
B. Distinguishing Growth and Development from Maturation
C. Various aspects of Growth and Development.

A. Growth and Development — Meaning and Distinction

Mostly, these two terms are used interchangeably and taken as synonymous terms. Both relate to the measurement of changes which occur in the individual after conception in the womb of the mother. Change is the law of nature. An individual starting from a fertilized egg, turns into a full-fledged human adult. In this turn-over process he undergoes a cycle of changes brought about by the process of growth and development in various dimensions — physical, mental, social, emotional, etc. Therefore, in the wider sense, both the terms growth and development can be used for any change brought about by maturation and learning (formal as well as informal education) and essentially is the product of both heredity and environment.

In the strict sense of terminology, these two terms have different meanings that can be put in the way given ahead.

Growth	*Development*
1. The term growth is used in purely physical sense. It generally refers to an increase in size, length, height and weight. Changes in the quantitative aspects come into the domain of growth.	1. Development implies overall changes in shape, form or structure resulting in improved working or functioning. It indicates the changes in the quality or character rather than in quantitative aspects.
2. Growth is one of the part of developmental process. In strict sense, development in its quantitative aspect is termed as growth.	2. Development is a wider and comprehensive term. It refers to overall changes in the individual. Growth is one of its parts.
3. Growth may be referred to describe the changes which take place in particular aspects of the body and behaviour of an organisation.	3. Development describes the changes in the organism as a whole and does not list the changes in parts.
4. Growth does not continue throughout life. It stops when maturity has been attained.	4. Development is a continuous process. It goes from womb to tomb. It does not end with the attainment of maturity. The changes, however small they may be, continue throughout the life span of an individual.
5. The changes produced by growth are the subject of measurement. They may be quantified and are observable in nature.	5. Development, as said earlier, implies improvement in functioning and behaviour and hence brings qualitative changes which are difficult to be measured directly. They are assessed through keen observation in behavioural situations.

(*Contd.*)

Growth	*Development*
6. Growth may or may not bring development. A child may grow (in terms of weight) by becoming fat but this growth may not bring any functional improvement (qualitative change) or development.	6. Development is also possible without growth as we see in the cases of some children that they do not gain in terms of height, weight or size but they do experience functional improvement or development in physical, social, emotional or intellectual aspects.

Hence observed in minute details, both growth and development show differentiation. But in wider and practical sense both terms are used to denote the changes in the organism's physical as well as functional behaviour. These changes which cover physical, emotional, intellectual and social aspects of a human life are roughly divided into four major classes by Mrs. Hurlock (1956, p. 2-3): (i) Changes in size; (ii) Changes in proportion; (iii) Disappearance of old features; (iv) Acquisition of new features.

All these types of changes have qualitative as well as quantitative aspects and hence generally, growth and development go hand in hand. And it is in this sense, that the two terms are to be used collectively. Both, taken together, explain the total changes-functional as well as constitutional changes — in the body and behaviour of the individual with the lapse of time after the conception. In this text, we would like to use these terms in synonymous sense for convenience.

B. Distinguishing Growth and Development from the Term Maturation

Meaning of the term Maturation

Maturation is known for its uniqueness and specificity as a natural process for the growth that takes place within an individual. It was A. Gessel, who used the term maturation in the field of child development in 1919. The changes brought out by maturation are said to be the result of unfolding and ripening of inherited traits and are relatively independent of activity, practice or experience. We can take the help of some well known definitions of the term maturation for knowing and understanding well about its meaning and nature. Let us reproduce a few of them for this purpose.

Mc Geoch (1942): Maturation includes any change with age in the conditions of learning which depends primarily upon organic growth factors rather than upon prior practice or experience.

Thompson (1979): "Maturation" is a name for the growth process during which a structure or function is more and more becoming adult, that is "mature".

A. Gesell (1929): Maturation is the maturity and firmness of the nerves and muscles brought out by the internal mechanism of the body quite independent of the impact of the environmental factors external to the organism.

H.J. Eysenck *et al.* (1972): Maturation is an autonomous process of somatic, psychological and mental differentiation and integration spread over developmental stages and phases which condition and build on one another in the course of time; as a result of this process the individual growth is completed and consolidated somatically, maturally and spiritually as well as socially and he can thus adapt to life.

A.T. Jersild *et al.* (1975): Maturation is the process by which underlying potential capacities of the organism reach a stage of functional readiness. This process involves both the changes in structure that come with growth and the progressive exercise of structures that provide ground work for later performances.

Biggie and Hunt (1968): Maturation is a developmental process within which a person, from time to time manifests different traits, the blue prints for which have been carried in his cells from the time of his conception.

The definitions cited above may help us in drawing following conclusions about the meaning and nature of maturation.

- Maturation in its purest sense is the result of the mechanism of heredity. Heredity contributions decide the course of the changes (behavioural and developmental) observed in the children since their conception in the womb of the mother.
- The effect of the process of maturation continues throughout the developmental period i.e. upto the end of the period of adolescence.
- Maturation helps the children to get matured in terms of their growth and development in all the various aspects — physical, motor, mental, social, moral and spiritual for playing the role of a matured adult in their lives.
- As a natural phenomenon of growth and development, maturation helps in the development of inner potential of the human organisms making them ready and capable of reaching the heights or attaining possible milestones of their personality.
- Maturation is essentially linked with one's organically internal growth processes that are primarily or momentarily, independent of environmental factors external to the organism.

In this way, *maturation as a term and concept stands for a natural and spontaneous process of growth and development guided through the genetically controlled internal mechanism of an organism (quite independent of the impact of training or experience) responsible for bringing changes (behavioural and developmental) with the passage of the time during the developmental age.*

Effect of Maturation on Growth and Development

1. As one grows in age, he or she is naturally bound to be accompanied with some changes in his body, mind and behaviour purely because of the phenomenon of maturation. This is more clear and revealing in the case of lower species like birds and animals. Let us have a look at examples from our environment around us. A bird conceives and as a result lay eggs in its nest. If we observe, we find that after a few days, there are signs of life in those eggs. A little later young chicks come out from the eggs, jumping here and there, being fed by the parent birds but still unable to fly. However one day, we find that they have grown enough and developed the capacity to fly like the other grown-up birds.

2. Similarly, we observe in the case of tadpoles that as a result of maturation, *i.e.* natural process of growth and development, there is definitely a major change in their behaviour. They are able to swim and after sometime they begin to jump like an adult frog. What is observed in terms of their growth and development here can be purely attributed to the process of maturation. It is also true in the case of the young ones of animals. No training or experience is received by them in the beginning for growing and developing their abilities to walk and run like their adult parents. A baby deer is able to run quite fast just after its birth. How does it manage to eat grass and drink water, is just the result of the process of maturation as there is no such attempt of providing any formal experience or training to it by the parents or the other members of the species for the performance of such behaviour.

In this way, we can have enough evidence from the surrounding nature that explains the role of maturation in bringing desired growth and development in the behaviour and functioning of the small babies of insects, birds and animals.

3. In the case of human beings also, we may observe and notice the impact of maturation on the growth and development of the youngsters from their very birth in almost all the aspects and dimensions of their personality as illustrated below:

- With the passage of the time they grow and develop physically in their height, weight and body proportions and functioning of the internal and external organs. The process of maturation must help them in acquiring physical maturity and thus they turn into fully physically mature adults at the expiry of the period of adolescence.
- Same is true with the other dimensions of their personality as well. They grow and develop as mentally, socially, emotionally, morally and aesthetically mature personality at the time of acquiring adulthood. The process of maturation, *i.e.* an act of the natural growth and development helps them well in this task. However, the question here may arise as to whether the growth and development acquired in the case of human babies for turning them into a fully matured personality in terms of the mental,

social, emotional, moral and ethical standards is purely a function of the process of maturation or environmental influences, including training, or a combination of both.

• Definitely here the last one is the appropriate answer and as such it may be easily concluded that growth and development in the case of human beings for gaining maturity is a combined function of the process of maturation and learning. How does it becomes a combined function may be well illustrated through a number of instances described as follows:

(i) A child is not able to speak or utter words correctly until he reaches a certain stage or age in maturation. We can't expect a baby of six months to speak and utter words correctly even if he belongs to a very high hereditary stock (like the parents are too rich and scholars in the linguistic capacity, say Ph.D. in language) or is being constantly inspired and formally trained in speech. He has to grow and develop in the linguistic capacity in accordance with the maturation level he needs for doing so. In the natural process, he will learn to utter with the maturation of his vocal chords and other similar physical and mental functioning required for learning correct language. At the same time, it is also true that here we can't rule out the impact of favourable or unfavourable environmental influences, including schooling, formal or informal training, for acquiring proper and excellent linguistic ability.

A child at any stage of his schooling or life does not learn the language or develop his language ability just because he attains that stage. Definitely, the language is taught to him. The language which he learns is the one he hears and more specifically the one he gets through specific training. As a result, what a child acquires in terms of his language development at any stage of his life is a joint product of the natural process of growth and development, *i.e.* maturation and the environment influences including training.

(*ii*) What is true for language development is also true for the development of other mental functioning. The development of mental facilities like thinking, reasoning, problem solving, decision making, analyzing, synthesizing, discriminating, drawing inferences all need maturation as well as planned experiences and training on the part of the youngsters. Normally, we can't expect a child of tender age to be too logical, consistent, methodological in his approach and systematic in thinking and abstraction. He has to wait before he acquires the ability of abstraction, *i.e.* a certain stage of maturation, for developing his mental faculties enabling him to perform mental tasks requiring power of abstraction, creative, imagination, innovation and novelty.

(*iii*) In case of emotional development also, we can observe a similar phenomenon. A child develops in terms of emotional maturity on account of the process of maturation helped and influenced by the environmental influences. It is true that a child has to be a child in terms of his emotional behaviour. We can't expect him to behave like a grown-up adult. There is definitely an age characteristic emotional behaviour. That is why we can observe a definite pattern of emotional behaviour at each stage of maturation, *i.e.* infancy, childhood, pre-adolescence, adolescence, adulthood and old age. However, how one behaves and why one behaves under the influence of a particular emotion depends heavily on the impact of the environmental influences or feedback one gets from his formal or informal surroundings. The same is true for social, moral, religious or aesthetic standards and aesthetic sense from the individuals belonging to different stages of their maturation.

(*iv*) Surely age is a great factor. One learns and picks up so many things related to these aspects as he or she grows in age. Take the case of sexual development, a distinctly visible area showing the impact of maturation. As one grows in age, he or she is sure to pick up many things and practices related to sexual activities even without any prior experiences of formal training. Attraction towards opposite sex, to feel the necessity of the satisfaction of sexual urge are thus the peculiar developments that are bound to emerge as and when a child reaches the adolescence stage. However, his attitude and practices towards sex may now be coloured or influenced side by side by the exposures, experiences or formal / informal training he receives for doing so.

Thus, from the above discussion, it may be clear that growth and development in the various aspects and dimensions of the personality of an individual is very much helped and influenced by the process of maturation. As one grows in one's age he is helped by the process of maturation for being grown and developed into a full-fledged matured personality. However, how much maturity in the deeds and kinds is shown by an individual again depends upon the quality of experiences, environmental influences, formal or informal training, education, etc. received by an individual for this purpose.

C. Various Aspects or Dimensions of Growth and Development

If we use the term growth and development synonymously, the major aspects or areas, in which a human child goes ahead for his complete development, can be named as follows:

(a) Physical development
(b) Intellectual or mental development
(c) Emotional development
(d) Moral or character development
(e) Social development
(f) Language development

Let us see what we understand by these different aspects or dimensions of development.

(a) *Physical development.* The physical development of the individual includes the development of his internal as well as external organs.

(b) *Intellectual or mental development.* It includes the development of intellectual powers like the powers of reasoning and thinking, imagination, concentration, creativity, sensation, perception, memory, association, discrimination and generalization, etc.

(c) *Emotional development.* Under this aspect, starting with the basic instinct, the evolution of various emotions takes place and also the emotional behaviour is developed to the point of emotional maturity.

(d) *Moral or character development.* Moral or character development includes the evolution of moral sense and development of character. The individual develops his ethical and moral codes.

(e) *Social development.* Initially the child is selfish and antisocial. Gradually he is developed into a social being by learning to behave according to the rules and norms of his society and makes adjustment to it.

(f) *Language development*: It is the most important aspect of social development of a child. Initially when a child is born, she makes her own sounds and babbles but later on as she grows, she mimics sounds and words which subsequently transform into a language for communication with family and friends.

General Principles of Growth and Development

The changes brought about in the individual by the process of growth and development, tend to follow some well defined principles. These are known as principles of growth and development. These principles are being described below.

1. Principle of continuity: Development follows continuity. It goes from womb to tomb and never ceases. An individual starting his life from a tiny cell develops his body, mind and other aspects of his personality through a continuous stream of development in these various dimensions.

2. Rate of growth and development is not uniform: Although development follows continuity, yet the rate of growth and development is not steady and uniform at all times. It proceeds more rapidly in the early years of life but slows down into later years of infancy. Again at the dawn of puberty there is a sudden rise in the speed of growth and development but it is not maintained for long. Therefore, at no stage the rate of growth and development show steadiness. It rather takes place by fits and starts.

3. Principle of individual differences: According to this principle there exist wide individual differences among children with respect to their growth and development in various dimensions. Each child grows at his own unique rate.

4. Uniformity of pattern: Although development does not proceed at a uniform rate and shows marked individual differences, yet it follows a definite sequence or pattern and somewhat uniform in the offsprings of a species. For example, all offsprings of human beings begin to grow from head downwards. Similarly, the motor development and language development in all children seems to follow a definite sequence.

5. Development proceeds from general to specific responses: In all phases of child's development, general activity precedes specific activity. His responses are of a general sort before they become specific. For example, the boy waves his arms in general, random movements before he is capable of so specific a response as reaching. Similarly, when a new-born infant cries, the whole of the body is involved. With growth, the crying is limited to the vocal cords, eyes, etc. In language development, the child learns general words before specific. He uses the word daddy in greeting many men and it is only afterwards that he uses it for his father.

6. Principle of integration: Where it is true that development proceeds from general to specific or from whole to parts, it is also seen that specific responses or part movements are combined in the later process of learning or development. "Development," as Kuppuswamy observes, "thus involves a movement from the whole to the parts and from the parts to the whole" (1971). It is the integration of whole and its parts as well as of the specific and general responses that make a child develop satisfactorily in the various dimensions of his growth and development.

7. Principle of interrelation: The growth and development in various dimensions like physical, mental, social, etc. are interrelated and interdependent. Growth and development in any one dimension affects the growth and development of the child in other dimensions. For example, children with above average intelligence, are generally found to possess above average physical and social development. The lack of growth in one dimension, diminishes the bright possibility in other dimensions. That is why, the children having poor physical development tend to regress in emotional, social and intellectual development.

8. Development is predictable: With the help of the rate of growth and development of a child it is possible for us to predict the range within which his mature development is going to fall. For example, X-rays of the bones of the wrist of a child will tell approximately what his ultimate size will be. Similarly, the knowledge of the present mental ability of a child will help in predicting his ultimate mental development.

9. Principle of developmental direction: Kuppuswamy throwing light on this principle points out two specific facts concerning the direction of the development. He says that development is 'cephalo-caudal as well as proximodistal'.

By cephalo-caudal development he means that development proceeds in the direction of the longitudinal axis (Head to foot). — First, the child gains control over his head and arms and then on his legs so that he can stand.

According to the proximodistal tendency of the development, it proceeds from the centre to the periphery. In the beginning child exhibits its control over the large fundamental muscles but afterwards due to growth and development of smaller muscles he can exhibit more refined movements.

For example, control over fingers comes after the control over the arm and the hand.

10. Development is spiral and not linear: The child does not proceed straightly on the path of development with a constant or steady pace. Actually he makes advancement during a particular period but takes rest in the next following period, to consolidate his development. In advancing further therefore, he turns back and then moves forward again like a spiral.

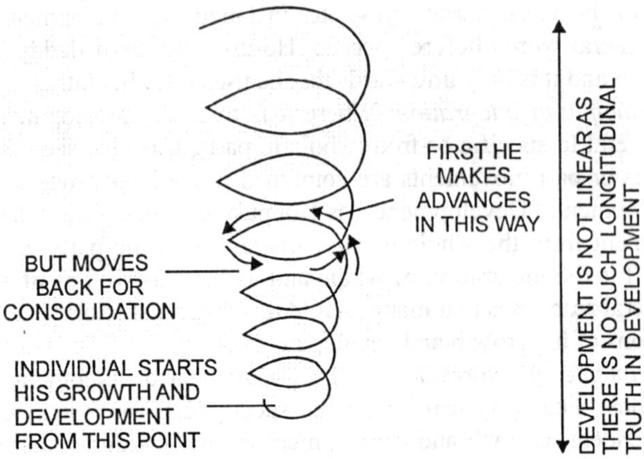

Figure 1.1: Development is spiral not linear

11. Growth and development is a joint product of both heredity and environment. Child at any stage of his growth and development is a joint product of both heredity and environment. His growth and development in any dimension at all times is directly or indirectly influenced by the forces of heredity and environment.

Educational Implications of the Principles of Growth and Development

The above mentioned principles of growth and development carry wide educational meaning for the children, parents and the teachers. It can be explained in the following way:

1. Knowledge of the principles of growth and development tells us that there are wide individual differences among the children with respect to their rate of growth and development. Therefore, we must pay attention to their individual pattern and growth rate while planning the course for their education and development.

2. Its knowledge helps us to know what to expect and when to expect from an individual child with respect to his physical, mental, social development, etc. at different stages of development. The correct knowledge of the growth trend of a child helps the parents and teacher not to under or over-estimate the future competency or expectancy of their child.

3. It helps us to know the direction as well as the general pattern of development. It guides us to locate the degree of abnormality in our

children and students and to take like-wise remedial steps. The knowledge that development starts from whole to parts and then from parts to whole helps us to plan the learning procedure and set the learning methods accordingly.

4. Principles of inter-relation and interdependence of the various aspects of growth and development help us to aim for the harmonious growth and development of the personality of the child and warn us not to develop a particular aspect at the cost of one or the other.

5. The knowledge of the uniformity of pattern with respect to growth and development makes it possible for the parents and teachers to plan ahead of time for the changes that will take place in their children. Children will also get benefitted if they can be acquainted with these changes beforehand.

6. The knowledge that heredity and environment both play a joint role in the process of growth and development helps us to pay sufficient attention over the environmental conditions in upbringing the children.

In this way the knowledge of the principles of growth and development helps much in the well-being of the youngsters.

2

Stages of Growth and Development

Meaning of Stages of Growth and Development

For human organism life starts from a fertilized ovum in the womb of the mother. Not only before birth, but also after birth to many years the child is a helpless organism until or unless he is helped by the continuous process of growth and development and attains maturity. When one attains maturity he is ceased to be called an adolescent and labelled as an adult member of the society. He is supposed to play a responsible role in the society. Before being called as adolescent, he is named as child or infant, etc. All of these names — infant, child, adolescent and adult, etc. are linked with various stages of growth and development through which the child passes from birth to death.

There are certain common developmental or practical characteristics belonging to each stage. The human organism shows peculiar quantitative and qualitative changes in his body and behaviour with the help of which we can say at what particular age an individual belongs to which definite stage of his life.

If we also include the pre-birth period, the life span of a human organism can be divided, conveniently, into the following stages:

Name of the Stage	*Period and approximate Age*
1. Pre-natal (Pre-birth) stage	From conception to birth.
2. Stage of Infancy	From birth to five years
3. Childhood stage	From 6 to 12 years or in strict sense up to the on-set of puberty.
4. Adolescent stage	From the on-set of puberty to the age of maturity (generally from 13 to 19 years).
5. Adulthood	From 20 years and beyond or in strict sense from the age of attaining maturity till death.

We do not claim the absolute rigidity in the above classification in terms of either the division of life span into above mentioned stages or the duration of period, mentioned against them. There are certainly great individual differences and so, we should not imagine that every child will necessarily have each stage according to the period indicated above.

From the angle of school education, the first and the last stage serve no useful purpose. Therefore, in this text we will confine our attention to the remaining three stages of development.

How our development goes on with various stages of our life, it must be quite interesting thing to be known. Let us try to discuss the main characteristics of the pattern of development during the above most educative stages of our life-infancy, childhood and adolescence.

A. Stage of Infancy

The special features of the developmental trend and behaviour pattern at this stage are the following:

(1) Rapid growth and development: Infancy is the period of rapid growth and development. Inner as well as outer organs develop rapidly at this stage. There is rapid growth in terms of height, weight, and size. There is rapid development of emotions and almost all the emotions are developed in the child during this stage. This stage is marked by intensive motor activity and restlessness.

(2) Dependence: An infant depends upon his mother, father and other family members for the satisfaction of his basic needs. He is a helpless creature and can move and function only with the help of others. Even for the emotional satisfaction, he depends upon others. He expects that everybody around him should love him and give him his entire affection and attention. He wants to love and to be loved and in this exchange he totally depends on the mercy of others. In this way the child at this stage is dependent but as he moves into the later years of his infantile behaviour he slowly proceeds towards independence.

(3) Self-assertion: Although the child is a helpless one and depends upon others for the satisfaction of his needs, he is quite self assertive. He tries to dominate his superior and elder ones. His wishes must be fulfilled. He thinks he is always right and all around him should obey him. He is the prince although without crown and tries to assert himself all the time in all situations.

(4) Period of make-believe and fantasy: Infants live in the world of their own creation. This is a period of rich but baseless imagination. As in this stage the infant has limited potentialities and aspires more than what he can actually get in actual life, he compensates himself in fantasy and make-believe.

(5) Selfish and unsocial: In infancy the child is almost completely ego-centric and selfish. He does not want to share his toys or give any of his possessions to any one else. He wants to have all the things, even love, admiration and affection reserved for him. He does not care for the social and moral codes and principles and places his self interest at the premium.

(6) Emotionally unstable: Infancy is the period of violent emotional

experiences. The emotions at this stage are marked by intensity, frequency and instability. They are spontaneous and the infant is hardly able to exercise control over them. He is not able to hide his feelings and in this way, the emotional expression of the infant is generally in the overt form.

(7) Characteristics of mental development:

(i) *Developing curiosity and questioning attitude:* At this stage the child is very much curious about knowing so many things around him. The world and the environment is new for him. He is in the habit of questioning like what is this, why does it happen or not happen, etc. His queries are virtually endless. Answers do not interest him as much as asking questions. His speed of questioning is so rapid that he does not bother to wait for the previous answers.

(ii) *Intellectually not developed:* The child at this initial stage is very immature in intelligence. He lacks in reasoning and abstract understanding. He can think only in concrete terms and is not developed in abstract reasoning and thinking. The powers of observation, perception, concentration, etc. are also not developed.

(iii) *Rote memory:* The child though not developed much intellectually has a very good memory. But this memorization is without reasoning, it is purely a rote memory. He can cram and reproduce the matter easily.

(iv) *Creativity:* The period of infancy is also characterized by the tendency of creative impulse in the child. He develops a creative attitude and often engages himself in making or collecting so many things. He tries to take satisfaction in realizing that he can make, construct and perform the activities as his elders do.

(v) *Time concept is not developed:* For the child at this stage, the divisions of time such as yesterday, today, tomorrow, month, year, etc. are meaningless as he has not yet developed the concept time.

(8) Sexual development: Although the sex organs at this stage are not developed, yet the sex tendency is in a continuous stage of development. The findings of Psycho analysis like Freud and others have clearly shown that the sexual life of the infant is as rich as that of an adolescent. An infant passes through the three stages of sexual development — stage of self-love, homosexual and heterosexual. At this initial stage, the child derives pleasure from his own body by sucking his thumb or touching the sex organs. Later on he seeks the satisfaction of his sex impulse outside and develops sentiments of love for the mother or father depending upon his sex. Finally, the child develops heterosexual tendency and in this respect the male child gets itself attached to the mother and the female child to the father.

B. Stage of Childhood

Main Characteristics

When the child completes his five years and steps into school going age, this period of childhood starts. It goes upto the on-set of puberty. During this period significant changes in the sphere of physical, intellectual, emotional and social aspects take place. The main characteristics of development during this stage can be named as follows:

1. *Period of slow and steady growth:* Where the infancy is the period of rapid and intensive growth, the stage of childhood is the characterized as the period of slow, steady and uniform growth. Development rate, although continuous and uniform, is very slow at this stage.

2. *Independence:* Whereas an infant looks for help in every sort of work, even if he is able to do it independently, the child at this stage desires independence. By acquiring experiences and developing physically, intellectually and socially he tries to adjust himself in his environment. In fact at this stage he feels more at home with the world and takes satisfaction by doing his work with his own efforts. He becomes increasingly independent of his parents whom he considers merely, convenient persons to provide food and shelter.

3. *Emotional stability and control:* Childhood in the emotional aspect is the period of stability and control. Intense emotional outbursts which usually find their expression in motor activity and physical form during infancy are rarely repeated at this stage. The child learns to hide his feelings. He can exercise control over his emotions and express them in appropriate and socially approved ways. His emotional behaviour is not guided by instinctive causes but has an appropriate rationale behind it.

4. *Developing social tendency:* In contrast to an infant who is egocentric, the child at this stage, develops social tendencies and picks up so many social virtues. He likes to play in group and shares his toys with others. Feelings of mutual cooperation, team spirit and group loyalties are developed among children of this age. This period of childhood is often named as gang-age as the child of this age is always a member of some group and develops a very strong sentiment for the group. He is so much loyal to his group that he sometimes even does not mind the displeasure of his parents and teachers.

5. *Realistic attitude:* Child at this stage begins to accept and appreciate the hard realities of life. He, no longer remains in the own world of make-believe, fantasy and fairy-tales. He is now a perfect realist in place of imaginative idealist. He begins to take a close interest in the world of realities and tries to adapt himself in the real environment.

6. *Formation of sentiments and complexes:* Infancy is the age of innocence. The child at this stage in not in the habit of hiding his feelings and checking his emotions. Therefore, no complexes are formed at this stage whereas childhood stage gives birth to so many complexes due to inhibition, repression, etc. At this stage of infancy, emotional behaviour does not turn itself into a permanent structure for giving birth to sentiments. But at this stage of childhood emotional behaviour gets itself structured into

sentiments. Various sentiments like religious, moral, patriotic and aesthetic sentiments begin to develop at this stage. The formation of such sentiments leads towards character development.

7. Sexual development: With regard to sexual development, this stage is called 'latency period'. Sexual energy, generally, at this stage remains dormant but emerges with great force at the end of this stage. The sexual behaviour of the children at this stage is characterized by the development of an attitude of antagonism and indifference towards the opposite sex. While at the infancy stage the boys and girls play together, the children at this stage like to play with the members of their own sex. Due to their varied interests they gradually develop a general attitude of antagonism towards the opposite sex. As a result of this antagonistic behaviour the two sexes naturally draw apart. Even when brought together in family gatherings, boys and girls of this age are barely civil to one another. Sex antagonism is more pronounced in boys than in the case of girls. They do not want anything that resembles a girl. In the case of girls the attitude of antagonism, generally, takes the form of indifference. They try to ignore the boys in place of tormenting, teasing and interfering with their play.

8. Intellectual development: This stage is the period of intellectual advancement. The rate of intellectual development is quite rapid at this stage which resembles the rate of physical growth at infancy. At this stage the child acquires new experiences and tries to adapt himself in his environment and prepares himself to solve the problems. His power of reasoning, thinking, observation, concentration, perception, imagination, etc. are developed. He cannot very well go with abstract thinking. He develops the concept of length, time and distance and learns to express himself in various ways.

9. Development of interests and aptitudes: In childhood the child's field of interests widens and he shows special aptitudes, likings and dislikings towards the things and work. The children of this age are usually extravert and are very fond of excursions and visits. They develop interest in reading various types of books. Radio, television drama and movies hold a strong appeal for them. They are interested in everything which is mysterious and romantic. Wide differences in the interest pattern can be seen among boys and girls. Boys are interested in the activities requiring fearlessness, courage and adventures while girls are inclined towards the activities requiring tenderness, softness and other feminine characteristics.

C. Stage of Adolescence

The word 'adolescence' comes from the Latin verb 'adolescere' which means 'to grow'. So, the essence of the word adolescence is growth and it is in this sense that adolescence represents a period of intensive growth and change in nearly all aspects of child's physical, mental, social, and emotional life. It is very crucial period of one's life. The growth achieved, the experiences gained, responsibilities felt and the relationships developed at this stage destine the complete future of an individual.

Who is to be called an Adolescent?

When does this crucial period start and end in one's life? Who should be labelled as an adolescent? These are some pertinent questions which should be answered at this stage.

Technically speaking, a child is described as an adolescent when he achieves puberty, that is, when he has become sexually mature to the point, where he is able to reproduce his kind. He ceases to be an adolescent when he has acquired maturity to play the role of an adult in his society or culture. Maturity, as the term used here, does not mean mere physical maturity, it also implies mental, emotional and social maturity.

It is very difficult to point out the exact range of the adolescence period in terms of chronological years. Achieving puberty and becoming mature cannot be tied to a universal span or period. Therefore, the range of adolescence, not only differs from country to country but varies from community to community and from individual to individual. In general, girls become sexually as well as socially mature at an early age. The standard of living, early or late marriage, health and climate, the cultural traditions and environment, attitude towards sex, the role expected from the child at different ages, are some of the other factors which control the dawn of puberty and attainment of maturity by children.

In our country, in comparison to western countries, the period of adolescence starts early as Indian children achieve puberty earlier, because of the favourable climatic and cultural factors. Also it ends earlier due to early attainment of maturity whereas in the western world "the adolescence extends roughly from 13 years of age till 21 for girls and 15 till 21 for boys", (Hariman, 1946: 3) in India it usually ranges from 13 to 19 among boys and from 11 to 17 among girls.

The above classifications of the range for the period of adolescence are not rigid. There are wide individual differences. However, with a view of a rough estimate for universal applicability, with regard to span of adolescence the adolescents can be referred as teenagers — the individuals having chronological age between 11 to 19 years.

Significance of the Study of Adolescence

You may be somewhat curious for knowing that why is it so that in your syllabus special emphasis is laid on the study of adolescence. How is it so important for a secondary teacher training course? In what way is it going to be useful for you to deal with your students? Let us try to seek answers of these questions which are more or less related to the significance of the study of adolescence to you as a secondary school teacher.

The reason for confining your syllabus to the study of adolescence lies in the fact that you are being prepared as a teacher of secondary or at most higher secondary classes to teach the students ranging in the age group 11 to 18 years. This means you are supposed to deal with the adolescents and therefore you need to be familiar with the development pattern of these children along with their specific needs, characteristics and problems. In the page to follow in the chapter, we are going to discuss on these issues. The knowledge of such study will definitely help you in dealing with your adolescent students, especially in the following ways.

1. You will be knowing that adolescence is a period of intensive growth and development with respect to children's physical, cognitive, social, emotional and sexual aspects of their personality. Normally what should be expected from the children in terms of their growth and development under various aspects of their personality, will be known to you and must be able to help your students to achieve their maximum in terms of their growth and development.

2. Adolescence is said to be a stage of great stresses and strains. The children of this age are quite perplexed and worried about their somatic variations and sudden changes in their total appearance, behaviour and attitude of the others towards them. They are worried about the sudden changes in their sex behaviour, sex related physiological and psychological problems etc. The study of adolescence will make you able to understand the stresses and strains of this age and devise means for helping them to pass through these stresses and strains.

3. Adolescents are said to be quite touchy, moody and sensitive. They are very conscious about their self respect. The study of their behaviour and characteristics will make you able to deal with them properly.

4. Adolescence is the age of action having varied interests and tastes. It is the age of poets, writers, scientists, creative artists, athletics and martyrs. The knowledge of this fact will require from you to recognize the abilities and talents of your students, give them proper opportunity for the nourishment of their interests and abilities so that the tremendous energy of this age may get a constructive channel.

In this way the study of adolescence will definitely help you in dealing with your adolescent students with a clear cut objectives of helping all round growth and development.

Pattern of Growth and Development during Adolescence

As said earlier, the human growth and development takes a spiral form and not linear. Therefore, within the alternate stages of life, we find a sort of repetition and resemblance of characteristics. The old adults are often found to behave like children. In adolescence also we find a sort of repetition and recapitulation of what has been done during infancy. The observation of Ross (1951: 145) reflects the above idea when he says, "Adolescence is best regarded as a recapitulation of the first period of life, as second turn of the spiral of development." Like infancy the adolescence is the period of too much restlessness and disturbance or as Stanley Hall regard it "a period of great stress and strain, storm and strife."

Let us see how far these observations are true. The adolescence's growth and developmental pattern along with the peculiar characteristics of this age can help us in understanding our adolescent. In the following lines, we will make an attempt in this direction.

(a) Physical development during adolescence

During adolescence, the physical growth and development reaches to its peak and human body finds its final shape. The maximum limit with regard to increase in size, weight and height is achieved. Bones and muscles increase to the greatest possible extent leading to a great increase in motor activity. The growth and function of all other outer and inner organs also reaches to its maximum and almost all the glands become extremely active at this stage.

There is a growth of hair under arms and around genital organs. Boys and girls develop the characteristic features of their respective sexes. There is the roundness of the breasts and hips among the girls and the decoration of the faces with beard and moustaches among the boys. There is a distinct change in voice among the two sexes. While the girls' voice acquires shrillness and becomes sweet, the boy's voice deepens and becomes harsher. The girls begin to menstruate monthly during this period and the boys have nocturnal emissions (discharge of semen during sleep) accompanied by erotic dreams. In this way physiologically, the boys and girls attain all the male and female characteristics respectively during this age and prepare themselves for being called men and women or gentlemen and ladies.

(b) Emotional development and changes

Emotional development reaches its maximum during adolescence. It is the period of heightening of all emotions like anxiety, fear, love, anger, etc. Once again like an infant an individual experiences emotional instability and intensity during adolescence. The physical growth and development being maximum, the strength of the boys gives opportunity for maximum motor activity. Therefore, in matter of emotional expression and experiences the adolescence provides the highest peak. At no stage the child is so restless and emotionally perturbed and touchy as in adolescence. He is too sensitive, inflammable and moody. In the words of Ross (195': 147) "the adolescent lives an intensely emotional life, in which we can see once more the rhythm of positive and negative phases of behaviour in his constant alternation between intense excitement and deep depression." This is why the period is often designated as a period of stresses and strains.

In this way as Ross clarifies, the adolescence are not consistent in their emotional expressions. Their emotions fluctuate very frequently and quickly. The current of emotional flow in the adolescence is too intense. It is very difficult to put check on the emotions during the peak of adolescence. In fact, during adolescence emotions take their roots into sentiments. Self consciousness, self respect and personal pride is too much increased. Group loyalty and sentiments of love etc. are developed which make an adolescent sentimental and passionate. What he feels, he feels it very strongly and when be reacts, he reacts vigorously.

(c) Social development and changes during adolescence

Adolescence is the period of increased social relationships and contacts. Whereas a child cares very little for the society, an adolescent develops a good amount of social sense. He ceases to be ego-centric, selfish and unsocial. Now he wants to mould his behaviour according to the norms of the society.

The social circle of an adolescent is very wide. Contrary to childhood, he becomes interested in opposite sex. The friendships are no longer nominal. He believes in making intimate friendship and attaches himself closely to a group. Peer group relationship controls the social behaviour of this age. The child develops a strong sense of loyalty towards group. He wants to be accepted by the group of which he is a member. The rejection is costly as it creates so many adjustment problems.

Another significant change in the social aspect of the child during adolescence lies in his relationships with his parents and the family. Now there is a craving for independence. He wants that his personality should be recognized by the parents and elderly members of the family. He must not be treated as a child. He gives more importance to the values and beliefs maintained by his peer group than the advice of his parents. There may even be hidden or open rebellion, if the parents try to impose their opinion and values on their adolescent children.

(d) Intellectual development and adolescence

Adolescence is the period of maximum growth and development with regard to mental functioning. Intelligence reaches its climax during this period. Intellectual powers like logical thinking, abstract reasoning and concentration are almost developed up to the end of this period. An adolescent learns to reason and seeks answer to 'how and why' of everything, scientifically. His power of critical thinking and observation is much developed. He does not try to follow the beaten track. He is almost critical of everything. He develops a fine imagination. Writers, artists, poets, philosophers, and inventors are all born in this period. Improper channelization of imagination and dissatisfied needs may turn an adolescent into day-dreaming. Therefore, a great care is to be taken for properly cultivating their power of imagination.

Hero worship is most prominent in this period. Adolescents, generally, love adventures, wandering, fairly tales and develop interest in reading such books. Their area of interest is actually widened. Adolescence is the age of action. According to the difference in tastes and temperaments, nearly all the adolescents have some or other hobbies and strong likes and dislikes for the world of nature, man and things.

(e) Moral and religious development

With the development of social and civic sense, the children during the period learn to behave according to the norms of their society and culture. Also the group sense makes them follow some moral or ethical code. It prepares a stage of proper moral development. The formation of strong sentiments during this period intensifies the process of moral development. The character by which we know a person in his life, to a great extent, is the product of the experiences gained, complexes formed and sentiments made during this age.

The impact of religion and religious practices is also felt for the first time at this age in one's life. An adolescent tries to talk about God and religion. He often engages himself in the discourse about philosophical concept like Soul, Brahm, the meaning of life, the question of death, etc.

(f) Sexual development and adolescence

Sexual development reaches its peak during adolescence. The adolescent is sexually mature. In fact, the whole personality structure and behaviour of the adolescent is dominated by sex. During adolescence the sexual development like infancy goes into three stages as described ahead.

(i) *Stage of auto-erotism or self-love:* At this stage the young boys and girls fall in love with themselves. They try to take pleasure with their own bodies. Self decoration and enjoying it before mirror is their common practice. Self-enjoyment by indulging in masturbation is also prevalent at this stage.

(ii) *Stage of homo-sexuality:* At this age boys and girls are attracted toward the members of their own sex and seek gratification from each other's body by grouping them in two or three at one time.

(iii) *Hetero-sexual Stage:* At this age boys and girls are seen attracted toward each other. They are keen to make friendship or establishing even sexual relationships with the members of the opposite sex.

Special Characteristics of Adolescence
(With Reference to the Needs and Problems of Adolescents)

After acquainting ourselves a little with the growth and developmental pattern of the adolescent, it is worthwhile to point out some of the special characteristics of adolescence. Adolescence often termed as the age of storm and stress, has so many conflicting situations and problems of adjustment which need a careful study. Let us think over the origin of such problems and try to analyse the specific needs and demands of adolescents.

(1) *Perplexity with regard to somatic variation:* Every adolescent has more or less difficult task of adjusting to 'somatic variation' which may occur during or after puberty. As said earlier, during the period of

adolescence maximum physiological changes take place. These rapid changes create problems for the adolescents in the following way:

(a) The flow of blood during menstruation creates worries among the girls and gives birth to so many fears and anxieties. Similarly, the discharge of the semen during nocturnal emission among the boys horrifies them. They become quite perturbed about the loss of fluid. These particular physiological changes bring so many complexes in the minds of the children. It makes them introvert and secretive.

(b) There are always individual differences among the human beings and so one cannot deny the possible differences with regard to bodily development, look and appearance among the adolescents. The adolescent with his nearly developed body, is constantly making comparisons between himself and his contemporaries. Differences are almost certain to cause him some anxiety. Particularly, they are concerned with height, weight, fatness, thinness, facial blemishness, largeness or smallness of the hips and breasts in girls and of the genitals in boys.

For both boys and girls, appearance and bodily condition, which is not in keeping with what is considered the norm, will cause some anxiety. Girls want to look feminine and be attractive to boys. Boys want to look manly to gain prestige with other boys and particularly with girls. To be reasonably satisfied with one's physical appearance, thus becomes an important task for an adolescent. He has a need to become accustomed to new bodily changes. Any deviation from the norms and standard of the peer group can produce complex in the mind and make him maladjusted.

(2) Intensification of self-awareness: Self-consciousness is too much developed in adolescence. There is a strong desire in an adolescent that his or her bodily changes should be noticed by the elders as well as by the members of his own age-group. Adolescence can be described as an age of self-decoration. Boys and girls pay more attention towards their dresses, make-up, manner of talking, walking, eating, etc.

In fact, there is a craving for recognition in adolescents. Every adolescent desires that he or she should be a centre of attraction for the opposite sex and his her abilities, intelligence, and capacities should be recognized by the peer group and elders. Moreover, the adolescents are too much sensitive, touchy and inflammable. They aim to maintain at any cost their concept of themselves and whenever possible to enhance their status among their peers. An attack on their phenomenal self invites strong reactions and behavioural problems. It makes an adolescent either aggressive or withdrawn depending upon the circumstances.

(3) Intensification of sex-consciousness: Sex consciousness becomes too intense at this time. Most of the adolescents' problems are concerned with the sudden functioning of their glands, secretion of sex hormones and the awakening of the strong sex instinct.

Firstly, menstruation and ejaculation through natural occurrences at puberty give a shock to most of the adolescents. Afterwards every adolescent feels a sort of strong sensation in the sex organs. This makes to motivate him in seeking satisfaction through masturbation and homosexual relations. In the third stage of their sexual development the adolescents are attached towards the opposite sex. Sex sensation combined with curiosity about sex draws the members of the two opposite sex nearer and nearer. This nearness is sometimes developed into relationships and intercourse and creates so many problems and complexes for the future.

These activities create so many worries and complexes in the minds of the adolescents. They become perturbed and develop a sense of guilt. In most of such cases they express the opinion that by acquiring these habits they have ruined their lives and they will now remain unfit for any future sexual life.

(4) Independence v/s Dependence: The adolescent is on the boundary line of childhood and adulthood. So, he is typically a person who needs security, guidance and protection like a child and independent views, maturity of opinion and self-support like an adult. He is still immature. His abilities and capacities are still in the process of growth and development. He depends for the satisfaction of his so many needs — physical, emotional, etc. — on his parents and elders. The emotional instability of his behaviour and difficulty in coming in terms with the somatic changes makes him quite restless and often insecure.

He needs security and complete freedom from unnecessary worries and anxiety at this stage and in this way he is once again in the search of mother's lap and father's affection. Also, his intense love for thrill and adventure, coupled with his uncontrolled emotions, needs somebody to guide him, and to check his unbridled flow of energy.

On the other hand, as his social circle is widening, he tries to emancipate himself from the care and look after of his parents and elders. He thinks himself a mature and full-fledged adult. He reacts strongly when the parents and the elders consider him still a child. He tries to assert or show that he is now a mature person and not a child as they think of him. His opinion should now be given weightage. He has every right to give suggestions and directions in family matters. He can very well manage his own affairs and the elders should not interfere unnecessarily. He begins to feel ashamed and embarrassed for the protection and care shown by the parents.

Not only he suffers from the duality in his behaviour, but also the parents themselves are not decided about the roles of their child at this age. Sometimes, they expect him behave as an adult and at other times, they treat him as a child. Therefore, the poor adolescent is caught between the role of the child and the adult. He possesses a strange mixture of the needs for dependence and independence which creates conflicting situations and problems for him.

(5) Peer-group relationship: Peer group relationship plays a substantial role in the life of an adolescent. He goes away from his parents and elders and spends much of his time with members of his peer group. He values the ideals of the group and develops a sense of loyalty towards it. He is now directed by the standard and norms of his peer group and pays least attention to the desires and advice of his parents and elders. He is more concerned with gaining prestige and recognition in the eyes of his peers. Every child wants at this stage that he should be fully accepted by his peers. Nothing can be more devastating to adolescent than to be rejected by his age-mates. There is sure to exist a difference in the opinions, views, likings and disliking of the elders and adolescents. It is here that the difficulty arises. The adolescents find themselves the victims of the conflicting demands of social and cultural norms of adults and their peer group and they often become confused and perplexed with regard to any decision making.

(6) Idealism v/s *Realism:* A typical feature of adolescence lies in the interest of the adolescent in ideals. He desires to help in the creation of an ideal society. He is very critical of the existing circumstances and happenings and thinks of bringing reform. He often engages himself in asking such questions: Whither is the world going? What is the meaning of our life? What is God? What is humanity? Why are there so many sufferings and inequalities? In this way he tries to place himself on a superior level by searching some lofty aims and ideals and wants a set of moral principles he can understand as well as some guiding principles by which he can operate.

But in this search of idealism he goes away from realism. In the attempt of touching sky from the ground he is deprived of the support which is available from the ground. In fact, lack of experience makes him somewhat unrealistic. He tends to accept the impossible. When it is not attainable he becomes quite disturbed and unreasonable. Many of the adolescents turn themselves into problem youths. Some of them become pessimistic and believe in destroying whatever comes in way of realising their dreams. Some turn into withdrawn and daydreamers. They begin to roam in their own world of imagination, make-believe and fairy-tales and thus have possibility to turn into maladjusted personalities.

(7) Vocational choice and need of self-support: The adolescent's strong desire is to achieve self-sufficiency and make himself quite independent like an adult member of the society. Also the life ahead demands from him that he should prepare himself for the future vocation which he wants to adopt. Therefore, the period of adolescence requires from the individuals to take a decision about their vocations. Vocational decision is an important one for an adolescent and he often finds himself not quite upto the mark in making a right choice. Emotional instability, lack of experience and maturity prove as obstacles in the right choice. Moreover, his interests, aptitudes and abilities are in the process of making yet. This uncertainty

about the interests and abilities makes him quite puzzled. Therefore, the adolescents want proper guidance and advice with regard to their interests, aptitudes and vocational choice.

If we try to make close analysis, we can find that the adolescence is like a crossroad which provides an opportunity for the adolescents to choose and proceed in wrong as well as in right direction equally. It has every chance of turning adolescents into maladjusted personalities the chief cause of which is the frustration of needs and conflict of motives. At the adolescent age there emerges new physical, social and emotional needs. With regard to physical needs the adolescent needs to become accustomed to new bodily changes and desires to have other's notice that such changes have occurred.

In the social aspect he has a strong need for the belongingness to a peer group. Emotionally, he needs to the loved, accepted and admired. He needs security, freedom from anxiety and recognition of self. There is striving for independence from parental control and a struggle for making the active sexual instincts and urges satisfied or sublimated within the norms of the society and culture.

All this demands proper direction and guidance to the adolescents. The educational process, the parental care, the efforts of the teachers and the environmental conditions — All should be so designed as to bring proper growth and development of the adolescents and channelization of their energies into proper direction.

Differences in the Trends of Growth and Development of Boys and Girls in Adolescence

Differences in the trends of growth and development of boys and girls can be located as under.

Girls reach puberty about a year or two earlier than boys do. Consequently growth spurt occurs earlier in girls than in boys. Therefore between the age 12 to 14 they are found to be taller and heavier than boys. But they are again surpassed by the boys. By the end of adolescence, the young men are generally higher and heavier than the young women.

Boys and girls develop the characteristic features of their respective sexes. There is roundness of the breasts and hips and thinness of the waste line among the girls and growth of facial hair and the development of larger muscles in the upper body among the boys. There is distinct changes in the voice among two sexes. While the girl's voice acquires shrillness and becomes sweet, the boy's voice deepens and becomes harsher. Regarding primary sex characteristics the development in girls involve the development of ovaries, uterus and vagina, and the beginning of menstrual periods. While in boys, it brings the growth of the scrotum, testes and penis and the ability to produce sperm. There is also occasional discharge of semen during sleep accompanied by erotic dreams among boys.

In the matter of physical strength and stamina, the adolescent boys in general show marked superiority over the adolescent girls.

Like physical growth and development, the girls demonstrate more intelligent behaviour in the early adolescence than the boys. However, in the field of abstract thinking boys are seen usually ahead to the girls. Moreover, there seems not much significant difference in the intellectual functioning of the adolescent boys and girls and it can never be stated that adolescent girls are inferior to adolescent boys in intellectual functioning or vice versa.

In moral development also, there seems no significant difference in the trend of growth and development of adolescent boys and girls except that girls are more likely found to focus on the needs of others, to be concerned about social relations, and to take other points of view into account where boys tend to deal more narrowly with rules and moral issues and focus on individual rights and self-fulfillment.

In the areas of interests and likings there seems some observable difference among boys and girls. Boys take interest in the activities and play which are considered to be more masculine and involve more physical strength and stamina. The girls take interest and prefer light games and exercises. They exhibit wide areas of interests than the boys. Their tastes are more refined than the boys. They are more inclined to literature, fine arts and aesthetic activities. They show more inclination towards reading romantic novels, poems, literature, etc. and take interest in self-decoration as well as beautification of the home, schools and surroundings. On the other hand, boys exhibit more interest in outside activities, outdoor games and difficult adventurous risky tasks.

There seems difference in the emotional make up of the adolescent boys and girls. In comparison to boys, girls in our culture are found more sensitive, emotional and sentimental. Kindness, sympathy, tolerance and other tender feelings are more intensely shown by the girls than the boys.

In our culture outward manifestation of their sex feelings are usually prevalent in boys than the girls. Although girls are attracted to boys, but they do not make it public as boys do.

Usually girls are found more expressive. It is rather difficult for them to hold a thing or idea with them. They are in the habit of expressing and disclosing it. While the boys are more secretive and seclusive. May it be the cause that girls can release their tension easily through such expression than the boys.

However, the demonstration of such behaviour and trends of growth and development by the adolescent girls and boys can't be taken as universal. It differs from culture to culture, place to place and situation to situation. With the change in attitude towards girls and improved rearing practices, the gulf regarding the developmental and personality characteristics between the boys and girls, is getting narrower day by day and now there is hardly any area left where girls cannot be seen to surpass the boys.

What can the Teachers, Parents and School do for Adolescents?

The needs of the adolescents have to be satisfied and their problems are to be realized in a proper way in order to help them in growing and developing properly. The task is serious and desires all dimensional efforts. Below some of these efforts are mentioned:

(1) To have the proper knowledge of adolescents' psychology: Adolescence is the bridge between childhood and adulthood. The behaviour of the adolescent and his personality needs a careful study. It is essential to have the knowledge of the adolescents' psychology in order to understand them. What are their specific needs? What type of changes do take place during this period? What are the problems faced by the adolescents? How should they be treated? All this is essential to be known by the parents, teachers and administrators who have to deal with them.

(2) Providing suitable environment for proper growth: As we know, the growth stops at the end of adolescence after attaining maturity. Adolescence is the stage where maximum growth takes place. For getting maximum, what one can get with respect to physical and mental growth, suitable environment should be provided by the parents and the teachers at home as well as in schools. Adolescents must be provided with balanced diet. Their eating habits should be properly checked up. They must be given knowledge of health, personal hygiene, cleanliness, various diseases and their prevention, etc. to keep them fit for growing. Adequate provision for physical exercise and activities should be made in the school curriculum and necessary facilities should be provided.

(3) Rendering proper sex education: Sex plays very dominant role at the age of adolescence. The rapid physiological changes, the secretion of sex hormones, the sudden awakening of sex instinct and urges — all necessitate the provision of adequate sex information and education for adolescent. The following things may help in this direction:

(i) They should be helped in making adjustments with regard to their new bodily changes and somatic developments. Girls should know that flow of blood during menstruation is not a disease. It is a natural process which prepares them for becoming mothers. In a similar way the occasional discharge of semen during sleep among the boys is not in any way harmful to them and should not be in any way a cause of worry. The boys should be told all about this.

(ii) Their curiosity of sex also needs satisfaction. For this purpose the parents and the teachers should provide adequate information regarding the sex hygiene and physiology, the process of the birth of a baby, the hazards of immature and before marriage intercourse, etc. in a very frank, scientific, judicious and impersonal manner.

(iii) The sex instinct and urges also need to be cared properly. There should be proper sublimation of sex instinct and channelization of sexual energy. Forceful inhibition and taboos, and restrictions imposed in this direction bring disastrous results. With the provision of wide field of interests, a network of co-curricular activities and social situations, the boys and girls should be given a chance to know and work shoulder to shoulder with each other. This will remove their so many misconceptions about each other and will lead to their healthy adjustments.

(4) Proper dealing with the adolescents: Recent researches in the field of Adolescents' Psychology have revealed that the adults, the parents, elders and the teachers — and their unreasonable ways and points of view are the real problems of adolescence. They are in the habit of criticising the adolescents and always impose their authority and assert their likings and dislikings. They forget that there is a generation gap between them and adolescents. In dealing with them the parents and the teachers should realize that the demands of their peer group are more important than their own expectation.

Secondly, in the adolescents there is a craving for recognition and they also try to maintain their self-prestige and status among their peers. They assert that they are now mature individuals. Their opinions should be valued and they should be given a patient hearing. Therefore, it is badly needed on the part of the teachers as well as parents that they should stop treating the adolescents as children and give them due recognition. Their opinions should be invited and they should be given opportunities for free expression. They must refrain from activities damaging to the pupil's self-concept. The adolescents must not feel that they are insulted and their phenomenal self has been attacked unnecessarily. The teachers and parents should stop murmuring and criticising the attitudes and actions of the adolescents blindly. Youths are more in need of models and critics. The elders must give a deep consideration to adolescents' needs and problems. It is futile to punish misbehaviour. The root causes should be removed.

(5) Training of emotions and satisfaction of emotional needs: The age of adolescence is marked by too much intensity, force, instability and immaturity of emotions. The adolescent youths are highly inflammable and restless. Their emotions can be aroused with a slight provocation. The political parties and opportunist leaders can easily befool them and use them in destroying national property. Therefore, there is a strong need of emotional education to the adolescents. Their emotions should be properly trained and their emotional energies should be diverted towards the constructive ends.

Moreover, the adolescents suffer from some emotional hungers. They have a strong desire to love and to be loved. They need to be accepted by their age mates and every adolescent aspires that he should be admired and praised. He needs that he should be given freedom to proceed in his own way and adopt his own style of life but on the other hand, needs protection, shelter and affection of the parents, elders and teachers. He becomes disturbed if he is not provided proper security and freedom from anxiety. They parents and the teachers should take care of these needs of the adolescents. They must be given what they need in terms of their emotional requirements.

(6) To take care of the special interests of the adolescents: The adolescence is the age of wide interests and aptitudes. There are wide individual differences among the adolescents with regard to their special interest and aptitudes. A great care should be taken to locate the special interests and aptitudes of the adolescents. According to their interests and aptitudes they should be provided with learning experiences and opportunities for participation in co-curricular activities. The curriculum should provide the open choice for various subjects and activities according to the tastes and temperaments of the adolescents.

Their thirst of curiosity, wandering and adventure should be quenched through excursion, N.C.C., mountaineering, scientific exploration, etc. The love for humanity and ideals should be utilized in rendering social services and community services in the neighbourhood and distressed areas. In brief, the adolescents should be provided with useful activities according to their interests so that they can be constantly busy and their mind pre-occupied with healthy and constructive ideas.

(7) Providing religious and moral education: One of the causes of increasing restlessness, indiscipline, dishonesty, and aimlessness among the youth of India is that there is no proper provision of religious and moral education in our system of education. Ours is a secular state and therefore the doubts are expressed in the provision of religious instruction inside the schools. But it is a false fear standing on erroneous grounds. Actually the roots and the goals of all the religions are one and the same. If we try to do away with the rituals, the essence of all the religions is morality. Therefore, it is the education for morality and character formation, which is to be provided by religious education and every school, home and other social agency can work in this direction. The parents, teachers, social workers and administrators should join their hands in creating suitable atmosphere and offering opportunities of practising moral qualities.

As mentioned earlier, adolescents have great attraction for ideals. Therefore, in the religious instruction provided to them, the emphasis should be shifted from the rituals to ideals. By nature the adolescents are the hero worshippers. If we provide them with the selected examples of saints and prophets from all religions, their interests can be better served as they will imbibe many of the ideals of their heroes.

In this way, religious instruction and moral education can play a leading role in the proper development of adolescents. But it should never be confined to a mere communication of knowledge about morals. Moral habits are always caught from the environment. Example is always better than precept. The teachers, parents and elder members of the society should set examples before the adolescents and should join their hands creating suitable atmosphere for practising moral qualities.

(8) Provision for vocational education: There is a strong desire of achieving independence in adolescents. Economic factors obstruct their

way. Therefore, they are worried for acquiring self-sufficiency in economic aspect. What occupation should they choose, how can they earn their livelihood are some questions, the answers of which they try to seek. Here arises the need of proper vocational guidance and vocational education for them. The youths of today are bewildered and aimless because of the indefiniteness of their vocation. The education imparted to them does not provide jobs and occupations. Therefore, the strong need of today is to provide job oriented and vocation based practical education of the adolescents. The government, society, parents and the teachers should make their efforts in this direction,

Caring for Adolescents

1. To have the proper knowledge of adolescents' psychology
2. Providing suitable environment for proper growth
3. Rendering proper sex education
4. Proper dealing with the adolescents
5. Training of emotions and satisfaction of emotional needs
6. To take care of the special interests of the adolescents
7. Providing religious and moral education
8. Provision for vocational education
9. Arranging guidance services

Fig. 2.1: Caring for Adolescents

(9) Arranging guidance services: Lack of guidance creates aimlessness, indefiniteness and restlessness among the adolescents. The adolescents have their problems which need careful attention and proper solution. The adolescents are at the cross-roads of life. A slight mistake can lead them on the wrong path. Therefore, it is the utmost duty of the state, society and

school to provide proper guidance services to the students as well as to their parents. Guidance services should be organised in a proper form both inside the outside the schools. There should be well trained guidance workers and personnel. As far as possible, individual guidance should be provided.

The list of suggestions regarding the solution of the adolescents' problems and the satisfaction of their needs cannot be said as complete with above mentioned few points. The task is gigantic and requires strenuous efforts from all directions. Moreover, it is difficult to prescribe some common rule or formula for the direction and guidance of the adolescents with respect to their problems and needs. It is not a mass phenomenon. In actual sense there are no problem adolescents with problems. Therefore, the focus of guidance is always the individual and not the problem. Every adolescent is to be studied carefully as he requires special guidance and help for the solution of his problems and satisfaction of his needs.

3

Theories of Growth and Development

Introduction

We all have our origin from a fertilized ovum in the womb of our mother. It is the process of growth and development that has given us our shapes and sizes, abilities and capacities to function in physical, mental emotional, socio-cultural and moral ways. How this process of development in various aspects or dimensions such as physical, mental or cognitive, emotional, social, moral or linguistic is carried among the developing or growing children? What factors or things contribute or influence the development of children related to one or the aspects of his personality? The question like these have been a serious issue before the researchers and scholars in education psychology and sociology. As a solution, they have arrived at their own ideas, principles and developmental theories. We would be discussing a few of these developmental theories in this chapter known as:

A. Piaget's Theory of Cognitive Development
B. Erickson's Theory of Psycho-social Development
C. Kohlberg's Theory of Moral Development
D. Freud's Theory of Psycho-sexual Development

A. Piaget's Theory of Cognitive Development

Jean Piaget, a Swiss biologist later on turned into a cognitive and child psychologist, is known well for providing a stage theory of cognitive development for explaining the development of thinking in human beings from infancy to adulthood.

So keen was his interest in the study of cognitive and child psychology that he along with his wife (a former student of his at the Rousseau Institute) devoted almost all the precious years of their early married life to studying the cognitive development of their own three children by making them the subjects of their laboratory studies. As a result, today his theory of cognitive development has no parallel in the history of research in the field of developmental, cognitive and child psychology. For understanding this theory concerning the stages of cognitive development, let us first try to understand the major theoretical premise on which the theory stands.

Piaget's Theoretical Notions

Piaget designed a proper framework to understand the structure, functioning and development of the cognitive network of the human mind. He postulated that, like physical organs of the human body, there are two aspects of the human mind: one is referred to as cognitive structure and the other as cognitive functioning.

Cognitive Structure

Unlike other creatures, the human baby is born with a few practical instincts and reflexes such as sucking, looking, reaching and grasping. Therefore, the initial cognitive structure of infants is supposed to incorporate only those cognitive abilities or potentials which help them to do such acts such as look, reach out or grasp. Piaget named these abilities or potentials as *schemas* and termed them as the basic building blocks of our thinking. He defined them as the organized systems of actions or thought that allow us to mentally represent or "think about" the objects and events in our world (Woolfolk, 2004, p.30). Let us try to understand the meaning conveyed by the term 'schema' more clearly by referring to a particular schema like the 'sucking schema'. It refers to one's general cognitive ability or potential to suck objects. This schema is more than a single manifestation of the sucking reflex. It can be thought of as a cognitive structure that makes all acts of sucking possible. However, the description of this act of sucking differs in relation to contents *i.e.,* specific responses to specific stimuli such as the mother's nipple, a spoon, a toy, etc. We thus conclude that a schema represents a unit of one's cognitive structure in the shape of a general potential to perform a particular class of behaviours (like sucking, grasping, calculating, etc.), the content of which is related to the conditions that prevail during any particular manifestation of that general potential.

The various schemas with their contents thus form the basic structure of the human mind. The earlier schemas represent those reflexes and instincts that are biologically inherited. However, as a child grows, with the interaction of physical and social environment, he is able to form different schemas, resulting in changes and modifications in his cognitive structure.

Cognitive Functioning

The structure of an organism is said to play a decisive role in its functioning. Therefore, what is available to an individual in terms of his schemas decides how he is going to respond to the stimuli present in his physical or social environment. On the other hand, the individual has to adapt to his environment for survival as well as proper growth and development. The key to his cognitive development thus lies in his constant interaction with an adaptation to his physical and social environment. The task of such adaptation is carried out through the processes of assimilation and accommodation.

Assimilation refers to a kind of matching between the already existing cognitive structures and the environmental needs as they arise. In a situation where a six-month old infant is given a new toy it is likely to respond by putting the toy in his mouth. This is assimilation, as what the child did was to assimilate, incorporate or fit ideas about the new toy into already existing cognitive structures about old toys. His cognitive structure about old toys revolved around the sucking schema, therefore, he at once responded by performing the act of sucking.

Now, in case the new toy is too big to be picked up and placed in the mouth, it will certainly need a change or modification in the already existing cognitive structure. The child will have to change his old ways of thinking and behaving in order to adapt or adjust to the new situation. Consequently, now instead of sucking, the child may respond by pushing or grasping the toy. This is called *accommodation* as one tries to accommodate or adjust to new ways of thinking and behaving in place of assimilating or behaving in the same old fashion. Thus, whereas in the process of assimilation, one's responses are supposed to bank upon one's past experiences and already compiled stock of information, in the process of accommodation one has to learn new ways of thinking and behaving by making changes or modifications in one's existing cognitive structure. For instance, when the child is offered milk in a tumbler instead of the feeding bottle, first he tries his old way of behaving, *i.e.,* sucking. Afterwards, as a result of accommodation he picks up the new ways and consequently makes the necessary modification in his old cognitive structure.

Parallel to the concept of the processes of assimilation and accommodation linked with the process of the child's cognitive development, Piaget postulated the concept of *equilibration.* He asserted that the process of assimilation or accommodation helps the organism to adjust or maintain a harmonious relationship between himself and his environment. This adjustment mechanism was called equilibration by Piaget. It can be defined as an innate tendency or continuous drive on the part of an organism to organise its experiences (through assimilation or accommodation) for obtaining optimal adaptation to the changing demands of its environment by maintaining a proper balance between its cognitive structure and the changing demands of its environment. In fact, it is the need of seeking optimal adaptation or maintaining balance between himself and his environment that makes an individual feel uncomfortable and start reorganising his cognitive structure for equipping himself with new ways of thinking and behaving.

In this way Piaget highlighted the role of the following factors in one's cognitive make-up and its functioning:

1. The biologically inherited reflexes and mental dispositions as the fundamental cognitive structure.

2. The changes and development brought about in the cognitive structure through maturation (i.e., the process of natural growth).
3. The changes and development in the cognitive structure brought about through experiences (interaction with the physical and social environment) involving the processes of assimilation, accommodation and equilibration.

Stages of Intellectual Development

As already pointed out, Piaget, on account of his biological background, traced the initiation of human cognitive development in terms of biologically inherited ways of interacting with the environment. He further postulated that the changes and developments in one's cognitive structure are brought about by interaction with one's physical and social environment. This task is carried out through the mechanism of equilibration, resulting in constant organisation of one's cognitive structure by the interplay of accommodation and assimilation. This task of constant organisation of the mental structure is an individual phenomenon; we may, therefore, find wide differences between children in terms of possession of cognitive abilities. However, as Piaget concluded, this organisation of the mental structure in all children always takes place in a particular order involving definite stages of intellectual development. Thus, although children of the same age may differ in terms of possession of mental abilities, the order, in which the abilities evolve, and the pattern of development are quite constant and universal. Let us discuss this pattern of intellectual development in terms of the four developmental stages suggested by Piaget.

Sensori-motor Stage (From birth to about two years)

Piaget called the first stage of intellectual development the sensori-motor stage because (a) it is characterized by the absence of language, and (b) it is limited to direct sensory and motor interactions with the environment. The cognitive development at this stage occurs along the following pattern:

1. At birth the infant exhibits a limited number of uncoordinated reflexes such as sucking, looking, reaching and grasping.

2. During the next four months the uncoordinated reflexes are coordinated into simple schemas providing the child with a general potential to perform certain classes of behaviour. For example, the infant now tries to suck anything which is put into his mouth, stares at whatever he sees, reaches for everything and grasps all that is put into his hands.

3. By the age of eight months the infant is able to react to objects outside himself. He begins to realize that the objects around him are separated from himself and they have their independent and permanent existence. Prior to such development his view of the environmental objects is quite transitory, *i.e.,* what is out of sight is purely out of mind. For example, if the infant is playing with a toy and you pick it up, hide it somewhere while allowing the

child to watch your act of hiding the toy, he will at once forget about it. For him the toy placed under a blanket or hidden somewhere has disappeared and is no more. With the passage of time, gradually the concept of object permanence evolves in the cognitive structure of the infant. He begins to realize that the objects continue to exist even though he cannot see or experience them. Thus, he begins to search for the objects that are hidden. For example, if you hide a toy in the blanket, the infant will try to lift the blanket and search for the toy. In case you have shifted it somewhere, he will proceed to investigate its whereabouts under the assumption that the object has its permanent identity. When he does so we may infer that the child has been able to see or experience the object in his mind by making its mental image. Now he can proceed to the next stage of intellectual development involving the symbolic world of language by leaving behind the pure sensory or motor exploration.

4. Another significant achievement for the child of sensory motor stage according to Piaget is that by the end of the period of infancy he may step into logical goal-directed actions. Throwing light on this aspect Woolfolk (2004) writes *"Think of the familiar container toy for babies. It is usually plastic, has a lid, and contains several colourful items that can be dumped out and replaced. A six month old baby is likely to become frustrated trying to get to the toys inside. An older child who has mastered the basics of the sensori-motor stage will probably be able to deal with the toy in an orderly fashion by building a "container toy" scheme, (1) get the lid off, (2) turn the container upside down, (3) shake if the items Jam, (4) watch the items fall. Later on the child is also soon be able to reverse this action by refilling the container*" (p. 32-33).

Pre-operational Stage (about 2 to 7 years)

While stepping into this stage, the child begins to replace direct action in the form of sensory or motor exploration with symbols. The learning of the language provides him with a good tool for thinking. He begins to utter worlds to ask for something rather than just reaching out to get it. In addition to words, his thinking is also characterized by other symbolic representations or images of the things in the environment. This stage can be further sub-divided into (1) the pre-conceptual phase (approximately two to four years, and (2) the intuitive phase (approximately four to seven years).

1. Pre-conceptual phase: This is the period of the rudimentary concept formation and is characterized by the following features:

(a) In the early part of this stage, the children seem to identify objects by their names and put them into certain classes. However, they usually make mistakes in this process of identification and concept formation. For example, they think all men are '*daddy*', all women are '*mummy*' and all dogs are '*montu*'.

(b) Their mode of thinking and reasoning is quite illogical at this stage. It is neither inductive nor deductive but rather transductive in nature. For example, the child at this stage would reason like: as "cows are big animals with four legs and a long tail. This animal is also big and has four legs and a long tail, therefore it is a cow".

(c) Their thinking is sometimes too imaginative and far removed from reality. It may be seen in their play activities when a block of wood is turned into a riding horse or motor cycle and a doll into a baby. Moreover, at this stage they are unable to distinguish between living and non-living objects. For them the doll in their hands is a live baby who can cry, smile and sleep. Similarly the dreams they have are, for them, real and concrete events.

(d) The other major characteristic of the cognitive structure of the child at this stage is concerned with his egocentric nature. By egocentric Piaget means that the child can see the world only from his own standpoint. He considers that the sun and moon are following him, the rain falls to delight him, and obviously what exists in the external environment is specifically meant for him. He cannot think that people may have different opinions and differ in their modes of thinking and conclusions. He considers himself as the centre of a world of people who are supposed to perceive the things the way he does.

2. *Intuitive phase (approximately four to seven years)*: At this stage the child progresses towards the formation of various concepts at a more advanced level. For example, now he will agree that apples, oranges and bananas are all fruits despite the difference in their shape, colour or taste. But what he thinks or solves at this stage is carried out intuitively, rather than in accordance with any logical rule. Consequently, as Piaget concludes, the child's thinking at this stage in not logical and is full of contradictions. It is clearly reflected in the absence in him of the two main cognitive characteristics namely, reversibility (ability to reverse) and conservation (ability to see an object as permanent even though its arrangement or appearance is changed as long as nothing is added or taken away).

For example, when a child realizes that not only has he a brother but his brother also has a brother in him, it can be said that the child has developed the reversible quality in his cognitive operations. However, at the pre-operational stage children are seen not to possess the reversible characteristic in their mental functioning. For them moving from A to B may not carry the same meaning as moving from B to A.

Similarly, the thinking of pre-operational children at the intuitive stage is marked by an inability to conserve in terms of quantity as well as number as may be understood through the following experiments:

Experiment No. 1. A child belonging to the pre-operational age say five years old is shown two identical containers filled with the same quantity of coloured water. The child will agree that both have the same amount. Now the experimenter pours the water from one of the containers into a taller but narrower container and asks the child to compare the amount of water in this taller container with the amount in one of the old containers.

The inability to conserve in terms of quantity makes the child think that there is more water in the taller container even when the child has observed that the same amount of water has been poured into it (*see* Figure 3.1). The child in this experiment is likely to say that the taller container has more water because the level of the water is higher in this container. According to Piaget this happens because the child at this stage fails to realize that the amount or quantity of a material does not change with the change in the shape or appearance of its container. In other words, the child belonging to the preoperational stage shows a marked inability to conserve continuous quantity.

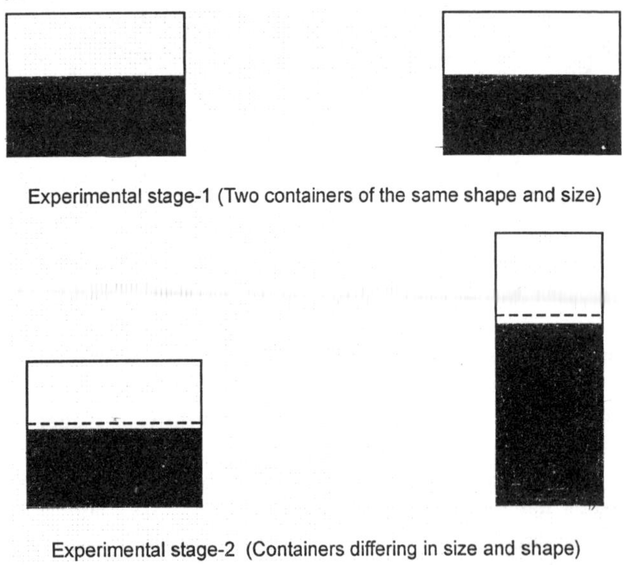

Fig. 3.1: Experiment demonstrating inability for conservation in terms of quantity.

Experiment No. 2. A child is shown two sets of beads arranged in one-to-one correspondence. The child is asked if the beads in the two rows are equal in number. The child would say that they are. The beads in one row are then spaced further apart (or spaced closer together) and the child is then asked to tell which row has more beads.

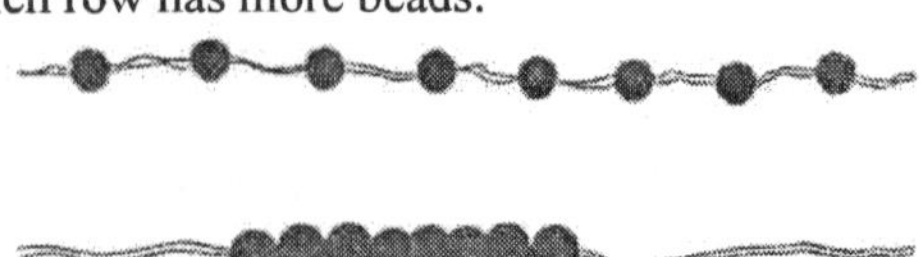

Fig. 3.2: Experiment demonstrating inability for conservation in terms of number.

Here with reference to Figure 3.2 the child belonging to the pre-operational stage is likely to say that the bottom row has more beads. What leads the child to think in such an illogical manner? The answer according to Piaget lies in the fact that the concept of the conservation of numbers is not yet developed in the child. He is therefore, unable to realize the simple fact that a mere change in appearance or arrangement of some objects cannot increase or decrease their number. As a conclusion it may be said in connection with intellectual development of the child belonging to the pre-operational stage that although the child's cognitive structure or thinking is seen to be operated through symbols instead of motor and sensory actions, yet his thinking at this stage is characterized as illogical and full of contradictions.

Concrete Operational Stage (about seven to eleven years)

This stage shows marked developments in the cognitive functioning of the child.

1. The child now learns to deal with concepts and ideas that exist only in mental terms. He can now think about things and figure out discrepancies and relationships.
2. He begins to think in terms of a set of interrelated principles rather than single bits of knowledge. As a result he can think in terms of systems.
3. His thinking becomes more logical and systematic. He can now make use of inductive and deductive approaches in terms of reasoning and arriving at conclusions.
4. The child now develops the ability to conserve both in terms of quantity and number of objects. He can now very well think that the change in appearance of an object does not alter either its quantity or its number.
5. The thinking of the child is no longer 'rigid' and 'irreversible'. A female child who has a sister now clearly realizes that her sister also has a sister.
6. The child now is no longer ego-centric in his thinking. He does not think of himself as the centre of the external world and does not perceive the world only from his own standpoint. He does not find it difficult to appreciate that other people have experiences, views and ideas that differ from his own.
7. The child now develops the abilities to deal adequately with classes. He can classify objects. He develops the ability of serialisation like arranging things from largest to smallest and vice versa. The number concept is also developed, but it all happens in a very simple concrete form.
8. The child now learns to carry out rather complex operations or tackle problems as long as they are concrete and not abstract. For example, the child now realizes the importance of cardinal numbers and ordinal numbers. He can operate symbolically by combining, reversing and forming associations among different objects.

In this way, the child reaches a satisfactory level in terms of intellectual development by his thinking becoming quite systematic and logical. However, what is done or thought by him at this stage is done purely on a concrete level. His thought processes are limited to real events observed or the actual objects operated by him. He is unable to think in abstract terms. In this way the concrete operation stage can actually be a pre-preparation for the final stage of formal operations mainly concerned with abstractions.

Formal Operation Stage (about 12 to 15 years)

The intellectual development and functioning takes a very sophisticated shape at this stage as the child learns to deal with abstraction by logical thinking. Actually he learns to utilize the tool of symbolism as effectively as possible in the process of thought and problem solving. The child now gets interested in forms. He begins to construct relationships between concrete operations and between symbols. Generalizations and framing of rules by operating in abstract terms become quite possible at this stage. The child now begins to appreciate that some hypothetical problems can be solved mentally by applying the same rules as would be applied to concrete problems. He begins to look at problems in many ways and explore various solutions but in a very systematic and logical way. For example, if a child of this stage is shown five colourless, odourless liquids in test tubes and is asked to find out what combination of the five will produce a brown liquid, he is likely to discover the possible combination by adopting a systematic approach, *e.g.*, combining the first and second, then first and third, then first and fourth and so on. Thus, it is quite distinctive in comparison to the children belonging to earlier stages of cognitive development who will simply resort to trial and error for finding the solution.

Moreover, the child's thinking at this stage does not remain only concrete but becomes hypothetical, with considerations given to the most unusual ideas. Hence, the creative aspects in the child are very much visible during this age not only in terms of concrete operations but also in terms of abstraction and pure imagination. For example, previous to this stage, if we were to ask a child to imagine he has three fathers, he might reply that it is no use imaging such a thing as one can only have one father. However, in the formal operational stage such thoughts involving unusual ideas are possible. Here one can imagine figures and shapes and can fly in the air without wings as is often done by children when studying poetry, algebra and geometry.

The other noticeable characteristic of this stage, as Piaget found, was the child's interest in dealing with things that do not exist in reality instead of the things concerning the present which are actually perceived by him.

In fact, Piaget was of the opinion that the thought processes and the intellectual functioning of a child at the formal operational period reflect the beginning of the most advanced stage in the functioning of his cognitive system. It provides a ladder to reach the limits of a person's intellectual development and actualize his potentiality to the maximum in the available circumstances. The high order of intellectual functioning developed through this stage, according to Piaget, is usually characterized by the presence of the most sophisticated cognitive abilities like the ability to (a) build up multiple hypotheses and a number of alternate solutions; (b) verify all possible solutions in a systematic and logical way; (c) generalize and arrive at abstract rules that cover many specific situations.

In this way, according to Piaget, after the expiry of the formal operation stage the child may reach full intellectual potential. He may discover the solutions of problems through mental manipulation of symbols by adopting a logical and systematic procedure known as scientific thinking and problem solving rather than a reflexive, motor or sensory manipulation as is done at the sensory motor stage; or by exposing his thinking operationally in more concrete terms as done at the concrete operation stage. It thus represents a stage which helps the child to attain mental maturity with respect to the development of his cognitive abilities.

Critical Evaluation of Piaget's Theory

Piaget's theory on intellectual development has been questioned and challenged on the following grounds:

1. Piaget's views on the pattern of intellectual development are not as uniform and universal as claimed by him. He based his theory on detailed observations of European children as they grew up in 1920s, 1930s and 1940s. The subsequent researches in Europe and outside have demonstrated significant deviations from the chronological ages linked with different stages of intellectual development by Piaget.

2. The Piagetian view that thinking proceeds in distinct stages has also been seriously challenged. It has been found that cognitive performance at particular ages is usually very inconsistent.

3. Piaget's claim that children below the age of concrete operations are incapable of logical thinking and are egocentric, has been refuted by a number of research studies. It has been established that children are able to both think logically and show sensitivity and concern for the feelings and viewpoints of others at very early ages.

4. The claim that a child is unable to perform an intellectual task like conservation at ages below those specified by Piaget has also been questioned. A number of studies have shown that it is possible to train children to carry out not only tasks like conservation but also very typical complex formal operations at ages below those specified by Piaget.

5. Piaget has linked biological maturation with the development of cognitive abilities and thus made a certain stage of maturation necessary for learning the cognitive task related to that maturation age. He is thus often blamed for being a pure nativist who gives singular importance to biological maturation for the intellectual development of the child. However, this criticism is one-sided, as Piaget believes that maturation works only as the

framework for intellectual development and the necessary material and means are supplied by one's physical and social environment. His stand on this issue may become quite clear through the following assertion of Inhelder and Piaget (1958):

> *"The maturation of the nervous system can do not more than determine the totality of possibilities and impossibilities at a given stage. A particular social environment remains indispensable for the realization of these possibilities. It follows that their realization can be accelerated or retarded as a function of cultural and educational conditions."*

If we examine the nature of the criticism levelled against Piaget's theory we find that most of it is one-sided. For example, as is clear from the above quotation, it is not true that Piaget's theory does not take the environmental experiences into account. Similarly, we can visualize that, while laying down different stages of cognitive development, Piaget does not mean that all children belonging to all cultures essentially pass through these stages in the chronological periods specified by him. As he gives due recognition to the forces of biological inheritance, maturation and environmental experiences in the formation and functioning of one's cognitive structure, the possibility in terms of variation in ages for reaching a particular stage of intellectual development cannot be ruled out. Consequently, the actual age at which certain types of mental abilities appear varies from child to child or from culture to culture. Irrespective of this acknowledgement linked with the individual differences with regard to intellectual development, the contribution of Piaget's theory can never be underrated. Whatever points we may raise against the universality and validity of his theory, it would always be remembered that intellectual development involves stages as specified by Piaget and occurs in the same order irrespective of the individual and environmental differences or geographical and cultural barriers.

Appreciation and Contribution to Education

Piaget, an acknowledged international authority in the field of child psychology and cognitive development, has contributed a great deal to the theory and practice of education. His contributions may be briefly summarized as follows:

1. Piaget interpreted and defined intelligence in a practical way. From birth onwards, the individual has to struggle for survival and seek adjustment with his environment. Intelligence in terms of his cognitive structure and its functioning helps him in this task. Therefore, the intelligence of an individual can only be assessed in terms of the nature of adjustment (balance between him and his environment) he is making at a particular time under the prevailing circumstances. This means that one's intelligence is a dynamic function. It really has some purposes or functions and it is these functions that help us to measure the intelligence of a person.

Interpreting intelligence in this way has led to intelligence tests being devised with emphasis on the mechanism of adaptation on the one hand, and maintenance of the balance between abilities and environmental demands for the development and welfare of the child on the other.

2. Piaget's theory has highlighted the importance of drives and motivation in the field of learning and development. It has utilized the concept of equilibration for this purpose by defining it as the continuous drive towards equilibrium or balance between the organism and its environment. Piaget's equilibration can be equated with Freud's sex gratification and Jung's self-actualization for activating one's behaviour.

3. Piaget's theory provides valuable information and advice on curriculum planning and structuring the schemes of studies. Since children of a particular region tend to reach a particular stage in their intellectual development at a particular age, what is to be planned in terms of their curriculum or scheme of studies must always be in tune with the expected level of their maturation and mental abilities. In other words, an ideal curriculum should provide the appropriate experiences at the proper time. For example, it is no use teaching world geography to students studying in first or second standard because at that age they have not yet acquired the necessary concepts like country, stage, or even city. Therefore, it is more appropriate to teach them local geography such as their neighbourhood, school, classroom and so on. Similarly, teaching algebra to the students of fourth or fifth standard is pointless as children of this age may not have acquired the ability to deal with abstractions. Piaget's theory may help in this direction by providing a suitable framework of the learning experiences in view of the cognitive development of the children and the needs of society.

4. The knowledge of Piaget's theory may prove quite valuable to teachers and parents for making them aware of the nature of the thought processes of the children at a particular level of maturation or chronological age. They may also get some idea of the changes that take place in the cognitive structure and functioning of their children. This type of knowledge may prove quite beneficial to them in dealing with the children and planning their training and education.

5. The major contribution of Piaget's theory is its analysis and suggestion of the optimal conditions for an individual's learning and development by introducing the concept of assimilation, accommodation and equilibration. According to Piaget, learning and development are the net result of interaction between a person's cognitive structure and his environmental experiences. For optimal learning to take place, the experiences or information presented must be of such a form and nature that it can be assimilated into the present cognitive structures, but at the same time different enough to necessitate a change in those structures calling for accommodation and resulting in new learning. Consequently, if the new

information or learning is completely unrelated to previous learning, it will certainly not fit in with the present cognitive structure and so would not be understood. On the other hand, if it is too simple or unchallenging, it will be completely assimilated and hardly any need for further learning will arise. Therefore, according to Piaget's theory, for acquiring learning it is essential that experiences or material presented to the learner are somewhat new and moderately challenging to initiate the phenomenon of accommodation but at the same time these experiences should be sufficiently linked and related with one's old learning so that they may be reasonably easy for being assimilated and understood by the learner.

6. Since the Piagetian theory considers both physical and social experiences as quite indispensable for one's intellectual development, it has placed a major responsibility on parents, teachers and others directly or indirectly connected with the education and welfare of children to arrange for the most appropriate and stimulating environment for their children.

7. Piaget's theory may be said to have the following implications vis-a-vis the children of nursery and elementary school:

(a) Since the children of this age are able to think only in concrete terms, it is advisable to allow them to experiment with materials in order to accommodate new understanding and to acquire new learning by themselves. For instance, to give the idea of the fractions 1 / 4, it would be best to cut an apple into four equal parts and then show one piece physically to show that the meaning of the fraction 1 / 4 is 'one out of four parts'.

(b) The teacher must try to emphasize discovery learning rather than teaching or telling each and every part of information to the students. They should try to set up environments in which the students can have a wide variety of experiences for self or discovery-learning.

8. Piagetian theory conveys that symbolic thinking adopted by children in their thought process after the sensory motor stage is not limited to the use of language only. There may be children who prefer to use images, relationships and other symbols instead of language as a tool for their thinking and may make better progress in terms of further learning and cognitive advancement. Therefore, the teaching-learning process should not be limited to the use of verbal communication, but should involve other symbolic expression and means for the communication of ideas suited to the circumstances and nature of the learner.

9. The last but not the least contribution of Piagetian theory is its emphasis on the individualization of education. It has advocated the need of child-centred education by saying that the educational experiences must be built around the learner's cognitive structure. What is suitable, appropriate and challenging to his cognitive structure must be given for him to acquire new experiences and develop his cognitive abilities. Since cognitive structures are sure to vary from child to child, in providing education, we have to think in terms of tailoring the educational material according to

each child's cognitive structure. For this purpose the teacher has to know the level of functioning of each student's cognitive structure and then plan for his further learning and cognitive development accordingly.

B. Erickson's Theory of Psycho-social Development

Eric Erikson was a native of Germany. He spent his early adult years studying art and travelling around Europe. A meeting with the famous psychoanalyst Sigmund Freud in Vienna led to an invitation from Freud to study psychoanalysis. It was a turning point of his career. He emigrated to America for this purpose and also to escape from the threat of Hitler. In America, he studied Native American traditions of human development and continued his work as a psychoanalyst. In 1950, he brought out his psycho-social theory — a developmental theory of the Eight stages of Man covering the entire life span rather than childhood and adolescent development like all other theories of development.

Introducing his theory, Erickson postulated that the development of an individual is the result of his interaction with his social environment. Right from his birth, his social development puts him under specific pressures or conflicts (called crises) by making specific demands at different ages or developmental stages of his life. The individual tries to meet these specific demands or resolve the crises by reacting psychologically in his own way, depending upon his circumstances. The complexity of the demands from society or social environment goes on increasing as the child advances on the ladder of growth and development. So, at each stage of his development, the child faces a new crisis, *i.e.* an issue that needs to be resolved at that particular stage of development. The way in which the 'crisis' of each stage is resolved has a major bearing on the development of one's personality which in turn is reflected as the positive and negative aspect of one's behaviour. Erickson discovered eight such issues or crises of life arising at different ages or periods of one's development and linked them with the eight stages of one's psycho-social development covering one's entire life span as outlined in Table 3.1.

Table 3.1: Age Span for the Stages of Psycho-social Development

Stage of Psycho-social Development	*Specific Age or Period*
Trust vs. Mistrust	Birth to 1½ years
Autonomy vs. Shame and Doubt	1½ years to 3 years
Initiative vs. Guilt	3 to 6 years
Industry vs. Inferiority	6 to 12 years
Identity vs. Role Confusion	Adolescence (12 to 20 years)
Intimacy vs. Isolation	Early adulthood (20 to 45 years)
Generativity vs. Stagnation	Middle adulthood (45 to 65 years)
Ego integrity vs. Despair	Later adulthood (65 years onwards)

The above division outlines the types of crises that need to be resolved at particular stages or periods of one's life. It also identifies the different stages of psycho-social development, *i.e.* the personality traits that are likely to develop at a particular stage. For example, one may go on acquiring positive traits like trust, independence, initiative, industry and identity, etc., to develop into a meaningful personality. On the other hand, one can develop into a troublesome, confused and doomed personality by failing to successfully resolve the crisis of one's age and developing negative traits like mistrust, shame, doubt, guilt feeling, inferiority and the like. Since these behaviour traits, modes of adjustment or psychological build-up are acquired through one's active interaction with the social environment, the stages of development are referred to as psycho-social development. These different stages of psycho-social development should not be considered to begin suddenly or end abruptly. In fact, one stage evolves into another through the whole life cycle and the crisis of issues not resolved during one stage is supposed to carry over into the stages that follow in one way or the other as revealed through the following discussion:

Stage I: The period of trust vs. mistrust (Birth to 1½ years)

In the first one and a half years of life, the infant is confronted with the crisis termed *trust* vs. *mistrust.* During this period the baby is completely dependent upon its mother or caretaker for the satisfaction of its needs. The way it is nourished, handled, protected and kept safe and comfortable at this stage may provide the baby with a sense of security or insecurity, a feeling of trust or mistrust in the mother or caretaker and ultimately in its surroundings. The sense of trust or mistrust with regard to the environment gained in this way at this stage of development may then be carried over to the stages of development to follow and consequently reflected in the developing personality.

Stage II: The period of autonomy vs. shame and doubt (1½ to 3 years)

Having gained a primary sense of trust and security with regard to his environment, in the second and third years of his life, the child now passes through the second stage of psycho-social development. With the newly developed motor or physical skills and language ability, the child now engages in exploring his environment and experimenting with his strengths and limitations for achieving a sense of autonomy and independence. The child now needs proper safety measures against the risks involved in activities like walking, running, pulling, and handling the objects of his environment or in terms of learning undesirable language but this does not mean that he should be denied a reasonable degree of freedom to acquire a sense of independence. Within the bounds of safety, he must be provided adequate opportunities for the acquisition of a sense of autonomy and knowledge about his limitations.

Children who are denied the opportunity to develop a sense of independence by over-protective, harsh or restrictive parents begin to doubt their ability and ultimately begin to feel embarrassed or ashamed in the presence of others. However, the development of the sense of doubt and shame within reasonable limits is not harmful. A healthy sense of doubt helps the child to set his own limits and the development of shame helps him to develop a sense of right and wrong. Therefore, at this stage of psycho-social development, the child needs to be helped in striking a balance between the conflicting needs of his social environment to acquire a sense of autonomy and develop a sense of doubt and shame for the adequate development of his personality.

Stage III: The period of initiative vs. guilt (3 to 6 years)

The third stage of psycho-social development between three to six years of age is characterized by the crisis of initiative versus guilt. Equipped with the sense of trust and autonomy the child now begins to take initiative in interacting with his environment. He asks questions about each and everything, explores his environment ceaselessly, and engages in planning and carrying out activities of various kinds. The extent to which the initiative for carrying out physical and mental exploration is encouraged or discouraged by the parents and the available social environment, goes a long way in developing ability in the child to initiate plan and carry out these activities in later life.

In case the child is discouraged from taking the initiative by his parents and guardians not having faith in him, or is pulled down by unhealthy criticism, punishment or rebuke for minor failures, the child is sure to develop a sense of guilt leading to hesitation, indecision and lack of initiative in planning and carrying out his life activities. Although in case of failure he feels a reasonable amount of guilt for having failed to take the initiative at the right time or made mistakes in planning and carrying out his activities, this enables him to learn from his failures. However, to allow this to develop into a guilty conscience is harmful to the development of the child's personality. Therefore, there is a need to resolve the crisis of *initiative* vs. *guilt* at this stage of psycho-social development and it can be properly done if we allow the child to experiment with his initiative by properly supervising and guiding his activities and encouraging him to develop a habit of self-evaluation of the results of his initiative.

Stage IV: Period of industry vs. inferiority (6 to 12 years)

Generally, by this age children begin to attend to school where they are made to learn various skills and the teachers as well as the school environment generate pressures on them to work hard in order to perform well. Parents also now begin to make demands upon the children to lend their hand with household duties or in some cases saddle them with occupational responsibilities. They also have to compete with their peers in terms of competence and productivity in school and other social situation. Now, in case the child performs well in school, home or in other social environments or is admired for his intellectual or motor pursuits he will be likely to develop a sense of industry filled with a sense of achievement. Such a child will consequently be motivated to work harder and achieve more in terms of competency and productivity. On the other hand, if his performance remains inferior to that of his peers or he does not satisfy his teachers and parents with his performance, he may begin to look down upon himself and develop a sense of inferiority.

The teachers and the school environment thus play a very significant role in helping the child out of the industry versus inferiority crisis. For the child, the school becomes the place where success and failure are defined. Therefore, it is the duty of the teachers and school authorities to structure their classroom and school environment in such a way as to help the students to maintain a positive attitude and view themselves as capable and valuable individuals.

Stage V: The period of identity vs. role confusion (12 to 19 years)

This stage, beginning with the advent of puberty, is marked with the crisis of *identity* vs. *role* confusion. Equipped with the sense of trust, autonomy, initiative and industry, adolescents begin to search for their own personal identity. The sudden changes in their bodies and mental functioning and the altered demands of society compel them to ask questions of themselves like, who am I? What have I become? Am I the same person I used to be? What am I supposed to do and in which manner am I to behave?

Erickson asserts that at this stage, the adolescent's search by questioning and redefining his own socio psychological identity established during earlier stages is definitely linked with (a) his sudden and rapid bodily changes, and (b) anxiety and pressures related to this need to make decisions about his future education and career. Consequently, the adolescent tries to search for his new role and identity. He experiments with various sexual, occupational and educational roles to understand who he is and what he can be.

The extent to which an individual is able to develop a sense of identity will depend upon the degree of success he achieves in resolving the crisis related to all the previous stages. Failure in resolving the crises of those periods would be likely, at this stage, to result in role confusion and consequently the individual will not be able to find himself. He may then feel completely bewildered, not knowing what to do and how to behave on his own. He may be unable to make the decision about his educational or professional career or about making friends. The lack of self-identification and role confusion may also lead to over identification with villains and clowns, showing a type of childish and impulsive behaviour or developing conformity in taste and style and intolerance of others. On the other hand, if the psycho-social development of the adolescent results in his achieving a sense of identity, it will result in the individual of the adolescent results in his achieving a sense of identity, it will result in the individual developing the required confidence in his ability to do things, make him properly balanced in terms of emotional reactions and will place him in harmony with his environment.

Teachers and parents can play a very constructive role in helping adolescents through this identity versus confusion crisis. The adolescents, craving for identity must be fully recognized and it should be clearly understood that adolescents want to be identified as adults and must, therefore, be treated as such and not as children as many teachers and parents tend to do. They should never be belittled or humiliated in front of their peers or anyone else for that matter. They must be assigned responsibilities independently or collectively and be trusted for their promises and conduct.

Stage VI: The period of intimacy vs. isolation (20 to 45 years)

This is the sixth stage of psycho-social development, and spans the years of early adulthood. During this stage the individual tends to develop a sense of intimacy or commitment to a close relationship with another person.

Throwing light on this aspect Erickson (1950), writes:

> *Thus the young adult, emerging from the search for and the insistence on identity, is eager and willing to fuse his identity with that of others. He is ready for intimacy, that is, the capacity to commit himself to concrete affiliations and partnerships and to develop the ethical strength to abide by such commitments even though they may call for significant sacrifices and compromises*

Thus, during this stage, the individual seeks to form close personal attachments by merging his identity with that of another person. The relationships develop into such a close involvement that he tends to risk even the loss of his ego or image as is evidenced in the harmonious relationships between husband and wife and intimate friends, and in the ideal relationship between a teacher and his pupil. The ultimate sense of intimacy is clearly visible in terms of the mutual identity experienced at the time of simultaneous organs in sexual intercourse with a loved partner of the opposite sex. Another form of such intimacy is seen in sacrifices made for one's close friends or for members of one's family.

The opposite of intimacy is isolation. When one fails to develop an adequate sense of intimacy by merging one's identity with that of another person or when relations deteriorate for one reason or another, one tends to develop a sense of isolation — a pulling away from relationships and breaking off of ties. Alternatives have to be developed for intimate relationships. It is essential to maintain equilibrium in such cases as the deviation from or denial of intimate relationships is costly in terms of a normal and happy life. This does not mean, however, that isolation is altogether undesirable or harmful. A certain degree of isolation is crucial to the maintenance of one's individuality and the development of one's personality in the desired direction, but if it exceeds certain limits, it may become a serious handicap to the establishment and maintenance of close ties and may lead to loneliness and self-absorption. The crisis of *intimacy* vs. *isolation* needs to be resolved by striking a balance between the two contradictory needs — the need for intimacy and the need to maintain one's individuality. The degree to which one succeeds in resolving this crisis is said to secure one's adjustment with one's self and the world one lives in.

Stage VII: The period of creativity vs. stagnation
(Middle adulthood — 45 to 65 years)

An individual's life up to this stage is taken up with trying to establish himself in a professional career. Now, he needs to satisfy his need for generativity, a concern to establish and guide the next generation. This is realized through nurturing his own children, guiding and directing other young people and by engaging in some kind of creative, productive or fruitful activity that may prove beneficial to society. Instead of caring only for himself or for those in his family or friends who are close to him, he participates in the welfare of the future generation as represented by his own children, pupils, subordinates and young people in general. This is, in fact, an effort at extension of one's self and its merger with self or others in society.

As opposed to the sense of generativity, there is a tendency on the part of the individual to become egoistic and selfish. This leads to stagnation and personal impoverishment. Although it would be quite natural to pause in one's life's work to reflect upon, evaluate and consolidate one's achievements and to regroup one's energies for future productivity, an excess of this habit may result in self-indulgence and psychological invalidism. A balanced adjustment between the extremes of the need for generativity and the need for inactivity is thus required so that in the time of inactivity one may become more energetic and be able to put renewed efforts into rendering service to society and future generation.

Stage VIII: The period of ego-integrity vs. despair
(Old age, about 65 onwards)

This stage of psycho-social development is associated with later adulthood or old age. Although the precise commencement of old age cannot be determined because some people remain physically and mentally active well into their eighties and nineties, others feel, look and act old even in their fifties, yet biologically speaking, old age may be said to begin when people cease to reproduce.

During this last stage of psycho-social development one is confronted with the final crisis of one's life span, termed *ego-integrity* vs. *despair*. Ego-integrity refers to the integration or culmination of the successful resolution of all the seven previous crises in the course of one's life. The successful resolution of the previous crises provides a sense of fulfilment and satisfaction to one's ego. When one reflects on one's past and feels satisfied over what has been done, one is sure to develop a positive outlook about oneself and the world around. A person with a developed sense of ego-integrity is at peace with the life he has lived and has no major regrets over what could have been or for what should have been done differently. On the other hand, persons who have not been able to successfully resolve the previous crises of the developmental stages are sure to feel differently. They look back on their lives with despair and feel dissatisfied with the way they have lived their lives. The thought that they now have no time left for changing the course of their lives and doing what should have been done, makes them feel miserable and, consequently, they are doomed to develop a deep sense of despair. These people can become desperately afraid of death. On the other hand, people who have no regrets for the way their lives have been lived and who have an admiration or love for their ego are easily able to accept the inevitability of their death and live life as fully as they can till their last breath.

At the same time, despair is not the absolute negative aspect of one's personality. To feel satisfied or dissatisfied about one or the other issue is common and natural. One may regret many mistakes and deficiencies of one's life, but this should not be stretched to the point where one develops a sense of disaffection with one's ego and begins to hate oneself and then sink into a state of utter depression. It is, therefore, essential to strike a balance between the conflicting needs of ego-integrity and despair and to successfully resolve the final crisis of one's life resulting in a well-balanced optimistic outlook for oneself and the outside world in order to live the remaining days of one's life as gracefully and productively as possible.

In a summarised form, Erickson's stages of psycho-social development covering entire life span of an individual may be represented in the manner given ahead.

Table 3.2: Erickson's Stage of Psycho-social Development along with the Needs and Expectations from the Individual

Stages of Psycho-social Development	*The Person and Specific Age*	*Needs and Expectations*
1. Trust vs. Mistrust	Infant (Birth to 1½ years)	Needs maximum comfort with minimal uncertainty to trust himself / herself, others, and the environment
2. Autonomy vs. Shame and Doubt	Toddler (1½ years to 3 years)	Works to master physical environment while maintaining self-esteem
3. Initiative vs. Guilt	Pre-schooler (3 years to 6 years)	Begins to initiate, not imitate, activities; develops conscience and sexual identity

(Contd.)

Stages of Psycho-social Development	*The Person and Specific Age*	*Needs and Expectations*
4. Industry vs. Inferiority	School age child (6 years to 12 years)	Tries to develop a sense of self worth by refining skills
5. Identity vs. Role confusion	Adolescent (12 to 20 years)	Tries integrating many roles (child, sibling, student, athlete, worker) into a self-image under role model and peer pressure
6. Intimacy vs. Isolation	Young Adult (20 years to 45 years)	Learns to make personal commitment to another as spouse, parent or partner
7. Generativity vs. Stagnation	Middle Age Adult (45 to 65 years)	Seeks satisfaction through productivity in career, family, and civic interests
8. Integrity vs. Despair	Older Adult (65 years onwards)	Reviews life accomplishments, deals with loss and preparation for death

Kohlberg's Theory of Moral Development

Lawrence Kohlberg a psychologist belonging to the University of Harvard, was born in 1927, grew up in Bronxville, New York. In his later student career, he stayed on at Chicago for graduate work in psychology, at first thinking he would become a clinical psychologist. However, he soon became interested in Piaget and began interviewing children and adolescents on moral issues as an extension of the Piaget's work on children's moral reasoning and development. As a result of his study he got success in putting forward a theory of the development of moral judgement. The sample of his study consisted of hundreds of children belonging to different ages of childhood and adolescence from different family set ups, cultures and countries.

In his concept of morality, and moral judgement it may be seen that he differs from the popular view that children imbibe the sense and methods of moral judgement from their parents and elders by way of learning. According to him *as soon as we talk with children about morality, we find that they have many ways of making judgements which are not internalized from the outside, and which do not come in any direct and obvious way from parents, teachers and even peers* (Kohlberg, 1968). Going further he clarified that internal or cognitive processes like thinking and reasoning also play a major role in one's moral development, *i.e.* the way children make moral judgement depends on their level of intellectual development as well as on their upbringing and learning experiences.

For studying the process of moral development in human beings, Kohlberg first defined *moral development as the development of an individual's sense of justice.* For estimating one's sense of justice he concentrated on one's views on morality with the help of a test of moral judgement consisting of a set of moral dilemmas. For instance, should a man who cannot afford the medicine of his dying wife needs, steal it? Should a doctor mercy-kill a fatally ill person suffering terrible pain? Is it better to save the life of one important person or a lot of unimportant persons? For the purpose of creating interest among the children he interviewed, he tried to put before them these moral dilemmas in the form of story or narrative descriptions like below.

Heinz Steals the Drug

In Europe, a woman was near death from a special kind of cancer. There was one drug that the doctors thought might save her. It was a form of radium that a druggist in the same town had recently discovered. The drug was expensive to make, but the druggist was charging ten times what the drug cost him to make. He paid $200 for the radium and charged $2,000 for a small dose of the drug. The sick woman's husband, Heinz, went to everyone he knew to borrow the money, but he could only get together about $1,000 which is half of what it cost. He told the druggist that his wife was dying and asked him to sell it cheaper or let him pay later. But the druggist said: "No, I discovered the drug and I'm going to make money from it." So Heinz got desperate and broke into the man's store to steal the drug-for his wife. Should the husband have done that? (Kohlberg, 1963, p. 19)

After putting such dilemma before the subject, he persuaded him to respond. However, Kohlberg was not really interested in whether the subject says "yes" or "no" to this dilemma, he wanted to know the reasoning behind the answer that can reflect his level of moral reasoning needed to assess the subject's level of moral development. For this purpose, he went ahead to put the question like "Why do you think Heinz should or should not have stolen the drug?" For further probing he planned to ask questions like "Do you think that Heinz had a right to steal the drug?" "Was he violating the druggist rights?" "What sentence the judge should give Heinz, once he was caught?" In this way, many of such questions were there with Kohlberg for finding out the reasoning behind his subject's answers.

Finally with the help of the analysis of the responses Kohlberg got from his subjects, he came to the conclusion that like the Piagetian stages of cognitive development, there also exist universal stages in the development of moral values, and the movement from one stage to another depends on cognitive abilities rather than the simple acquisition of moral values of one's parents, elders and peers. He then identified three levels of moral development, each containing two stages as shown in Table 3.3.

Table 3.3: Kohlberg's Three Levels and Six Stages of Moral Development

Level I	**Pre-moral or Pre-conventional Morality (Age 4 to 10 years)**
Stage 1:	The stage of obedience for avoiding punishment
Stage 2:	The stage of conforming to obtain rewards and favours in return
Level II	**Conventional morality (Age 10 to 13 years)**
Stage 3:	Good Interpersonal relationships (The stage of maintaining mutual relations and approval of others)
Stage 4:	Maintaining social order (The stage of obedience for avoiding censure by higher authority or social systems)
Level III	**Post-conventional morality involving self accepted moral principles (Age 13 or not until middle or later adulthood or never)**
Stage 5:	Social contract (Stage of conforming to the democratically accepted laws and mores of community welfare)
Stage 6:	Universe ethical principle (Stage of conforming to the universal ethical principles and the call of one's conscience)

Let us now briefly discuss these levels and stages of morality.

Level I. Pre-moral or Pre-conventional Morality (4-10 years)

At this level, the child begins to make judgements about what is right or wrong, good or bad. However, the standards by which he measures the morality are those of others. He is persuaded to take such judgements either to avoid punishment or to earn rewards. Development of morality at this level usually follows the following two stages:

Stage 1. Obedience and Punishment Orientation

In the beginning, the child's morality is controlled by the fear of punishment. He tries to obey his parents and elders purely to avoid reproof and punishment. Actually the Kohlberg's Stage 1 resembles the Piaget's first stage (Heteronymous Stage of morality) of moral reasoning. The child assumes that powerful authorities hand down a fixed set of rules which he or she must unquestioningly obey. To the Heinz dilemma, the child typically says that Heinz was wrong to steal the drug because "It's against the law", or "It's bad to steal", as if this were all there were to it. When asked to elaborate, the child usually responds in terms of the consequences involved, explaining that stealing is bad "because you'll get punished" (Kohlberg, 1958).

Stage 2. Individualism and Exchange

At this stage of the moral development children begin to recognize that there is not just one right view that is handed down by the authorities. Different individuals have different viewpoints. "Heinz," they might point out, "might think it's right to take the drug, the druggist would not." Since everything is *relative,* each person is free to pursue his or her *individual* interests. One boy said that Heinz might steal the drug if he wanted his wife to live, but that he doesn't have to if he wants to marry someone younger and better-looking (Kohlberg, 1963, p. 24).

In this way, the second stage of the pre-moral or pre-conventional level, children's moral judgement is based on self-interest and considerations of what others can do for them in exchange or return. Here they value a thing because it has some practical utility for them. They obey the orders of their parents and elders and abide by some rules and regulations, because it serves their interests.

Level II. Conventional Morality (10-13 years)

At this level of moral development also, children's moral judgement is controlled by the likes and dislikes of others — the conventions, rules and regulations and the law and order system maintained within society. Stealing or mercy-killing would thus be judged wrong because it is considered wrong by society at large and by the legal system. In this way, the conventional level of morality may be regarded as the level where the child identifies with authority. It is characterized by the following two stages:

Stage 3. Good Interpersonal Relationships

In the early years of the second level of moral development, the child's moral judgement is based on the desire to obtain approval of others and avoid being disliked by being declared a good boy or a good girl. For this purpose he begins to judge the intentions and likes or dislikes of others and acts accordingly. As concluded by Kohlberg, children of this stage of moral development believe that children should live up to the expectations of the family and community and behave in "good" ways like a good boy or good girl. Accordingly as Kohlberg discovered many of his subjects argued that Heinz was right to steal the drug because "He was a good man for saving the life of his wife simply because no husband would have sit back and watched his wife die." As example, Kohlberg quotes the response given by his subject Don (aged 13 years) as below.

> *It was really the druggist's fault, he was unfair, trying to overcharge and letting someone die. Heinz loved his wife and wanted to save her. I think anyone would. I don't think they would put him in jail. The judge would look at all sides, and see that the druggist was charging too much. (Kohlberg, 1963, p. 25).*

Kohlberg concluded from such responses of his subjects that by responding in such a way, they were demonstrating the level of their conventional morality because it assumes that the attitude expressed would be shared conventionally by the entire community — "anyone" would be right to do what Heinz did.

In case we try to find similarities and dissimilarities between the Piaget's theory of moral development and Kohlberg's theory of moral development, we can fairly analyze that there lies substantial similarities between Kohlberg's first three stages and Piaget's two stages being covered during the entire period of childhood. In both the developmental theories, we may observe the similar sequence characterized with a shift from unquestioning obedience to a relativistic outlook and to a concern for good intention on the part of wrong doers. The difference lies in the fact where in Kohlberg's theory these shifts occur in three stages rather than two as emphasized in Piaget's theory of moral development.

Stage 4. Maintaining the Social Order

According to Kohlberg, Stage 3 reasoning works best in two-person relationships with family members or close friends, where one can make a real effort to get to know the other's feelings and needs and try to help. At Stage 4, in contrast, the respondent becomes more broadly concerned with *society as a whole.* Now the emphasis is on obeying laws, respecting authority, and performing one's duties so that the social order is maintained. In support of his conclusion Kohlberg again cites the responses of his subjects to the Heinz story. Many of his subjects were found to utter that they understand that Heinz's intention or motive was good but they cannot condon the theft. What would happen if all of us started breaking the laws whenever we felt we had a good reason? The result would be Chaos; society could not function.

In this way the children reaching the moral Stage 4, begin to take moral decisions from the perspective of the society as a whole. At this stage children's moral behaviour and judgements are governed by conventions as well as the laws and mores of the social system. The standards of others are now so established that it becomes a convention to follow them. The children now follow the rules and regulations of society and take decisions about things being right or wrong with a view to avoiding censure by the elders, authorities or the social system.

Level III. Post Conventional Morality Involving Self-accepted Moral Principles (Age 13 and afterwards)

This marks the highest level of attainment of true morality as the controlling force for making judgements now rests with the individual himself. He does not value a thing or conform to an idea merely because of consideration of the views of others, conventions or the law and order system of the society but because it fits onto the framework of his self-accepted moral principles. However, to reach this level is not an ordinary thing. One may be able to attain it in the beginning or middle of his adolescence or it may be postponed for him till the middle or later adulthood or he may never attain it in his life time. This highest level of moral development is also characterized by two separate stages as described below.

Stage 5. Social Contracts and Individual Rights

At Stage 5 as Kohlberg concludes, individuals begin to ask. "What makes for a good society?" They basically believe that a good society is best conceived as a social contract into which people freely enter to work toward the benefit for all. They recognize that all rational people would agree on two points (*i*) getting certain basic rights, such as liberty and life, to be protected, and (*ii*) needing some democratic procedures for changing unfair laws and for improving society. In support of his conclusion Kohlberg quotes the responses of his subjects to Heinz dilemma. Many of his respondents make it clear that they do not generally favour the breaking of laws; laws are social contracts that we agree to uphold until we can change them by democratic means. Nevertheless, his wife's right to live is a moral right that must be protected.

In this way, at this stage the individual's moral judgements are internalized in such a form that he responds positively to authority only if he agrees with the principles upon which the demands of authority are based. The individual at this stage begins to think in rational terms, valuing the rights of human beings and the welfare of society. For example, at this stage in reference to the rights of the human being, the decision about mercy-killing may be left to the individual who is suffering, and if so needed, the concerned laws may be amended for the welfare of society at large.

Stage 6. Universal Principles

This stage of moral development is the highest stage or perfection achieved in terms of moral reasoning and development of morality. In propagating his theory of moral development, Kohlberg believes that there must be a higher stage of moral development — as just conceived by him through his Stage 6 — which defines the principles by which we get the type of justice as conceived by the great moral leaders like Mahatma Gandhi and Martin Luther King. The principle of justice is universal and requires us to treat the claims of all parties in an impartial way, respecting the dignity of all people as individuals and humans. According to Kohlberg, we can reach this stage in case we begin to look at a situation purely through one another's eyes. Take the case of Heinz dilemma, reaching this stage would essentially require that all parties — the druggist, Heinz, and his wife — try to view the things from other perspectives for seeking justice and fair solution of the problem. As a result, in the end, they would all agree that the life of the wife must be saved by sacrificing the narrow interests related to money or conventional laws.

In this way at the Stage 6 of our moral development the controlling forces for making moral judgements are highly internalized. The decisions of the individual are now based upon his conscience and the belief in universal principles of respect, justice and equality. He does what he, as an individual thinks right regardless of legal restrictions or the opinion of others. Thus, at this stage people act according to the inner voice of their conscience provide evidence of sharing, helping and defending the victims of injustice and lead a life that they can without self-condemnation or feeling of guilt or shame.

From the above discussion of the Kohlberg's stages of moral development, it is clear that although children begin to think about morality in terms of justice or right and wrong at a very early age, yet they have to wait until adolescence or adulthood for the dawning of the stage of true morality. Also, it is not essential that all people pass through the third level of moral development. Most adults are not able to cross the second level and few can reach Stage 5, and among these there are very few who, being intellectually quite sound, can think rationally and base their moral judgement purely on the dictates of their conscience at the risk of life and property.

Evaluation of the Kohlberg's theory of Moral Development

Appreciation

Kohlberg's theory of Moral Development is appreciated on the following grounds:

1. Kohlberg is the first psychologist who tried to present a comprehensive stage theory of moral development by stating that the development of moral reasoning is characterized by a series of qualitative distinctive stages. He claimed that an individual progresses through them in order, without skipping any. Each of the Kohlberg's stage builds upon the foundation laid by earlier stages but reflects a more integrated and logical consistent set of moral beliefs than those before it (Ormond, 2003, p. 88).

2. Kohlberg's theory of moral development provided an unique description for explaining the progression to higher stages of our moral reasoning by taking into account Piaget's stage of cognitive thinking or logical reasoning. Kohlberg proposed that advanced moral reasoning (Post conventional reasoning) requires formal operational thought for abstract understanding of the purpose of the laws and rules to help society run smoothly (Kohlberg, 1976). Hence, the post conventional level of morality does not appear until adolescence (the concrete operational stage of their cognitive development). In this way, for the development of his theory of moral reasoning, Kohlberg tried to adopt the base provided through Piaget's stages of cognitive thinking. Consequently, it appears that development of moral reasoning and cognitive thinking travel side by side. However, in his theory of moral development while explaining advanced moral reasoning Kohlberg put up a different view. He asserted that progression to an advanced stage of cognitive development does not guarantee equivalent moral development. One may have a quite develop cognitive structure and functioning, but it is not essential that he must demonstrate the same higher level of his moral reasoning in tune with his higher cognitive development. It was thus a unique feature in the moral development theory of Kohlberg in its assertion that it is quite possible to be logical operational in logical reasoning but preconventional in moral reasoning implying that cognitive development is a necessary but insufficient condition for moral development to occur (Ormrod 2003, p. 90).

3. In addition to make use of the Piaget's stage of cognitive thinking or logical reasoning for building his sequential stages of moral reasoning, Kohlberg also tried to make use of Piaget's concept of disequilibrium as an instrument or explanation for the development of advanced moral reasoning among the children. As we know Piaget proposed that when a child is unable to assimilate the new learning, he experiences a state of disequilibrium, which makes him eager to expand his ways of thinking and reasoning to accommodate and learn the new thing. Following the foot step of Piaget, Kohlberg in his theory of moral development advocated that one progresses to a higher stage of moral development only when he faces disequilibrium by realizing that his beliefs about morality are unable to address the events and dilemma he is experiencing at present. In this way, Kohlberg theory of moral development produced a unique way of presenting certain problematic situations or dilemmas before the growing children for letting them experience disequilibrium and gradually restructure their thoughts about morality for moving to the subsequent higher stages of moral development.

4. Kohlberg's theory of moral development provided substantial weightage to the role of experience, modelling and social interaction in the development of morality among children. It emphasized that morality is a learned behaviour and moral reasoning is developed through successive stages with close interaction of child's individuality with his environment — particularly social and cultural.

5. The Kohlberg's theory of moral development has been able to suggest and expect from the individuals to demonstrate a higher stage of moral reasoning where they no longer accept their own society and existing rules but think reflectively and autonomously for bringing changes to make the society progress and humanity flourish. In this way, his theory may provide enough ground to work its way towards the thinking of the great men like Socrates, Martin Luther King and Mahatma Gandhi and thus inspiring us to proceed toward the challenging vision of our highest moral development.

Criticism

Kohlberg's theory of moral development has been the subject of criticism highlighting its fallacies as below:

1. An important limitation of Kohlberg's theory of moral development lies in the fact that it deals with moral reasoning rather than with moral behaviour. Many individuals at different stages of the moral development may be found to demonstrate similar type of moral behaviour and individuals at the same stages may behave morally in different ways. In practice, there may be a quite weak link, between moral reasoning and moral behaviour. A child may have reached a higher stage of moral reasoning as established by Kohlberg through the analysis of the responses to the presented moral dilemmas but it is not essential that he should also behave and demonstrate morality suitable to this moral stage. Thus, children might learn so many things about moral decisions or moral reasoning at various ages, but what they do may be another matter. Therefore, it can be

properly said that Kohlberg's theory is not able to provide a proper answer for the simultaneous development of moral reasoning and moral development across the various ages.

2. Kohlberg through his specific stages of moral development has tried to draw a line among the types of moral development reached by the individual at the different ages. In practice, however, the picture regarding such fixed pattern across the varying ages involving different individuals may not be so clear. An individual at one period of his life span may be found to demonstrate more than one type of morality — pre-conventional, conventional or post conventional depending upon the situation he faces for doing so. In this way, contrary to Kohlberg's assumption, moral behaviour is more context or situation oriented than the age specific moral development attained by the individuals.

3. Kohlberg's theory is also criticised on the ground that young children are probably more advanced in their moral reasoning then established by Kohlberg. Even pre-schoolers have some internal standards of right and wrong, regardless of what authority figures might tell them and regardless of what consequences certain behaviours may or may not bring (Smetana, 1981).

4. It is also said that Kohlberg's stages are culturally biased. It is argued that how stage model based on the Western philosophical model can be applied to non-western cultures without considering the extent to which they have different approaches and outlooks towards morality. It is also doubtful to apply this model to the moral developmental pattern found in the children belonging to traditional village and tribals cultures.

5. Carol Gilligan (1987), believes that Kohlberg; theory is sex biased as it does not adequately describe female moral development. Gilligan observes that Kohlberg's stages were derived exclusively from interviews with males and therefore reflect a decidedly male orientation. She charges that Kohlberg's stages focus on the issues of rights and rules, fairness and justice but omit other aspects of morality especially compassion and caring for those in need that are more characteristic of the moral reasoning and behaviour of females.

6. Kohlberg's concept of the post conventional morality has also been a subject of severe criticism. Kohlberg's has advocated for the morality of consciousness or autonomous thinking on the part of the individuals reaching the post-conventional level. Practically it is nothing but a sort of an open war with the established ethical codes and organized functioning of the society. If everybody acts according to the morality of his own, then certainly there will be a chaos. It is absolutely dangerous for people to place their own principles and ethics above society and the law. Moreover, everybody cannot be so worthwhile and selfless as the great thinkers and reformists like Martin Luther King or Mahatma Gandhi, therefore, it is unwise to preach and advocate for the development of such unbridled level

of consciousness and morality among the individuals.

7. Lastly, it can also be said that Kohlberg's theory of moral development is not so comprehensive as claimed to provide answers for all the moral dilemmas and thus is not able to guide our moral reasoning to face all the situations in our life without ambiguity and confusion. It has its weakness and limitations like other theories of development. Although Kohlberg claims that his Stage 6 of moral development is capable of equipping an individual with the decision making tools needed for the toughest moral dilemmas. However, in practice there may lie many issues that the principle of justice arrived at this stage frequently fail to resolve. One such issue may be abortion. Justice for whom and in what ways, is the issue that can hardly be resolved properly at the satisfaction of all the parties involved. The decision have to vary with the situation. In this way, the stages described in Kohlberg's theory are certainly not aimed for providing a ready made answer to the moral dilemmas. These represent particular mode or pattern of moral reasoning at the specific ages and thus can never be thought as universally applicable to provide solution to all types of moral issues raised in varying situations.

However, on the basis of the criticism, laid down above, it should not be assumed that Kohlberg's theory is to be discarded or it has little significance for understanding the mechanism of moral development among human beings. Despite the criticism, that there is no doubt that Kohlberg's accomplishment in bringing his theory of moral development is great. His theory offers valuable insights into the nature and development of moral reasoning among children and adolescents. He has not just expanded on Piaget's stages of moral judgement but has done so in a quite convincing and appropriate way by having a beautiful blend of individualistic and socialized trends of constructive approach for the development of moral reasoning on the part of human beings.

Educational Implications of Moral Development Theory

The moral development theory provided by Kohlberg has enough potential to direct and guide the way of teachers and parents for helping the children develop morally by highlighting some of the essential facts like below:

1. The moral development is essentially a learned phenomenon. As Kohlberg (1968) asserts the stages of moral development are not the product of maturation. The sequence related to development of moral reasoning do not simply unfold according to genetic blueprint. It is therefore much needed on the part of we elders that we should never blame heredity for the child's level of moral reasoning and moral development.

2. The child at his early years of development (infancy and early childhood till the age of 4 or 5 years) is neither moral or immoral but is essentially non-moral in the sense that he has no moral thinking regarding good or bad of an act. He may pick up the things belonging to others without feeling any need of asking or informing them about it simply due to

the reason that he feels nothing bad or wrong in doing so. Since no moral sense or reasoning lies with the children of this age, we elders should behave accordingly without blaming them for their act of disobedience, unsocial or antisocial behaviour as these children are quite ignorant about the goodness or wrongness of their behaviour.

3. The children belonging to Kohlberg's first three stage of moral development believes in the eternal nature of the rules and the authority of the elders. They want to obey their orders and rules without questioning their validity. Accordingly we elders must be quite cautious in putting rules and regulations before the children belonging to this age span. The rules once made should not be altered then and there. The children without any discrimination should be made to follow them. It is essential at this stage because, children have not attained enough mental maturity for deciding at their own that what is sight or wrong for them. It is in the interest of the children, their peers, parents, teachers and community as a whole that they should be made to observe the rules and regulation regarding their appropriate individual and social behaviour.

4. The children prior to their entry into the age of adolescence can only grasp the concrete ideas and form related to morality. At this stage, for them examples are always better then precept. In childhood, therefore, they should be presented with models of appropriate behaviour by the elders for being observed and imitated. The abstraction regarding moral reasoning or concept is out of reach to the children belonging to the development period of childhood. It is therefore futile to expect from them to talk about soul, the fruits of Karma, rudiments of religion and God, etc.

5. With the development of their intellectual abilities, older children belonging to adolescence stage now no longer believes in the eternity or non-changing pattern of the rules. They can't be expected to obey the elders and observe the set rules silently as happens in childhood. They need reason and satisfactory answer to their question "why". Therefore, we should be quite cautious in emphasizing about the rules and moral conduct at this stage. Rather making them follow the rules and ethical norms blindly, they should be told about the significance of such behaviour from the individual as well as social point of views. They should be allowed to ask questions and remove their doubts about the appropriateness and inappropriateness of their behaviour in practising morality at home, schools and other social situations. Discussion and debates on the moral issues should also be encouraged and children need to given opportunities as well as freedom to reason about the prevalent social and ethical norms for their better adoption in their lives.

6. The parents and teachers should also recognize the importance of the principle of reciprocity as believed by the individuals in their period of childhood. If you do good to others, others also behave with you nicely. Judging the impact of a bad act or foul saying on one's self may force the

children to behave in a proper way. If one thing is pinching them, it will do the same to others. Stimulating and encouraging such thinking and feelings on the part of children may help them to imbibe and practice good things.

7. Kohlberg strongly emphasizes that the goal of moral education is to encourage and help the individuals to develop to the next stage of moral reasoning and morality. According to him the most common tool for doing this is to present a "moral dilemma" for making the child confronted with a situation involving his moral reasoning and judgement. The child may adopt view, characterizing his developmental age but may not be able to resolve the moral dilemma, he may then be forced to adopt the moral reasoning belonging to the next stage of moral development. Kohlberg's device of inducing conflict, resembles equilibration model emphasized by Piaget. When a new thing does not fit into the existing cognitive structure through assimilation, one has to go for the due enlargement of his cognitive structure for doing away with the state of disequilibrium. In this way, both the moral development theories (given by Piaget and Kohlberg), urge to adopt a cognitive conflict inducing approach for helping the child to move further on the higher stages of his moral development. In this method, teachers are urged to lead discussion groups in which children have a chance to grapple actively with moral issues. For the proper inducement of cognitive conflict, it is well cared to encourage arguments that belong to one stage above those of most of the class. Since students do not find sufficient, the level of moral reasoning which they presently have with them for resolving the confronted moral issue, they will be stimulated and interested in the acquisition of the moral reasoning belonging to the higher stage of their moral development and this will definitely help them in their pursuit of higher and higher moral development.

8. Kohlberg's theory of moral development inspire and motivates us that it is quite possible to attain the true morality characterized with selfless feelings of doing good to others, adherence to the principles of equity, equality, moral justice and human rights being preached and practised by the great men of the history like Gandhi and Martin Luther King. Students, for this purpose, should be exposed to the lives and works of the great social reformers, freedom fighters, social revolutionaries, philosophers, and religious figures. They should also be given reasonable freedom to express their original ideas and views about the prevalent social structure, laws and ethical norms along with their zeal to replace them with some suitable ones. May be that there may be a quite few to attempt to reach this highest stage of moral reasoning but surely there are the ones who are responsible for leading the society and humanity to a more illuminated path and certainly we should make provision for them in our system of education.

Freud's Theory of Psycho-sexual Development

The famous psychologist Sigmund Freud (1856-1939) is well known for providing us a theory of children's development popularly named as the theory of psycho-sexual development. Let us try to know the essentials related to this theory of psycho-sexual development.

According to Freud, sex is the life urge or fundamental motive in life. All physical pleasures arising from any of the organs or any of the functions are ultimately sexual in nature. Sexuality is not the characteristic of only the grown-up. Children from the very beginning also have sexual desires. This, he termed as infantile sexuality. A child passes through the following different stages with respect to his psycho-sexual development:

1. The Oral State: According to Freud, mouth represents the first sex organ for providing pleasure to the child. The beginning is made with the pleasure received from the mother's nipple or the bottle. Thereafter it is used to derive pleasure by putting anything, candy, stick, his own thumb, etc.

2. The Anal Stage: At this stage, the interest of the child shifts from the mouth (as the erotogenic zone) to the organs of elimination, *i.e.*, anus or the urethra. He receives pleasure by holding back or letting go of the body's waste material through the anus or urethra. This stage, generally, ranges from two to three years.

3. The Genetic Stage: Duration of this phase, in the development of the child, ranges from 4 to 6 years. At this stage the child's interest gets shifted from the eliminating organs to the genitals. The children now come to note the biological differences between the sexes and derive pleasure by playing and manipulating the genital organs. This type of awareness about sex organs according to Freud, may give birth to a number of complexes.

4. The Latency Stage: This period starts from six or seven years in the case of girls and seven to eight years in the case of boys and extends upto the onset of puberty. At this stage, boys and girls prefer to be in the company of their own sex and even neglect or hate the members of opposite sex.

5. The Phallic Stage: Puberty is the starting point of the phallic stage. The adolescent boy and girl now feels a strange feeling of strong sensation in the genitals and attraction towards the members of the opposite sex. At this stage they may feel pleasure by self-stimulation of the genitals, may fall in love with one's own self by taking interest in beautifying and adorning their own body organs and may take interest in making sexual relations with the members of opposite sex. In this way their behaviour is now centered round the satisfaction of the sexual needs either through homo-sexual or hetero-sexual relationships.

In this way Freud tried to adopt a somewhat different and unique approach for knowing and understanding the development of children interim of their Psycho-sexual behaviour. The views expressed by Freud in his psycho-sexual development theory have been quite controversial and often criticised much on account of his over emphasis and undue importance to sex. However, many of his views, especially related to infantile sexuality and colouring everything related to children's development with the expression of sex desire or motive were quite indigestible to the contemporary psychologists including his own discipline like Alfred Adler and Carl Jung.

However, irrespective of all these things, due credit is also given to Freud for highlighting the role of sex in one's live in terms of shaping his psycho and behaviour and outline the developmental path of the children determined through his or her basic instinct and drive. Thus his theory of psycho-sexual development may be well credited, in fact, for opening a new chapter in the history of sex education by —

(a) Discussing the stage of psycho sexual-development.
(b) Emphasizing the need for spontaneous expression of the sex instinct, and
(c) Changing the general attitude towards sex by treating it as a natural, essential biological function instead of regarding it as shameful, dirty or bad.

4

Physical and Motor Development

Children's Physical Development

Physical growth and development refers to a process which brings bodily and physiological changes — internal as well as external — in an organism from the conception till his death. Generally these changes take place in the following dimensions —

(*i*) *In his gross physical structure of physique*: It involves changes in terms of height, weight, body proportions and general physical appearance.

(*ii*) *In his internal organs*: It involves changes in the functioning of glands, nervous system and other body systems — circulatory, respiratory, digestive, muscular, lymphatic and reproductive.

The process of physical development plays a significant role in the proper adjustment and progress of an organism. In the beginning the infant is quite helpless. He depends upon his parents and other members of the family for the satisfaction of his bodily needs. As a result of the changes brought by physical growth and development, his body organs become adaptable to his increasing body needs and gradually he is developed into a mature responsible adult.

The General Pattern of Human Physical Development

Although there are wide individual differences among the human beings and therefore, it is not possible to describe a perfect general pattern of the growth and development, yet physical growth and development seems to follow, to some extent, a general pattern which can help us to think about some definite structural changes in the case of normal children at each stage of their growth and development.

Below we try to summarize this general pattern of physical and development along with definite structural changes.

1. Increase in Height and Weight

On the average, at birth a baby is about 19 or 20 inches in height and between 7 and 8 pounds in weight, boys being slightly taller and heavier. During the first two years, there is rapid increase in both height and weight. There is a steady and slower growth from the third year till the on-set of puberty. By five years the height of the child, approximately becomes almost double and he acquires almost five times his birth weight. During the period of adolescence we again find a sudden increase in both height and weight. Girls reach puberty about a year or two earlier than boys do. Therefore, between the age 12 to 14 they are found slightly taller and heavier than boys. But they are again surpassed by the boys. By the end of adolescence, the young men are generally higher and heavier than the young women. Generally both men and women get their maximum height and weight upto the end to adolescence. But there are very much variations in weight as it is more susceptible to environmental influences. Therefore, it is no surprise to note the sudden increase or decrease in weight in later years after attaining maturity.

Weight of the brain increases rapidly in the early years of life. By the time the child completes the age of four his brain gains almost 80 per cent of its final weight, another 10 per cent being added by the time he completes his eight years. By the 20th year, the brain gains almost all its weight.

Age	*Height (in cms.)*		*Average Weight (gms.)*	
	Girls	*Boys*	*Girls*	*Boys*
Below 3 months	55.0	56.2	4.2	4.5
3 months	60.9	62.7	5.6	6.7
6 months	64.4	64.9	6.2	6.9
9 months	66.7	69.5	6.6	7.4
1 year	72.5	73.9	7.8	8.4
2 years	80.1	81.6	9.6	10.1
3 years	87.2	88.8	11.2	11.8
4 years	94.5	96.0	12.9	13.5
5 years	101.4	102.1	14.5	14.8
6 years	107.4	108.5	16.0	16.3
7 years	112.8	113.9	17.6	18.0
8 years	118.2	119.8	19.4	19.7
9 years	122.9	123.7	21.3	21.5
10 years	128.4	124.4	23.6	23.5
11 years	133.6	133.4	26.4	25.9
12 years	139.6	138.3	29.8	28.5
13 years	143.9	144.6	33.3	32.1
14 years	147.5	150.1	36.8	35.7
15 years	149.6	155.5	38.8	39.6
16 years	151.0	159.5	41.4	43.2
17 years	151.5	161.4	42.4	45.7
18 years	151.7	163.1	42.4	47.4
19 years	151.7	163.4	42.4	48.1

Source: Growth and Development of Indian Infants and Children, Technical Report Series No. 18, Indian Council of Medical Research, 1972.

2. Changes in Body Proportions

The child does not only grow in size but also shows a marked change in the proportion of the different parts of the body. For example, the head constitutes about one-fourth the height of the body at birth, its size is relatively much larger than the arms and legs. As the child grows older, the proportion of the head decreases and by the end of adolescence it becomes one eighth of the body. In addition to head, the other body parts, legs, arms, torso, etc. also show changes in proportions as the child requires them more and more in his adaptation to coming life.

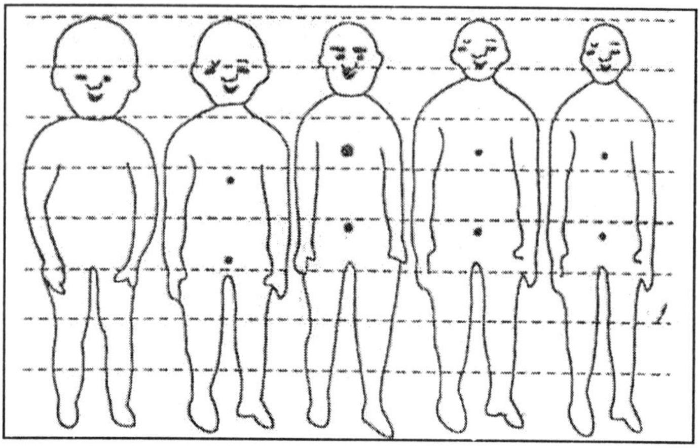

Fig. 4.1: Changes in body proportion from birth to twenty five years (Adapted from "Psychology in Education" by Sorenson, Herbert)

3. Anatomical Development

The bones of a child are not smaller in size than the bones of an adult, but they differ also in composition. The child's bones contain, relatively, a great amount of water and smaller quantity of mineral matter than do those of the adult. They are more soft and more blood flows through them than through the bones of an adult. This accounts for their greater reliability. But it also increases the chances of bones deformities and infection.

As regards the eruption of teeth, it has been found that most of the children acquire their milk teeth by the time they are two years of age. Near the end of the fifth year, the permanent teeth begin to appear the growth of which acquires a long time. The last four of the permanent teeth, the wisdom teeth, erupt between the age of seventeen and twenty five years, if they appear at all. Girls usually show more advanced teeth growth than the boys except in the case of wisdom teeth, where boys are usually ahead of the girls.

4. Development of Internal Organs

From birth onward, the internal organs of the child's body undergo constant development. As a result the child's body systems show desirable change in order to satisfy the growing needs. Below we consider the growth and development of these internal organs.

(i) *Nervous System.* It show a rapid growth during the prenatal period and the first four years after birth. Before birth the development consists primarily of increase in the number and size of nerve cells. Because no new cells are formed after birth, therefore the development in the first four years consists of the development of immature cells present at birth. After the age of four years the growth of the nervous system proceeds at a relatively slow rate.

(ii) *Muscular System.* Muscular system also shows a remarkable development, although no new muscle fibres develop after birth. The muscles of the child are more delicate and less firmly attached to the bones than are adult muscles. But gradually the muscles get themselves changed in shape, size and composition and become firmer and stronger.

(iii) *Circulatory and Respiratory Systems.* Lungs as well as heart are very small in early childhood but gradually they grow in volume as well as in weight and reach to the maximum upto the end of adolescence. They also show desirable improvement in their functioning. The veins and arteries do not follow the same growth pattern as that of the heart and lungs. Prior to adolescence, they grow rapidly, whereas they show little growth during adolescence.

(iv) *Digestive System.* The young child has a small tubular shaped stomach in comparison with the bag like shape stomach of the adults which not only holds a large amount of food but which also empties more slowly. Therefore they require more feeding in the earlier years of their life than they will need later. In addition to the greater quantity of food, they need food with essential energy value for their rapid growth and development.

(v) *Lymphatic System.* It is involved in the elimination of waste and the destruction of bacteria in the body. From birth onward this system shows the sign of rapid development until it reaches to its maximum between the age of 11 and 12 years, when the death rate is about the lowest. After 12 years it decreases rapidly.

(vi) *Reproductive System.* The development of sex organs shows a peculiar trend in contrast with the overall growth and developmental pattern. Their rate of development is very slow during early childhood but picks up its speed as the child advances towards adolescence and becomes almost developed upto the end of adolescence.

The minute observation of the above mentioned pattern can reveal the following important facts regarding the general trend of physical growth and development —

1. It is very rapid from birth to the age of two or three years.
2. Then, it continues at diminished rate till the beginning of adolescence.
3. The first three years of adolescence are marked as the years of rapid

growth and development.

4. This is followed by a period of slow growth and development to the time of maturity.

Factor Affecting the Children's Physical Development

The physical development of an individual is conditioned by both heredity and environment. Some of the important hereditary and environmental factors which influence the process of physical development are —

1. The traits and characteristics inherited at the time of conception.
2. Single birth or multiple births.
3. The physical as well as mental health of the mother during pregnancy.
4. Nutrition received by the embryo within the womb of the mother.
5. Normal or abnormal delivery.
6. Conditions and care at the time of delivery.
7. Look after of the baby and its mother.
8. Nutrition received by the child after birth.
9. Presence or absence of physical defects.
10. The living conditions — physical, social and cultural.
11. The opportunities of recreation, self expression, play and exercise.
12. Presence or absence of illness and diseases.
13. Emotional and social adjustment of the child.
14. Adequate or inadequate rest and sleep.
15. Proper or improper medical care.

Importance of Physical Development and its Educational Significance

All the aspects of the children's development — physical, intellectual, emotional, social, moral, etc. are closely interlinked. The development of any one of these aspects affects the development of the other. Physical growth and development is not an exception. Certainly, it influences the development in other directions. For example, development of the nervous system influences the development of intellectual powers. Emotional and social adjustment is also linked with physical development. While the children having normal physical growth find development are accepted by their age group, the physical deviates — who are very small, very large, too fat or too thin etc. — remain isolated. They are often nicknamed, ridiculed and denied participation in the play and recreational activities enjoyed by their age associates. It brings serious maladjustment and personality problems. The young child is intelligent enough to becomes aware of the fact that he differs in appearance and physical abilities from other children. His attitude towards self is injured and self confidence is shaken. In this case either he becomes shy and timid or becomes aggressive in order to compensate for his inferiority feelings.

Moreover upon the balanced development of the internal as well as external organs depends on the balanced functioning of the body systems. The functioning of the body systems decide the interest, attitude and the total behaviour of an individual. For example, glands and their functioning affect his emotional behaviour to a great extent. Similarly, his anatomical development, the development of circulatory, respiratory systems, etc. give the person the required abilities for participating in various motor activities.

In this way physical development influences the total make-up of an individual and thus needs a very careful attention. It can help the teachers to achieve one of the most important aims of the educational process — to bring an all round balanced development in the personality of the child. Therefore the knowledge of the process of physical growth and development is very essential for a teacher. Specifically it can serve him in the following ways —

1. He can be aware of the physical deviates, their psychology and problem of adjustment. Consequently he can help them in their social and emotional adjustment as well as in school learning.
2. The children are the back bone of a nation's strength. Their health and proper physical development is an asset to the progress of the country. Our schools have to play decisive role in the task of physical welfare of children. The teacher with the knowledge of physical developmental process can render valuable help in this direction.
3. Needs, desires, interests, attitudes and in a way the over all behaviour of an individual is controlled, to great extent, by his physical development. Therefore at a particular age level what would be the expected behaviour of the child of that age group can be estimated through the physical growth and developmental pattern. For example, with the study of the trend of the physical development in adolescence, one can be aware of their growing physical, emotional and social needs. Accordingly, adolescents can be helped by the teacher in the adjustment to their rapid development and changes.
4. Study of the pattern of physical development helps us in knowing what can be expected normally from the children at a particular age level. In turn experiences, methods and techniques of teaching, timetable, text-books, aid material, seating arrangement and learning environment, etc.

In this way we can see that the knowledge of the process of the physical development helps the teacher in the realization of his objectives. By its knowledge, he does not only become equipped for setting his programmes according to the needed requirements of his students but can also help them in improving their health and attaining proper physical strength and abilities.

Children's Motor Development

Meaning of Motor Development

Motor development in general, means the development of motor capacities and abilities of an individual. Motor capacities and abilities as Crow & Crow (1953) define stand for *"the various kinds of bodily movements that are made possible through the co-ordination of nerve and muscle activity."* (p. 34)

As examples, of these bodily movements we may cite a number of activities concerning conative aspects of the human behaviour like walking, running, jumping, swimming, grasping, throwing, catching, writing, using tools and equipments, etc. We may easily observe that a new born child or an infant is quite helpless with regard to the performance of these activities. His such helplessness can be very well identified. He can see but can not stare or focus at a particular object. He may remain lying down but can not crawl, stand or walk. He is unable to grasp and hold the things and engage himself in the individual or collective play activities. He is so much helpless in his motor capacities that he could not even manage his urgent affairs like passing out stool and urine, protection from harmful situations and satisfying the need of food and water. However, with the passage of time, he is able to gain control over his neuromuscular apparatus as a result of the maturation and art of learning the various motor movements and develop his motor abilities and capacities so much so that he is able to perform many complex motor activities demanded by his environment. Now he does not remain helpless but gains confidence. This change in the motor abilities and capacities of the child is brought by a developmental process known as motor development.

Therefore as a term motor development, in general, may be referred to the development of motor activities *i.e.* development of control over bodily movements. Since this control is a natural outcome of the gross as well as finer co-ordination of the nervous and muscular system, the term motor development according to E.B. Hurlock (1987) may be properly defined as *"the development of control over bodily movements through the co-ordinated activity of the nerve centers, the nerves and the muscles."* (p. 138)

The control over bodily movements requiring gross or finer co-ordination of the nervous system and muscular system, thus constitute the subject of the process of motor development starting from the very early stage of one's life and goes on till one has a will and strength for acquiring such control for the acquisition of motor abilities and skills.

How this development process goes on at the different stages of life, what are its general characteristics and principles etc. and how this development is useful for the individual child are some of the basic questions that need to be answered for understanding the mechanism of motor development going on in our children. Let us try to seek answers for these queries in the subsequent discussion carried out in this chapter.

How does Motor Development take place in the Growing Children?

Watching a small baby taking his or her first step while sitting on a sofa to your outstretched arms is something that you will probably always remember and talk about proudly by utterances like "look, Anita took her first step last week." Why not? It is a quite significant milestone in the motor development of your child. Like this, there happens a variety of milestones related to gross and fine motor development of the youngsters that are not only fascinating but are in fact very much essential for the survival, adjustment, welfare and progress of the child in the existing and coming days of his life. Motor development is an essential as well as universal phenomenon in the sense that each new born baby passes through it as a result of the close interaction between his hereditary endowments and environmental influences. Yet even though each child is different, generally children attain the major milestones with regard to their gross and fine motor development at a fairly predictable order in the subsequent ages of their development. For the clarity of the discussion here we would be discussing development of Gross motor and Fine motor skills side by side in the period of infancy, childhood and adolescence.

Motor Development in Infancy (from birth to two years)

In infancy the new born baby demonstrates quite significant changes, as he grows in age, in terms of his gross and fine motor ability and skills in the various areas and aspects. The motor development and activities performed by the infants may be seen to follow the usual law of developmental direction emphasizing that motor development goes from head to foot *i.e.* the development of strength, co-ordination and reflexes-starts with the head and gradually works down to the trunk, arms and legs. Consequently, we would like to discuss the motor development and activities of the infants in relation to such downward development.

A. Motor Development and activities in the region of head

1. Eye co-ordination:

During few hours after birth the new born baby has quite poor eye coordination but in a few months the baby becomes quite capable in demonstrating various motor abilities related to eye co-ordination such as focusing his eyes on the stationary and following his eye on moving objects.

2. Control and movements of head:

- During the first month of life, the baby has little control of his head. It lags when you lift him to a sitting position. It is for this reason you should keep one hand behind the baby's head when you pick him up.
- Between one and two months of age, the baby is able to raise his head up above a flat surface. As he continues to grow, he can hold his head up longer.
- At three months, the baby's head still bobs when he sits, but he is beginning to hold his head erect. When laying on his stomach, a baby three to four month old can raise his head and chest well above the mattress, supporting his weight on his forearms.

B. Development and activities of trunk

- When the baby is about four or five months old, he will probably roll over the first time, usually from the belly to the back, it is therefore advisable not to leave the baby alone at this time on a table or bed. Before long, if you put the baby on his back, he may roll over on his stomach and get on his hand and knees, as though ready to crawl. While lying on his back, he may lift his head and shoulders as though he is trying to sit up.

- During the age of 5 to 8 months the baby is able to pull himself to a sitting position when someone lifts his hands and he can sit alone for about half an hour if he is well propped. Some placid infants, particularly if they are plump, will lie on their back a little longer and do not sit alone with support until the seven months or so.
- By nine or ten months, an infant can crawl on his stomach or hands and knees. And he can support his weight by holding on to the sides of his cot or playpen.
- During the age 9 to 12 months the baby reaches out into his environment, not only with his hands but with the whole body. He can sit, lie on his back and then sit again. Most babies of this age can pull themselves to a standing position without help. In the beginning, he may not know how to sit down again.

C. Development and activities of the arms and hands

- The three months old baby plays with hands as with a toy. At around four months of age, the baby can bring his hands together in front of him and before long actively suck his thumb.
- Although, at about three months the baby does have an ever increasing amount of arm and hand movements but he still can not reach out and grasp and object as he is still not acquired the much needed eye-hand co-ordination for the former directing the activities of the latter.
- At the early stage of the acquisition of eye and hand co-ordination in the fourth months, the baby can only look to the objects but is not able to reach and grasp it. Later on as his eye co-ordination improves, he begins to reach the object for its grasping. As a result, by completion of four months, he can hold and shake a rattle.
- By the age of six months and so, the baby is able to reach for an object, grasp and then carry the object to his mouth.
- At six or seven months of age, the baby develops the ability to pass objects from one hand to another. The infant can grasp an object, move it over to the opposite hand and take hold of it.
- Initially infants grasp with the whole hand, (called a *palmar* grasp), latter, by about eight or nine months, the baby usually starts to develop the ability to use his thumb and index finger (called pincer grasp) to grasp small objects. And he uses both hands simultaneously-feeding himself a biscuit with one hand while he bangs his cup or plate with a toy held in the other hand.
- By about 9 to 12 months the baby learns to do many things with

hands and fingers like poking, pointing, touching, lifting, twisting, squeezing, picking up and dropping, etc.

- The child of 12 to 15 months of age gets joy from dumping items out of a bottle or box and may practice this skill by emptying waste-baskets and pouring liquids out of bottles. As well as being very active, the baby will sit for long periods of time, turning the pages of a magazine or picture book or playing with blocks and toys. He now also tries to assist in dressing and undressing himself, although his 'help' may lengthen the process.
- An average 18 months toddler generally can eat without help, drink from a cup, use a spoon, stack a few blocks and pretend to do housework.
- By the end of two years, the toddlers can perform some or the other delicate acts associated with co-ordination of fine movements like turning of pages and may enter well into the practice of toilet training.

D. Development and activities of legs

When a baby is just able to stand with or without support, he may be seen trying to begin his journey on foot by learning the skill of walking. The milestone earned by him in the field of locomotion with the use of his legs and foot may be summarized as below —

- In the beginning, during the age of 9 to 11 months he tries to walk while holding on to something for support with one hand. In the beginning they demonstrate a poor balance in terms of their walking movements. Throwing on this aspect Hurlock (1956: 147) writes —

    At first balance is poor. As an aid to maintaining equilibrium, the baby's arms are held outright, much like those of a tightrope walker or are pulled up to the body. The feet are turned outward and the legs are stiff. A rhythmic alteration of the two legs occurs. The head is held slightly forward and the baby looks straight ahead of him, instead of at the floor. This is necessary if balance is to be maintained, though it usually results in many falls.

- However, by their first birthday, usually most of the babies are able to walk properly with or without support and then later on in one or two months they may be seen to walk alone, with a new degree of confidence and independence.
- By the age 14 to 18 months the children's motor activities using their legs are reaching such a fine level of control that—
  (i) They start to run instead of walk. In fact, it may appear as though they are on the run constantly, going from room to room with frustrating speed.
  (ii) Besides, running in this style, they climb on to and off furniture and also may walk up and down stairs while holding your hand. It may also be seen that the children first walk up the stairs independently but are unable to get down without support.

(iii) It may also be seen that the children have acquired ability to balance on their feet in a squat position while playing with objects on the floor, walk backward and walk on tiptoe without losing their balance, stand and kick a ball without falling, stand and throw a ball and jump in place.

- Later on, by the second birthday, they begin to demonstrate their capability of getting up and down the stairs properly in a quite independent way besides climbing, getting down and sliding from some high or sliders.
- At two, toddlers can run well, throw a ball, scribble,
- By the end of the infancy the children are often torn between dependence and independence. They set out on their own to explore-climbing, walking, opening doors, trying to dress themselves and helping to feet them independently. But they still must be helped down from the steps they have climbed, protected from accidents and cuddled and cooed over when they scrape a knee.

Table 4.1: Motor Milestones — Gross and Fine Motor Development in Infancy

Motor skill	*Average age achieved*	*Are range in which 90 per cent of infants achieve the skill*
When held upright, holds erect and steady	6 weeks	3 weeks-4 months head
When prone, lifts self by arms	2 months	3 weeks-4 months
Rolls from side to back	2 months	3 weeks-5months
Grasps cube	3 months, 3 weeks	2-7 months
Rolls from back to side	41 / 2 months	2-7 months
Sits alone	7 months	5-9 months
Crawls	7 months	5-11 months
Pulls to stand	8 months	5-12 months
Plays pat-a-cake	9 months, 3 weeks	7-15 months
Stands alone	11 months	9-16 months
Walks alone	11 months, 3 weeks	9-17 months
Builds tower of two cubes	13 months, 3 weeks	10-19 months
Scribbles vigorously	14 months	10-21 months
Walks up stairs with help	16 months	12-23 months
Jumps in place	23 months, 2 weeks	17-30 months
Walks on tiptoe	25 months	16-30 months

(Adapted from Bayley, 1993).

Note: These milestone figures indicate the general trend, however, there exists individual differences with relation to age specific development.

Motor Development in Childhood (from 3 to 12 years)

As understood from the developmental milestones acquired during the infancy, the children entering the age three are equipped with necessary locomotion control and movement for carrying out the process of motor development with reasonable speed and efficiency as they have not to worry about staying upright, to move around in the environment, use the arms and hands in grasping, holding, pulling and performing their many age related activities. As a result of such development, the children at their pre-and latter childhood may be found to acquire various milestones regarding their gross and fine motor development as detailed below —

1. During 2-3 years, the children are generally found to demonstrate the following types gross and fine motor abilities.

(i) They walk more confidently and rhythmically in a quite hurriedly walking or running and sometimes changing it to running back to forth.

(ii) Engage in simple movements such as hoping, jumping throwing and catching (often with rigid upper body) and take pride and delight in performing these activities.

(iii) Push their tricycle or an riding toy with feet. At this stage they are in the habit of using little steering or pedalling for their tricycle.

(iv) Have the ability to pick up the tiniest objects between their thumb and index fingers for some time, but they are somewhat clumsy at it.

(v) Can build surprisingly high towers but not in a completely straight line.

(vi) While playing with a foam board or a simple puzzle they are rather rough in placing the pieces.

2. During 3-4 years, the children are still enjoying the same types of motor activities as they used to have earlier but at this age now they become more adventurous and thus are found to exhibit the following types of gross and fine motor development.

(i) Although they have been able to climb stairs previously with one foot on each step for some time, now at this age they begin trying to-be able to come down the same way.

(ii) They begin to jump on the spot, hope with flexing upper body and copying a circle etc.

(iii) They now begin to throw the objects with slight involvement of their upper body, however, they are still found to catch the ball by trapping it against their chests.

(iv) They demonstrate their ability to ride a tricycle by steering and pedalling it properly.

(v) They begin to demonstrate much more precision in their fine motor co-ordination. However, they may still feel trouble in building high towers with blocks with the hurry and impatience on their part.

3. During 4-5 years children are found to be more adventurous than they were at 3-4 years. At this age they are found to demonstrate the following types of gross and fine motor development.

(i) They can walk downstairs with one foot each step (alternating feet) and run smoothly.

(ii) They are able to gallop and skip with one foot.

(iii) They can throw ball with increased body rotation and transfer of weight on feet and are also to catch it with hand.

(iv) They ride on their tricycle by steering it smoothly and rapidly. The way a child uses a tricycle say a lot about his motor skills development during this age span. He is no longer a silent sitter or experimenting with pedals as he used to be at the age of three. Now he sees how fast he can make the tricycle to go without caring for the turn and obstacles in his path.

(v) Their fine motor co-ordination gets further improved resulting their hand, arm and fingers all move together under better command of the eye. As an example, the difference may be observed in relation to their dressing themselves. When a child is four he may begin to dress himself with little assistance from others.

4. *During 5-6 years* children become more active and stronger in terms of the development of their gross and fine motor abilities in the manner given ahead —

(i) They can run now more harder and enjoy races with each other and parents.

(ii) They are able to gallop now more smoothly and found to be engaged in true skipping and sideways stepping.

(iii) They show improvement in throwing and catching skills by displaying mature whole body throwing and catching pattern. Their speed of throwing also gets increased.

(iv) They now begin to ride on the cycle (small sized or with training wheel.)

(v) As a matter of further improvement in their fine motor co-ordination children now are able to use their hands more adroitly as tools. A child of six year can hammer, paste, tie shoes and fasten clothes. However, a child up to 5 to 6 years age is not ready for writing. The small muscles that control his fingers and hands are not developed well enough. He also does not acquire enough hand eye co-ordination at this age. For this purpose he has to wait a little more.

5. *During 7-12 years* when children are studying in the elementary school, they are found to demonstrate a quite reasonable development of their gross and fine motor abilities as summarized below —

(i) They gain greater control over their bodies and can sit and pay attention to the activities for longer periods of time. However they become more fatigued by long periods of sitting as they are not adequately matured in physical terms.

(ii) Their running speed is quite enhanced and they pay more attention and take more interest in the activities related to running, continuous fluid skipping, sideways stepping, jumping or bicycling without getting fatigued. Their skill regarding balancing on beam, throwing, catching, bating, kicking and dribbling improves in terms of body movements, technique, accuracy, distance and speed.

(iii) There comes a lot of improvement quite speedily in the fine motor abilities of the children during this age span. For example where at the age of four months, a baby could hold a block for a short time using his whole palm. Gradually, in the age span of seven the block moves over toward the thumb side of the hand and by eight or nine months, the baby uses just the thumb and first finger (also known as the forefinger) a more efficient and accurate way to handle objects.

(iv) Moreover, by seven years of age, children's hand become steadier and they begin to prefer a pencil to a crayon. A seven year old may concentrate hard when writing. He grips his pencil tightly and holds it close to the point. By the time he is eight years old, his hand-eye co-ordination and the small muscles in his hands and fingers are much better developed. As a result he may write more evenly and easily.

(v) At 10 to 12 years of age, they begin to show manipulative skills for the execution of the tasks and activities similar to the abilities of mature adult like such as using hands independently with more ease and precision, writing words with smaller spelling and smaller letter size, playing a difficult piece on a musical instrument and producing a fine quality crafts.

Table 4.2: Motor Milestones — Gross and Fine Motor Development in Childhood

Age	*Gross Motor Skills*	*Fine Motor Skills*
2-3 years	1. Walks more confidently and rhythmically, hurriedly walking or slow running.	1. Picking up the tiniest objects between thumb and index finger.
	2. Shows simple movements as hoping, jumping, throwing, catching (often with rigid upper body) and feeling delight in performing these activities.	2. Building high towers with blocks but not in a completely straight line.
	3. Pushing tricycle or any riding toy with feet using little steering or pedalling.	3. Rough in placing the pieces while playing on board or simple puzzles.
3-4 years	1. Climbing upstairs with one foot on each step and trying to come down stairs in the same way.	1. Feel trouble in building high towers with blocks due to hurry and impatience on their part.
	2. Begin to jump and hoping with flexing upper body.	2. Begin to demonstrate much more precision in their fine motor co-ordination.
	3. Begin to throw the object with slight involvement of their upper body and catching the object by trapping it against their chest.	
	4. Ride a tricycle by steering and pedalling it.	

Age	Gross Motor Skills	Fine Motor Skills
4-5 years	1. Walk down stairs with one foot each step (Alternating feet) and run smoothly. 2. Able to gallop and skip with one foot. 3. Can throw the ball with increased body rotation and catch ball with hand. 4. Can ride on tricycle by steering it smoothly and rapidly without caring for the turn and obstacles in his path.	1. Their hand, arm and fingers, all move together under better command of the eye. 2. Begin to dress himself with little assistance from others. 3. Begin to read and write letters onwards, colouring with crayons, sketching, dancing, acting (copying others), playing instruments and swimming according to their interests.
5-6 years	1. Can run now more harder and enjoy races with each other and parents. 2. Able to gallop more smoothly, true skipping and side ways skipping. 3. Shows improvement in throwing and catching skills. 4. Begins to ride on bicycle (small sized or with training wheels)	1. Able to use their hand more adroitly as tools. 2. Can hammer, paste, tie shoes and fasten clothes. 3. Show increase in the ability to read, write, colour, sketch, dance, playing instrument, swimming and acting etc.
7-12 years	1. Gain greater control over their bodies. Can sit and pay attention to the activities for a little longer duration. 2. Running speed is enhanced. They pay more attention and take more interest in the activities related to running, skipping, side ways stepping, jumping, swimming or bicycling without getting fatigued. 3. Improvement in throwing, catching, bating, kicking, dribbling, balancing on beam skill, etc.	1. Show advancement to handle objects in a more efficient and accurate way by using just their thumb and forefingers. 2. Show a great improvement in their hand eye coordination. 3. Show considerable fine movements with the use of the small muscles of their hands and fingers. 4. They become quite experts in the execution of the task and activities involving fine motor skills similar to the abilities of a mature adult.

Motor Development in Adolescence and Adulthood

Adolescence is said to be period of intensive growth and development in all the aspects and spheres of human growth and development including the motor development. The development and functioning of our gross as well as fine motor skills, thus, reach their peak at the end of adolescence and just a few years after that (mostly between the ages of 19 to 25). It is true for the average young adult and for outstanding athletes or sports personnel. It has been also commonly observed that there starts decline in the efficiency and output of the gross and fine motor abilities of the human beings as they step into their late adulthood. They begin to demonstrate decline in their moving / running, balancing, jumping and the co-ordination activities of the smaller muscles in terms of their speed, duration and precision.

Delayed Motor Development

Motor development, as already pointed out, follows a generalized pattern of growth and development in relation to the gross and fine motor abilities and skills of the children during the different ages of their development period. However, exceptions are there as some children demonstrate forwardness or backwardness in terms of the development of their gross and fine motor abilities and skills. To some extent such exceptions, within a reasonable limits of differentiation do not cause much trouble, however, deviation to a greater extent (especially on the side of retardation or delayed development) becomes a thing of concern to the parents, teachers and other persons interested in the welfare of the children. The children, who are the victim of their delayed motor development are found to be quite delayed in reaching the normal or generalized pattern of age specific milestones of their gross and fine motor development. It can prove harmful to the developing child in a variety of ways, mainly, as below —

- The delayed development is responsible to keep the child from reaching the stage of independent action when normally he is expected to do so.
- It affects their normal process of physical growth and development.
- It affects their social interaction with their peers and thus hampers their normal social development.
- The delayed motor development — gross and fine-puts obstacles in their normal mental development and functioning.

It affects adversely their socio-emotional behaviour. Because as a result of this early backwardness in the development of motor control, many young children develop feelings of inferiority which cause them to withdraw from the social group and this lays the foundation for unsocial attitudes and behaviour (Hurlock, 1956, p. 167).

Causes of Delayed Motor Development

The causes of delayed motor development in the children may be briefly outlined as below —

1. The improper growth conditions or inadequate nutrition received by the child in the womb of his mother.
2. Poor physical health of the child due to illness, malnutrition, glandular or chemical deficiencies and similar other reasons.
3. Inappropriate or abnormal size and body proportions of the child.
4. Low grade intelligence.
5. Improper or inadequate development of muscle control due to (i) lack

of adequate space for carrying out motor activities, (ii) Lack of proper facilities for play, exercise and other motor acts, (iii) lack of incentive, (iv) Lack of proper environment experiences, proper model for observation and imitation and timely training.

6. Improper effects of hampering or tight clothes and shoes.
7. Lack of proper tuning between learning or practising a motor skill and maturation.
8. Forcing a child for a skilled movement to extent of making him fearful or rebellion.

Importance and Educational Implications of the Knowledge of Motor Development

The knowledge of the nature and mechanism of the process of gross and fine motor development among the children may prove quite helpful to the parents, teachers, counsellors and other care takers of the children in a varieties of ways summarized as below —

1. They may be aware of the fact that motor development is essential for the all round balanced development of their personality as it works as a foundation and base for carrying out proper growth and development in physical, mental, social, emotional, moral and aesthetic development of the child.

2. There must be perfect co-ordination between the age specific maturation and acquisition of motor skills, the knowledge of this specific fact helps them to arrange for the proper learning or training experiences to the children at the very appropriate time.

3. The knowledge of the various laws and trends governing the gross and fine motor development of the children makes them quite knowledgeable about their expectations from their children about their general and specific acquisition or motor skills. It can then prove quite useful to them for the organization of suitable environment and learning facilities to their children for their proper motor development.

4. The knowledge of the factors responsible for the delayed motor development, may help them to take necessary preventive and curative measures.

5. There are some generalized milestones for the development of gross and fine motor skills among the children of various ages related to the different developmental periods like infancy, earlier and later childhood, adolescence, etc. These milestones in general may tell us in advance about the nature, characteristics and features of the children's motor development. Thus, what can be expected from growing child in general about his motor abilities is better known through the study of these age or stage specific milestones. Such knowledge may prove quite advantageous in the ways given below —

(i) We can be better prepared for providing our children the needed care, security and preventive safeguard for their adequate adjustment well being and progress. For example, if we know that during the first month of life the baby has almost no control of his head, then it would help us to take the needed precaution of keeping our one hand behind the baby's head while picking him up. Similarly, if we know that by the age of six months or so the baby is able to reach for an object, grasp it and carry it to his mouth, we would be quite cautious that baby should not put any harmful object in his mouth. Similarly, we can take a number of precautions for saving the children with their immature adventures for which they are not fully capable at a particular development period.

(ii) Besides taking precautions for protecting them from their untimely adventures the knowledge of these milestones can also prove helpful in our planning and providing needed facilities, congenial adequate environment, incentives, etc. for the expression of their motor potential and practice as well as exercise of their motor skills. We can plan for the needed learning experiences and training schedules, etc. for the children in a proper way in the light of these milestones.

(iii) A wise study and observations regarding the attainment of these milestones may also help us in educating ourselves that we should never feel too much anxious, over jealous and enthusiastic for the development of motor abilities and skills on the part of our children during specific ages of their developmental periods. These milestones are just only the guidelines telling us about the average gross and fine motor development of most of the children in a normal set up. The children may experience delayed development due to so many personal and environmental reasons. The variations in their developments to a moderate range is thus to be accepted by us without any anxiety. Every child possess his own individuality and certainly we should not thrust our own expectations on them with regard to their excelling in the motor skills related tasks and especially we should avoid putting unnecessary pressure on the children for the fear that they are not reaching the milestones marks.

(iv) Where the attainment of the laid down milestones should not be made a subject of utter concern and anxiety, but their values as providing red signal for getting us cautions about the nature of motor development of our children can not also be minimized. Milestones are helpful in the unlikely event that there really is something missing in a child. In this way the knowledge of the milestones can help us in timely diagnosis of the motor incapacities and disabilities of the children leading to the planning and implementing suitable special education programmes to them. For such diagnosis, you do not need to take into consideration the average age that children do certain things, but rather take into account the red-flag age (The age by which 90 per cent or more of healthy normal children are expected attain that milestone). Such comparison, then, may essentially help you to experience some doubt or concern about the normal motor development of your child and it is the time when you can approach the counsellor or doctor for the necessary help to your developing children.

6. Knowledge of motor development along with the milestones related to cross and fine motor skills may help the teachers, curriculum planners and trainers to plan for the suitable learning experiences, method and training techniques for helping the children in their proper education, development and efficiency gained in games and sports, craft and vocational activities.

Role Parents and Teachers in Providing Opportunities of Physical-Motor Development

Parents and teachers are the real well wishers and true helper of the developing children is seeking needful maximum development in terms of their physical and motor developments. Right from their early age as infants and toddlers parents can provide or organize needed physical activities in terms of children's play, physical exercises, games and sports for their developing children. After entering the school going age, the parents efforts are very much strengthened with the active cooperation of the school under the leadership of physical education teacher and trainers. The participation of the children in these activities may help the children in their proper physical and motor development in the following ways.

Role of Physical Activities in Children's Physical and Motor Development

Physical activities such as children's play, physical exercises, games and report, etc. may play a quite significant role in their physical and motor development in the manner summarized below.

(i) Children get valuable opportunities for keeping their muscles, and bones necessarily active, alert, flexible and strong in a proper way.
(ii) It helps them in getting extra nourishment to their skin.
(iii) It helps in beautifying and providing a good shape and structure to their physique and bodies. They can also be helped in increasing and balancing their heights and weights.
(iv) Internal organ and body system such as respiratory system, blood circulatory system, excretory system, digestive system, nervous system and glands, etc. all are necessarily activated and kept healthy by getting engaged in the play activities.
(v) It helps in the proper development and activation of the children muscular, nervous control capacity which in turn proves quite useful in their proper motor development.
(vi) These activities help a lot in attaining the level of the physical and motor development on the part of children required at one or the other ages or stages of their developmental period.
(vii) These activities help them in keeping their bodies fit, enjoying a healthy life and living longer.

Role of Parents

Parents are very much responsible for providing appropriate opportunities to their developing toddlers right from their earlier physical movements. They can help them in arranging for them suitable toys, play space and company of their peers along with hygienic environment and balanced diet for their proper physical and motor development. After entering into their school going age, it is the responsibility of the school for providing them needed opportunities in getting engaged in various types of physical activities including indoor and outdoor games, sports, physical exercises, etc. However, for playing such role on the part of the school and teacher for the physical and motor development of the children, they can be properly helped by the parents of the children. They can encourage their children for participating in physical activities games and sports, etc. being organized by the school. They themselves may lend their services for helping the school in the organization of these opportunities for the proper physical and motor development of their children.

Role of School and Teachers

The schools under the supervision and leadership of the teachers are required to have provision for a number of physical, motor activities and playing games in view of meeting the needs of health and Physical Education programs. In general these physical motor activities, play and games may be categorized and named as below.

(i) Various types of drill and marching activities
(ii) Calisthenics physical exercises.
(iii) Imitation activities like imitation of frog, rabbit, butterfly, lion, aeroplanes and train, etc. on the part of young children.
(iv) Yogic postures and asans
(v) Rhythmic like clapping with rhythm, tumbling and gymnastics
(vi) Indigenous or Indian games such as kho-kho and kabaddy, etc.
(vii) Minor games or indoor games such as carrom, chess, table tennis, ring, badminton, etc.
(viii) Athletic activities such as short sprints, 50 meters and 100 meters and relay races, jumps and throws, swimming and cycling.
(ix) Major games such as cricket, hockey, footboll, volleyball, basketball, lawn tennis, etc.
(x) Local play or free play activities of the children such as police-thief, lion-goat, *bole meri machhli kitna pani*, cat and mice, simple tag games, etc.

The organization of all the physical motor activities, play and games, need a careful consideration on the part of school teachers, instructors and school authorities. Let us think over this issue.

A. Selection

What type of physical-motor, play and games should be organized in the school, the decision in this regard should be based on the consideration like below.

- Availability of space and grounds
- Availability of material and equipments
- Availability of trained staff and personal
- Availability of financial resources
- Satisfying the varying interests, capabilities, age, gender of the children.
- Helpful in the multidimensional growth and development of the children.

B. Organization and Management

In the proper organization and managing various types of physical, motor activities, play and games in the school, the considerations like below may prove quite helpful.

- The children should be allowed to join the activities and games according to their interest and will.
- A proper provision should be made in the school time table for the organization of these activities / games.
- Proper facilities — physical and human resources should be provided by the school authorities for their organization.
- The children should be provided the needed opportunities and facilities for carrying out practice of the learned activities / games.
- Proper discipline should be maintained at the play / activities sites.
- The desired punctuality of the time and observance of rules and regulations should be properly enforced in the organization of these activities / games.
- The performance and participation of the children should be made a subject of appreciation and credit by making it mentionable in their certificates, cumulative records and profiles.

5

Emotional Development

Introduction

Emotional development is one of the major aspects of the human growth and development. Emotions like love, anger, fear, etc. play a great role in the development of a child's personality. Not only his physical growth and development is linked with his emotional make up but his intellectual, social moral and aesthetic development are also controlled by his emotional behaviour and experiences. The overall importance of emotional experiences in the life of a human being makes it quite essential to know about the emotions. What are these? What is their origin? How do they develop and influence the personality of the organism? What are the factors which are responsible for their proper or improper development and how can they be made more serviceable to the individuals and society?
Let us try to think about these issues.

What are Emotions?

Meaning of Emotion

Etymologically the word 'emotion' is derived from the Latin word 'Emovere which means 'to stir up', 'to agitate' or 'to excite'.

Woodworth by making use of this explanation has defined emotion as,

> *"Emotion is a 'moved' or stirred-up state of an organism. It is a stirred-up state of feeling that is the way it appears to the individual himself. It is a disturbed muscular and glandular activity — that is the way it appears to an external observer." (1945, p. 410)*

Crow and Crow have defined emotion in the following way.

> An emotion "*is an effective experience that accompanies generalized inner adjustment and mental and psychological stirred-up state in the individual, and that shows itself in his overt behaviour.*" (1973, p. 83)

Mc Dougall considering instincts as an innate tendency maintains that all the specific human emotions are derived from instincts. According to him an instinctive behaviour has three aspects.

(i) Cognition (Knowing)
(ii) Affection (Feeling or experiencing an emotion)
(iii) Conation (doing or striving)

When a child sees a bull coming towards her / him, s/he experiences an instinctive behaviour and undergoes the above three processes. Firstly, s/he perceives the bull, secondly s/he experiences an emotion of fear and thirdly s/he tries to run away. Therefore s/he concludes that an emotion is an affective experience that one undergoes during an instinctive excitement. S/he discovered 14 basic instincts. Each and every emotion, whatever it may be is the product of some instinctive behaviour. These instincts with their associated emotions can be listed as.

S. No.	*Instinct*	*Emotion accompanying it*
1.	Flight or Escape	Fear
2.	Pugnacity or combat	Anger
3.	Repulsion	Disgust
4.	Curiosity	Wonder
5.	Parental	Tender emotion, Love
6.	Appeal	Distress
7.	Construction	Feeling of creativeness
8.	Acquisition	Feeling of ownership
9.	Gregariousness	Feeling of loneliness
10.	Sex, Mating	Lust
11.	Self-assertion	Positive self-feeling or Elation
12.	Food-seeking	Appetite
13.	Laughter	Amusement

From the above definitions and derivation of emotion we can conclude the following important information about emotion.

1. The emotional experiences are associated with some instincts or biological drives. When the basic need is satisfied or challenged (the satisfaction is in danger), the emotions play their part.

2. In general, emotions are the product of perception. The perception of a proper stimulus (object or situation) is needed to start an emotional experience. The organic changes within the body (Favourable or unfavourable) may intensify the emotional experiences.

3. The core of an emotion is feeling. Which is essentially linked with some sort of impulsive act or urge to do. For the clarification let us try to differentiate between feelings and emotions.

Actually every emotional experience, whatever it may be, involves feelings-things of the heart. Feelings and emotions both are affective experiences. There is only the difference of degrees. After perceiving a thing or situation, feelings like pleasure or displeasure can be aroused. There may be some intensity or degree of strength in these feelings. When the feelings are so strong as enable to disturb or agitate the mind and can excite an individual to act immediately they are turned into emotions.

Therefore the urge to do or act (conative aspect) is the most important experience.

4. Every emotional experience involves many physical and physiological changes in the organism. Some of the changes which express themselves in overt behaviour are easily observable. Examples of such changes are the bulge of the eyes, the flush of the face, the flow of tears. The pulse rate, the beating of the heart, the choke in the voice, the fleeing from the situation or the attack on the emotion arousing stimulus. In addition to these easily observable changes there are internal physiological changes. Examples of such changes are changes in the circulation of blood, the impact on digestive system and the changes in the functioning of some glands like adrenal glands, etc.

These changes become so specific and distinguishable in the human being that a simple glimpse can enable us to detect a particular emotional experience in an individual and we can see whether he is in anger or suffers from fear, etc.

In addition to the above characteristics, the emotions have some more specific things to be told about. These are:

(i) Emotions are prevalent in every living organism.

(ii) They are present at all stages of development and can aroused in young as well as in old.

(iii) Emotions are the most individual and they differ from person to person.

(iv) Same emotion can be aroused by a number of different stimuli-objects or situations.

(v) Emotions rise abruptly but die slowly. An emotion once aroused tends to persist and leaves behind emotional mood.

(vi) Emotions have the quality of displacement. The anger aroused on account of one stimulus gets transferred to other situation. The anger on account of the rebuking by boss is transferred in beating the children at home.

(vii) One emotion can give birth to a number of like-wise emotions.

(viii) There is a negative co-relation between the upsurge of emotions and intelligence. Reasoning and sharp intellect provides a careful check on the sudden upsurge or emotions and on the other hand emotional experiences the reasoning and thinking powers are decreased.

Kinds of Emotions

If we try to analyse the impact of various emotional experiences upon the well-being of an individual, we came to the conclusion that the emotions have both positive as well as negative effects. Whether an emotion will prove to be helpful or harmful to an individual depends upon the following factors.

(i) the frequency and intensity of emotional experience.

(ii) the situation, occasion and the nature of stimulus which arouses the emotion.

(iii) Kind of emotional experience or emotions.

The last factor — the kind of emotional experience — counts much in this direction. Emotions, in general, can be categorized into two kinds:

1. ***Positive Emotions***: The pleasant emotions like affection (love), amusement, curiosity, joy and happiness which are very helpful and essential to the normal development are termed as positive emotions.

2. ***Negative Emotions***: Unpleasant emotions like fear, anger, jealousy which are harmful to the individual's development are termed as negative emotions.

By their nature of positiveness and negativeness it should not be assumed that all the positive emotions are always good and the negative emotions are bad. While weighing their impact, the other factors like the frequency and intensity, situations and the nature of stimuli should also be considered. Excess of everything is bad. Emotions with too much intensity and frequency whether positive or negative bring harmful effects. On the other hand the so-called negative emotions are very essential for the human welfare. The emotion of fear prepares an individual to face the danger ahead. The child who has no emotion of fear is sure to get injured because he has not learnt to save himself against a possible danger.

Emotional Development During Different Stages of Development

Development, in general, applies to the changes brought about with the passage of time. Emotional development in this respect reflects the following changes.

(i) There is a gradual birth of different emotions in an individual since his birth.

(ii) There are changes in the conditions or nature of stimuli that arouse the child's emotion.

(iii) There are changes in the manner in which the child expresses his emotions.

In the light of these changes we will try to discuss the process of emotional development during different developmental stages.

Emotional Development during Infancy

1. From his very birth, the infant cries and his bodily movements seem to give evidence of the presence of emotional element in him. What are the specific emotions, if any, which he experiences at this stage is a difficult question to be answered.

2. Truely speaking, as Mrs. Hurlock puts it, *"At birth and shortly afterwards the first sign of emotional behaviour is general excitement to strong stimulation. There are no indications of clear cut, definite emotional*

patterns that can be recognized and identified as specific emotional states. (1956, p. 216)

Thus, it is the stage of an undifferentiated excitement to any stimulus.

3. The stage of undifferentiated excitement is over in a very short time, when the general excitement becomes differentiated into simple responses that suggest pleasure and displeasure. The stimuli like sudden loud noise, wet, cold or hot objects applied to the baby's skin, feeling hungry and uncomfortable, etc. bring unpleasing responses. The stimuli like sucking, patting, and warmth, etc. bring pleasant responses.

4. The differentiation of general excitement into pleasant and unpleasant responses takes the following pattern according to Spitz.

> *"During the first two months pleasure and displeasure come in response to 'physical' stimulation. By the third month, pleasure is aroused by 'psychological' stimulation as shown in the baby's smile in response to human face. Slightly later displeasure can be aroused by psychological as well as physical stimuli as may be seen in the baby's reaction to being left alone."*
>
> (Hulock, E.B, 1956. p. 217)

5. As said above, before the age of six months the emotional behaviour is expressed through pleasant and unpleasant responses, that is, there are only two emotions (distress and delight) up to this stage. When the infant completes his six months, the negative emotions take the lead and gradually in the coming months, fear, disgust, anger, jealousy all are distinguishable. Between the 10th and 12th months the positive emotions like elation, love, sympathy, enjoyment all enter in the field. Up to two years, as the study of Bridges conducted in 1931 shows almost all the emotions, positive as well as negative, take their shape and become quite distinguishable.

6. There is continuous variation in manifestation of emotions during infancy. In the earlier months it is very difficult to have distinction on the basis of facial expression and bodily positions. Only the mothers can determine the causes of her child's crying and yelling. Later on gradually they become distinguishable. Moreover in the earlier months of infancy the child reacts more violently to emotionally disturbing situations, but as the infant approaches childhood, his crying, yelling and the vigorous movements of the body parts become less and less violent. Gradually with increasing age there is an increase in linguistic responses and a decrease in motor responses.

Emotional Development during Childhood

As said above, almost all the emotions make themselves distinguishable up to the beginning of childhood. Therefore, emotional development after the stage of infancy, concerns itself, only to the changes in the nature of situations or stimuli arousing emotions and the changes in the expression of emotional experiences. We find the following changes in the child during childhood.

1. In infancy the child is only concerned with his own well-being. Therefore, the emotions are generally aroused by the conditions which are related with his immediate well-being. But as he grows, his world grows larger and he has to respond to a variety of stimuli. During childhood peer group relationship and school atmosphere and other environmental factors influence his emotional behaviour. His emotions get linked with the new stimuli. At the same time he does not react to various old stimuli. For example, he does not show anger at being dressed or bathed, neither does he show any fear of strangers.

2. There is a remarkable change in the expression of emotional behaviour. In infancy this behaviour is usually dominated by too much intensity and is usually expressed through motor responses like crying, yelling, etc. But in childhood and specially in later childhood, the child tries to express his behaviour through reasonable means and is the result of many factors. In childhood the child is in a position to express his feelings through language. Secondly, he becomes social and realises that it may not be desirable or proper for him to show his emotions at all times. Thirdly, his intellect begins to play a proper role in exercising check over emotional outbursts.

In this way the child advances towards emotional stability and control and during the later period of his childhood, demonstrates an appreciable degree of control over his emotions.

Emotional Development during Adolescence

The emotional balance is once again disturbed in adolescence. The individual once again experiences the violent and intensive current of emotional experiences. With regard to emotional experiences, this is the period of intensive storm and stress. At no stage this emotional energy is so strong and dangerous as in adolescence. It is very difficult for an adolescent to exercise control over his emotions. The sudden functioning of sexual glands and tremendous increase in physical energy makes him restless. Moreover, adolescents are not consistent in their emotions, during this stage. Emotions during this stage fluctuate very frequently and quickly. It makes them moody. Sometimes they are very happy and at an other time they are extremely sad and all this happens in a very short time. So there is too much uncertainty in the nature of their emotional stages.

At this stage there is strong need of the training of emotions and proper channelization of emotional energy. The Hadow report has emphasized this need in the following words.

> *"There is a tide which begins to rise in the veins of youth at the age of eleven or twelve. It is called by the name of adolescence. If that tide can be taken at the flood and a new voyage begun in the strength and along the flow of its current, we think that it will move on the fortune." (Ross J.S. 1951, p. 153)*

Factors Influencing Emotional Development

The emotional development of the child rests on so many factors. The important ones are given below.

1. Health and physical development: Physical development and health has a positive correlation with emotional development. Any deficiency in physical side — internal or external — creates emotional problems. The children, weak in somatic structure or suffering from illness, are more emotionally upset and unstable than are children whose health is better. The normal functioning of the glands is very important for the balanced emotional development. Any abnormal increase or decrease in their power of secretion creates obstacles in the proper emotional development.

2. Intelligence: Intelligence, as the ability to make adaptation, has a significant correlation with the emotional adjustment and suitability of the child. Meltzer (1937) concluded that:

> *"There is less emotional control, on the average, among those of the lower intellectual levels than among children of the same age who are bright."* (Hurlock, E.B. 1956, p. 254)

An intelligent person, with his reasoning and thinking powers, exercises control according to the situation and make proper use of his emotions. At every stage the child's intellectual power guides and controls the emotional development of the child.

3. Family atmosphere and relationships: Emotional development is very much influenced by the family atmosphere and relationships. The emotional behaviour of the parents and elder members accompanied with the cordial atmosphere prevailed at home develop positive emotions among the children, while the conflicts, fights and tensions in family relationships give birth to negative emotions. Also the treatment, given to a child by the parents and the members of the family, influences his emotional development. The order of birth (whether the first or the youngest child), the size of the family, the socio-economic status of the family, the parental attitude (neglected, pampered and over protected child) all are the decisive factors in emotional bringing up of the child.

4. School atmosphere and teachers: The school life plays an important role in the emotional development of children. The healthy conducive atmosphere of the school always results in the balanced emotional development of children. All such things like the physical facilities provided in the school, the methods of teaching, the organisation of co-curricular activities and social life of the school, the relationship among the staff members and the head of the institution, the attitude of the teachers towards students and the self-example of the teacher's emotional behaviour, influence the emotional development of children.

5. Social development and peer-group relationship: Social development of children is closely linked to their emotional development. The more social is the child, the more emotionally adjustable he will prove. Socially rejected or maladjusted children always face difficult emotional problems. The maintenance of proper social relationships and acquisition of social virtues are the effective means for bringing essential modification in the emotional behaviour of the child. The proper social development can only bring the desirable and socially approved emotional development in children.

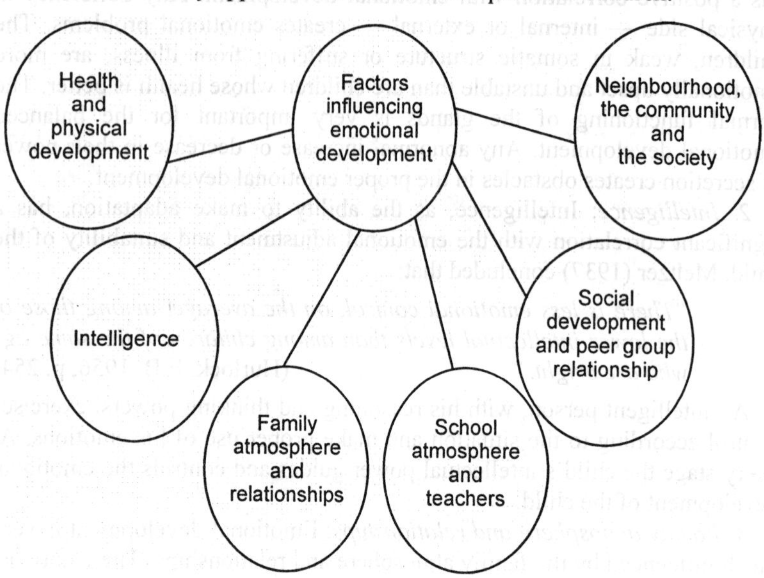

Fig. 5.1: Factors Influencing Emotional Development

6. Neighbourhood, the community and the society. The other social agencies like neighbourhood, the community and society, of which an individual is the member, also exert significant influence upon his emotional set-up. He picks up so many traits of his emotional behaviour from these surroundings. The brave community is sure to produce fearless and courageous children. The society where the elder members of the society unnecessarily exhibit emotional outburst of anger leads the youngsters to such negative development. Similarly, so many good or bad things related to emotional behaviour of an individual can be acquired through the impact of neighbourhood and the society.

In this way the factors influencing the emotional development of an individual can be labelled into two categories. In the first category there are personal factors like his physical, physiological, mental and social development. In the second category there are social factors like parents, family, school, neighbourhood, community and the society. Both of these factors exert a significant influence upon the emotional development of the child. While taking care of the proper emotional development of the child, the parents as well as the teachers should keep in view all the factors belonging to both categories.

Methods for the Training of Emotions

Emotions in their crude form are harmful to the individual and the society. One of the major objectives of any good scheme of education is to train and modify the emotions for the welfare of the individual and that of the society. The various methods employed for this purpose are:

1. Repression or Inhibition.
2. Industriousness or Mental Occupation.
3. Redirection and Sublimation
4. Catharsis.

1. Repression or Inhibition: Here the undesirable emotional behaviour of the child is checked by imposing restriction and giving punishment. No outlet or opportunity is provided to the child for the emotional expression. Rules and regulations are very strictly observed and the child is always required to express in socially desirable ways. Actually it is a negative method of exercising control over the emotions and in no way helpful for the healthy emotional development.

2. Industriousness or Mental Occupation: Another method for exercising desirable control over the emotions is to keep oneself busy in some constructive activities. Empty mind is said to be a devil's work-shop. Therefore, it is essential to have provision for co-curricular and leisure time activities for the balanced emotional development of the children.

3. Redirection and Sublimation: The direction of the flow of emotional energy is changed through the process of redirection and sublimation from an undesirable goal to a socially desirable one. In both these processes there is only a difference of degrees. Whereas, in redirection, there is no change in the nature of the emotion. Only the direction of the flow is changed. In sublimation, there is modification of original instincts or emotions. Sublimation changes the very form of the emotion.

As far as the method of controlling the emotions is concerned, redirection serves the best purpose. Like repression or inhibition it does not have negative effect upon the personality development of children. It does not destroy the emotion, but only brings desirable changes in the mode of its expression. If a child is very aggressive and displays emotion of anger frequently, his emotion of anger can be diverted towards the enemies of the country and the devils of the society. In this way this energy can be utilized in the defence of the country and for the weaker members of the society. Similarly, the sublimation of the love, in the cases of Tulsidas and Kalidas presents clear example of the role of sublimation in changing the emotional set-up of an individual.

4. *Catharsis*: In this method desirable channels are provided for the release of the emotional energy. In some way or the other, the individual is provided with the opportunity of self-expression so that the pent-up emotions get appropriate outlet. Under emotions the tensions are created in the minds of the individuals. By providing a proper outlet for emotional

expression, the tensions can be removed and he is made to feel better and lighter. To listen patiently, the verbal expression of an individual under emotion is the simplest catharsis process. The opportunity for self expression in the form of co-curricular activities, participation in festivals and fairs and rituals of the society — all provide means for the catharsis of emotional energy.

What can the teachers do in bringing Balanced Emotional Development of Children?

Role of education and specially of teachers in bringing balanced emotional development of children deserves special mention. The emotional development of children are influenced and controlled by so many factors. These factors have been mentioned earlier. Let us analyse the part played by the teachers in bringing balanced emotional development of children in the light of these factors.

1. Emotional development, as said earlier, depends upon physical and physiological development. Therefore, every care is to be taken for the proper physical development of children. Children should be made to learn the ways of healthful living. With due co-operation of the parents and the state authorities, children need to be cared for proper nourishment. The parents should be made aware of the physical weakness, deformities and illness of their children and necessary provision for the treatment should be made in the schools or state hospitals.

2. Home atmosphere exercises a good amount of influence over the emotional character of children. Therefore, teachers should seek active co-operation of the parents in making the atmosphere of the home suitable for proper emotional development. Parents and the elder members of the family should produce better examples of emotional expression before their children. They should try to develop healthy attitude towards their children and in no way spoil them by their own modes of behaviour. The teacher should try to know the causes of emotional maladjustment of children and find out how far home atmosphere and parents are responsible for this. Accordingly, he should take suitable step for the proper emotional development of children.

3. The teacher in the school, with the active co-operation of the authorities, should take care of the things given ahead.

(i) There should be an adequate provision of various co-curricular activities for the full expression and outlet of emotional energies of children.

(ii) Instructional methodology and curriculum should be dynamic, progressive and child-centred.

(iii) The children should get desired love and sympathy from the teachers. Their individuality should be respected and individual differences should be recognized. The teacher should see that the basic emotional needs of children are satisfied in the class-room or school.

(iv) With the help of positive methods of controlling and training the emotions, the emotional tension present in the minds of children should be removed and the creation of undesirable complexes should be avoided.

(v) Moral and religious training should form a part of the school programme. High ideas of life and moral principles should be made the guiding factors of the children's life.

(vi) Emotions are caught, they are not taught. Therefore, the teacher should refrain himself from any act or behaviour which can bring undesirable influence upon the emotional development of children. He must put his self example before children for the refined emotional expressions and behaviour.

(vii) Proper care should be taken for the balanced social development of children. The child should get due recognition in his group and in no case he should feel isolated or rejected by his peer group and classmates.

(viii) Teachers need to understand when behaviour is normal and when it is a symptom of something wrong. The causes for the emotional deviation should be sought and when behaviour is excessively immature, the service of a skilled guidance personnel should be obtained.

(ix) Teachers should recognize the place of emotion in the learning process. Balanced emotional feelings can serve as a tonic to the body and can make the learning an active and exciting experience. Therefore, the teacher, should make the child emotionally involved in his work.

6

Social Development

What is Social Development?

Human beings possess a unique characteristic which separates them from animal beings. Their behaviour is social. Society is as essential as food to them. They believe in the maintenance of social relationships and try to adjust with others. But this does not mean that the child is born with such social behaviours and social qualities. Like other aspects of growth and development, he develops the necessary social characteristics in him. *The process of the development of such qualities which brings desirable changes in his social behaviour is referred to as social development or socialization of the child.* Social development occupies very important place in the overall process of growth and development. We cannot even describe an individual a person if he has not passed through the process of social development or socialization.

Let us try to think over further. What does this term social development (also described as socialization) mean? Various thinkers have tried to define it. Some of the definitions are given below:

Sorenson — "By social growth and development we mean increasing ability to get along well with oneself and others." (1948, p. 50)

In this way Sorenson explains that during the process of social development there is a progress in the social abilities or skills of an individual. With these increasing abilities he tries to bring improvement in the maintenance of social relationships. He tries to mould his behaviour and seek adjustment and harmony with others.

Freeman and Showel — "Social development is the process of learning to conform to group standards, mores and traditions and becoming imbued with a sense of oneness, inter-communication and co-operation." (Hurlock, E.B., 1956, p. 257)

This definition lays stress on the following:

(i) Social development refers to the process by which a person acquires the necessary knowledge, skills and disposition that makes him an acceptable member of his own group.

(ii) It develops group loyalty and encourages mutual dependence, co-operation and cohesiveness.

(iii) It is the process which helps an individual to behave in accordance with social radiations and mores and thus makes him able to adjust in his social environment.

Mrs. Hurlock — "Social development means the attaining of maturity in social relationships." (1956, p. 257)

This brief definition carries a wide meaning. It asserts that as in the case of emotional development, the goal is to attain emotional maturity, similarly there in the case of social development, the goal should be the attainment of social maturity. An individual should have all the opportunities to modify or improve his social behaviour so that he may be able to maintain proper social relationships and can adjust himself to his social environment.

Garrett — "Socialization or social development is the process whereby the biological individual is converted into a human person." (1968, p. 55)

This definition is based upon the distinction between the term 'individual' and 'person'. We cannot name each and every body as person. The person always possesses some personality. The personality is the product of social interaction between him and his social environment. Socialization and social development — the process of social interaction — helps the individuals to attain essential personality characteristics.

In the light of all these views we can come to the conclusion that social development or the socialization is a process:

(i) which begins with the infant's first contact with other people and continues throughout life,

(ii) it is the net result of his constant interaction with his social environment,

(iii) it helps in learning and acquiring various social qualities and characteristics, and

(iv) with the result of such learning the individual becomes adjusted to his social environment and can maintain proper social relationships.

Social Development During Different Stages of Development

A. Social Development in Infancy

The behaviour of the human is not social at birth. He is too much self-centred. He is only concerned with the satisfaction of his physical need. He does not even distinguish between people and inanimate objects.

Social behaviour is said to be taking its birth when the infant first distinguishes between persons and objects. He is dependent upon the adults for the satisfaction of his needs, therefore, normally the baby's first social contacts are with an adult. Mrs. Hurlock in her book 'Child Psychology' has beautifully explained the process of social development during the first two years as a result of the contact with adults. Below we give the summary of her findings.

Duration of Age	Pattern of Social Behaviour
During First month	Cannot differentiate between the human voices and other noises.
Second month	Recognizes the sounds of human beings and gives smiles to the person.
Third month	Recognizes its mother and feels unhappy on separation.
Fourth month	Shows selective attention to the human face and feels happy in company.
Fifth month	Reacts differently to smiling and scolding and distinguishes between friendly and angry voices.
Sixth month	Recognizes familiar persons with a smile and shows definite expressions of fear of strangers.
Eighth and ninth month	Attempts to imitate the speech, simple acts and gestures observed in others.
Between the tenth and twelve month	Plays with his image and even kisses it as if it was another person.
At twelve month	Can refrain from doing things in response to 'no-no' or some other form of request.
At two years	Can co-operate with adults in a number of routine activities and becomes an active member of the family.

Social development of infants as a result of contact with other infants and children: With regard to an infant's social reactions to another infant or child it has been observed that his early behaviour is egocentric and selfish. He cannot share his toys with others. He wants to have all things for himself and does not tolerate any external interference. From the thirteenth to the eighteenth month the young child's interest shifts from play materials to the playmates. There is a decrease in fighting for toys and increase in co-operative use of them. Up to three years he learns to divide and share his possession with others and to co-operate with them. They are now in a position to engage themselves in the co-operative and organised plays activities. Up to seven years or so the children seek companionship regardless of sex of the other children. Usually the boys and girls play together at this stage.

Like emotions the early stage of social behaviour during infancy is characterized by negative social characteristics. Imitation, timidity, shyness, rivalry and desire for possession dominate the first two years of development. Between 2 to 6 years both negative and positive aspects of social behaviour are seen. Negativism, rivalry, quarrelling, teasing and bullying, co-operation, sympathy and social approval are some of the new social behaviours which are learned at this stage.

B. Social Development during Childhood

As we have seen that during the period 2 to 6 years a child progresses from being relatively unsocial to distinctly socialization individual. He learns to share, to co-operate and to do things with others. But the circle of his social contacts is limited at this stage. Therefore, we cannot expect much from him regarding his social development.

With the entrance in childhood most of the children begin to go to school. The area of their social contacts is now widened. We note the following changes in the social behaviour of a child:

1. This period is marked by greater degree of social awareness. There is a great expansion of child's social world. Most of the important types of social behaviour necessary to adjustment with others, begin to develop at this stage.
2. He tries to seek independence from his parents and other elders and spends less time with them. In actual sense he now drives no enjoyment from them. Thus, interest in playmates of his own age gets increased.
3. He becomes an active member of a 'peer group' and this group gradually replaces the family group in its influence over his behaviour and attitudes. The members of such a group are almost of the same age. They believe in group loyalty and thus try to conform to the rules and the values maintained by their group.
4. We find a sort of segregation among boys and girls of this age. They form their group among members of their own sex because of a definite and clear differentiation between their habits, interest and attitudes, etc.
5. The interests and values of the peer group often have a clash with the interests and values of the teachers and parents. The child at this age is caught between the two. On the one hand he aspires for the social values of his own group; on the other hand, he is equally anxious to win the love and affection of his parents as well as of teachers. Therefore, a proper balance between these two influencing forces — peer group, parents and teachers — is essential. Being neglected by either side he may develop himself into a maladjusted and antisocial personality.
6. Up to the end of the stage of childhood *i.e.* 11th or 12th year the child enters the peak of "gang age" with increasing loyalties towards his own gang and conflicts with other gangs, parents and teachers. The gang life develops so many good and bad social qualities in the child.

C. Social Development during Adolescence

Adolescence is a period of rapid changes and adjustments. In the social sphere also it holds a greater significance. The social development of this age is marked by the following characteristics:

1. Adolescence is marked with too much sex consciousness, sexual development and the accompanying attraction for opposite sex. Boys and girls of this age try to attract and hold the attraction of each other through their style of dress, manner of talking and other forms of social behaviour. They also try to seek friendship and even sexual relationships. In this way, the social behaviour pattern of the adolescence is almost dominated by sexual needs and desires.
2. During this stage group loyalty becomes very much pronounced. Like childhood, it does not confine itself to the gang only but extends to the

school, the community, the province and to the nation. Martyrs and patriots are the product of this age. Co-operation reaches its peak during this period and the individual are in a mood to sacrifice their own interest for the greater cause of the group, society and nation.

3. Adolescence is also marked with the increase in friendly relationships. The nature of friendship maintained at this stage differs much from that of childhood. While in the childhood the friends are generally chosen from the neighbourhood or class, in adolescence there is no such bar of distance. The adolescents tend to choose friends of their own age, mental level and from the same socio-economic group to which their own family belongs. Their friendships are based on their common interests, hobbies and skills or the satisfaction of their mutual needs and subsequently tend to last longer than the friendships made in early childhood. It sometimes ties them in life long relationships.

4. Adolescence is a period of intense emotions. Emotional behaviour dominates the social characteristics and qualities of adolescents. An adolescent is highly sensitive, idealist and social reformer by nature. He feels strongly for the weak and sufferers. He is always ready to do some sort of social and community service. From time to time he exhibits his desire for bringing reforms in the social set-up and is highly critical of social evils and injustice.

5. There area of specific interests and social contacts gets widened during adolescence. Besides individual characteristics the culture, socio-economic status of the family, sex education — all effect their social interest and contacts. We find too much diversity in the adolescents regarding their interests and sociability. While some are highly extrovert and sociable the others like to remain aloof and shirk from social contacts and participations.

In the end we can say that adolescence is a period of maximum social awareness, increasing social relationships and intimate friendships. During this age the individual is provided with wide area of interests and opportunities for making social adjustment and learning so many social qualities. During this age an individual prepares himself to play a role of adult in his social life. Up to the end to this stage, the social behaviour of the child becomes almost matured.

Factors Affecting Social Development

How to help the child in the task of his social development is a relevant question at this stage. In this task, the individual in addition to his own physical, mental and emotional development is helped by various social agencies. All these factors — personal and environmental — work together in influencing the social development of the child. What are these factors and how they influence the pattern of social development can be seen through the following discussion:

A. Personal Factors

1. Bodily structure and health: Development of social behaviour is influenced by the physique and health which one possesses. A healthy child with a normal physique develops self-confidence and a sense of self-respect. He has the strength and ability to make himself adjusted in the challenging social situations. He is always cheerful and co-operative. He is able to mix with the people and maintains proper social relationships. The child suffering from illness or having poor health or any physical deformities and defects develops the feeling of inferiority and feels difficulty in social adjustment. Therefore proper care should be taken for the balanced physical development of the children.

2. Intelligence: Intelligence is defined as the ability to make and take the right decision at a right time and the ability to adapt or adjust to new situations. These qualities are very essential for effective social behaviour. The more intelligent a person is, the more adjustable and social he will prove.

3. Emotional development: Emotional development of the child bears a positive correlation with the social development. Emotional adjustability and maturity is one of the very important elements of social maturity. The persons who can express their emotions in a proper degree at a proper time are found to possess a healthy social personality. Emotionally maladjusted personalities possess poor social qualities. Therefore due care should be taken for the training of the emotions of the child so that he may not feel any obstacles in the path of his social development.

B. Environmental Factors

1. Family atmosphere: Family is named as the most important primary agency for socialization of the child. The home atmosphere and the family relationships exercise much influence upon the social development of the child. The child learns the first lesson of social qualities from his parents. Consciously or unconsciously he imitates the behaviour of his parents and members of the family and thus picks up so many good or bad social characteristics which go with him even up to the end of his life. The size of the family the relationships within the family, attitude of the parents and family members socio-economic status and position of the family in the society — the traditions, culture, values and the ideals of the family — all influence the social development of the child.

The family which provides healthy social atmosphere and where basic needs of children are satisfied produces socially balanced personalities whereas in the homes where the family relationships are under strain and the elders possess negative social characteristics, the child is not brought up properly and consequently the socially undesirable and negative behaviour is produced among children. Therefore, it is essential to seek the active co-operation of the parents in providing suitable atmosphere at home for the proper social development of children.

2. The School and its atmosphere: Social development in children is greatly influenced by the social environment and functioning of the schools. The human relationships maintained by the school, the kinds of programmes and activities performed, its traditions, values and principles, the social qualities and behaviour of the teachers and school mates — all influence the social development of the child. The school, having a healthy social and democratic atmosphere inculcates so many social virtues among the students while a poor and unhealthy atmosphere of the school and the negative social behavioural characteristics of the teachers and schoolmates cast a bad influence upon the social behaviour of the child. Therefore, the teachers as well as the authorities should try their level best to make the school environment as healthy as possible for the proper social development of the children. They must produce good examples of social virtues and democratic living before children and through curricular and co-curricular activities, proper methods of instruction and personal contact, should help children in their proper social development.

3. Peer-group relationship and gang influence: The play mates, school or class mates also influence the social development of the child. He picks up the habits and social qualities of his companions. A good company helps him to learn good qualities while a bad company provides all opportunities to spoil him and turn him into anti social personalities. On the credit side, through peer group relationships and gang influence he learns to cooperate, to lead and follow, to think for a common cause and to adjust in the challenging social situations. It inculcates the sense of loyalty, sympathetic attitude and the willingness to obey the social rules and regulations.

Parents, teachers and other responsible members of the society should remain very careful to see that the child gets a healthy company. The negative influence of the peer group and the gang in the form of an unsocial behaviour for development of evil social characteristics should be checked. The child should be accepted by his peer group. He should get proper environment and opportunities to mix with his peers.

4. Community and neighbourhood: As the child grows older he comes in contact with the social circle of his neighbourhood and the community to which he belongs. The social interests habits and characteristics of the neighbours unconsciously and consciously influence the social behaviour of the child. Every community and the society is characterized by its unique cultural pattern, social mores, traditions and social characteristics. The child as a member of the community and the society picks up these things which go on shaping his social behaviour and influence his social development.

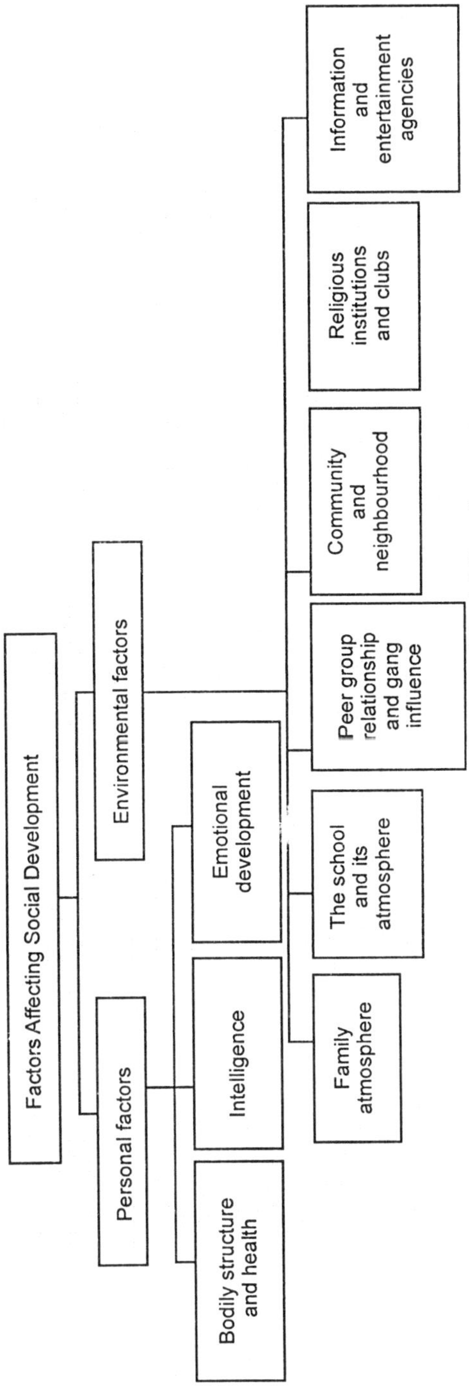

Fig. 6.1: Factors Affection of Social Development

5. Religious institutions and clubs. The social agencies like temple, church, social clubs, etc. also influence the social development of the child. These places serve as a meeting ground for the members of the society and help in developing social contacts and relationships. The social behaviour of an individual is greatly influenced by the traditions, values, ideals and social characteristics maintained by these institutions.

6. Information and entertainment agencies. Agencies like newspapers, Magazines, Radio, Cinema, Television, etc. also exercise their influence upon the social development of children. Sources of information constantly inform the readers, listeners and others about the changes in the social structure, customs, traditions and values and thus bring desirable changes in the social behaviour of individuals. The mass entertainment agencies like radio, cinema, television, etc. play a vital role in moulding and shaping the behaviour of the members of the society. The impact of these agencies in social life can very well be recognized. What a hero or heroine does on the screen is at once imitated. The values of the life, the style of living, the traditions and cultural pattern of the society all undergo a drastic change by the impact of these modern mass agencies.

These agencies should not be allowed to functions unchecked. Society or government should exercise a desirable control and check upon the functioning of these agencies so that no undesirable and anti social influence is left over the masses. Directly or indirectly these agencies should be made an important means for the assimilation of the social and democratic virtues among the citizens

The Place of Gender Roles in One's Social Development

Meaning of the term Gender and Gender Roles

Children's concept of gender in the schools is limited to view them as boys or girls or mark their gender in a prescribed form as male or female. However, in a more broader sense, technically and socially the term gender has been given definite meanings in the dictionaries and writings of scholars as well as world bodies as below.

Random House Dictionary (2017): Our conception of belonging to a particular gender originates from "the public image of being a particular gender that we present to others".

Oxford Dictionary: The term gender stands for "The role or behaviour learned by a person as appropriate to their gender, determined by the prevailing cultural norms".

Gupta, G.R. (2000): Gender can be defined as the commonly shared expectations and norms within a society about appropriate male and female behaviour, characteristics and roles. It may be taken as a social and cultural constructs that differentiate females from males and thus defines the ways in which females and males interact with each other.

These roles and expectations are learned and they can change over time as well as vary within and between cultures

The WHO noted: "The word gender is used to describe the characteristics, roles and responsibilities of women and men, boys and girls, which are socially constructed. Gender is related to how we are perceived and expected to think and act as women and men because of the way society is organized, not because of our biological differences."

In this way, the terms gender and gender roles stand intermingled. When we name a particular student as boy or girl, we have in our mind his or her gender classification in the form of male and female. In making such gender classification, we certainly perceive him / her in the light of the roles to be played by him or her as per expectations of the society. Usually these expectation are nothing but the stereotypes prevailing in the society about gender roles. But in practice the gender roles and expectations may or may not match the stereotypes associated with their gender roles. However, the gender stereotypes are found to cast a quite strong influence over the gender behaviour and roles. Therefore, it is quite essential for us to get acquainted with the term stereotypes, and their prevalence in home, neighbourhood and school for the male or female children.

Stereotyping — Meaning and Concept

As its etymological derivation, the term stereotype has been derived from a combination of two Greek words — "stereos" (meaning as firm or solid) and "typos" (meaning impression or opinion). Therefore, it tends to stand for "solid impression" or "firm opinion".

The terms stereotype and stereotyping have been variedly defined in the available dictionaries and writings of scholars. Let us try to have a glimpse of these definitions.

Stereotype — Definition

The American Heritage New Dictionary of Cultural Literacy (2005): It defines the term stereotype in the following two ways. (*i*) A too simple and therefore distorted image of a group, such as "Football players are stupid" or "The English are cold and unfriendly people". (*ii*) A generalize or usually exaggerated or oversimplified and often offensive, that is used to describe or distinguish a group.

Webster's Seventh New Collegiate Dictionary (1970: 860); Stereotype is "a standardized mental picture held in common by members of a group and representing an over simplified opinion, affective attitude or uncritical judgment (as of a person, a race, an issue, or an event)".

McGarty, Craig, *et. al.* (2002): In social psychology, a stereotype is a thought that can be adopted about specific types of individuals or certain ways of doing things.

Judd, CM. and Park, B. (1993): The thoughts and beliefs maintained about the people or issues. These thoughts or beliefs may or may not accurately reflect reality.

The definitions given above may help us in drawing following conclusions about the meaning and nature of the term stereotyping:

- Stereotyping reflects the oversimplified attitudes and feelings of the people in general towards specific types of individuals, groups and communities.
- It is the result of incomplete or distorted information accepted as fact without questions or putting into verification and critical judgement.
- It is responsible for breeding an antagonistic attitude, ill feelings and prejudices against the persons who are subjected to stereotyping.
- Under the influence of stereotyping, the victims (individuals or groups) may be found to suffer from: (i) the prejudices, isolation, discrimination, or marginalization on a group or community level, and (ii) anxiety of failure, inferiority complex and lack of confidence in terms of their adjustment and progress at the personal level.

Types or Forms of Stereotyping Behaviour

A stereotype is simply a widely held belief that an individual is a member of a certain group based on its characteristics. Due to the process of overgeneralization within social perception, stereotyping leads to a great deal of inaccuracy in social perception. Sex, race, age, sexual orientation, religion and physical ability are various categories which exist in stereotyping.

As an instance let us take into consideration the gender stereotypes.

Gender Stereotypes Experienced in Home, or Neighbourhood and School

- Girls like to be dependent, protected and looked after than the boys.
- Parents hold an opinion that their daughters need nurturing of passivity and dependency and their sons to be aggressive and independent. (Therefore they punish independence in daughters and passivity in sons.)
- Females are more conforming and more concerned about displaying socially desirable behaviour than males are.
- "Boys don't cry" and "Girls don't fight".
- Girls and females are most fit for doing household job and the boys and males for the outdoor work.
- Girls and females are talkative and are not fit for serious and responsible assignments.
- Girls are not supposed to study mathematics, sciences, computer, commerce and technical subjects. They are suitable for the study of humanity and languages.

- In work output girls and females are quite inferior and often lag behind their male counterparts.
- The girls are not supposed to take part in the games and play activities involving adventure, muscle power and stamina like wrestling, boxing shooting, paragliding and trooping, rock climbing, weight lifting, etc.
- Girls always surpass the boys in the demonstration of communication and social skills, musical and dancing abilities, aesthetic sense and artistic abilities.

Influences on Gender Roles

How the roles played by the children belonging to a particular gender — male or female get influenced by the environment or interactions experienced by him or her at home, school and society, maybe a thing of great importance for us. Let us try to know about such influences.

Parental and Family Influence on Gender Roles

The sense of knowing or considering one self as male or female (boy or girl) is primarily learned by a child through his / her exposure to the behaviour of his / her parents and family members toward the girl and boy child as well as through the observation of the role and activities performed by the male and female members of the family. The things like below in this concern may be found to influence his / her gender role in a quite effective way.

- From a very early age, parents and family members treat their male and female children in a quite different way. They are brought up in accordance with the specificities of their respective genders. Such as dressing them in gender specific clothes (including colour of the dress), providing them gender specific toys to play and expecting from them the gender specific behaviour.
- In most of our families in India, a clear cut gender bias and antagonistic attitude prevails towards the female child. While the birth of a son is celebrated in the family, the birth of a daughter is taken as a huge burden on the shoulders of the parents. All measures including the killing of girl child in the womb of the mother are undertaken by the families for preventing the birth of a girl child. Such antagonistic attitude towards a girl child does not stop but is rather enhanced after her unwanted entry into the family. It makes a girl child to get imbibed with a non-resisting nature, pessimism and tolerance for unjust, unfair and brutal behaviour towards them, a peculiar tendency and characteristic associates with her gender role throughout her life.
- Right from their early age, a girl child observes her mother, sisters and other female members of the family to get engaged in certain type of household work, wear particular type of dresses and talk as well as

behave in the way as expected from them for playing the female gender role. The same is true for a boy child who sees his father, brothers and other male members of the family and relations to demonstrate in their living and behaving the typical features associated with the role of male gender. The girl and boy children, then try to learn and imbibe such things in their behaviour and functioning for getting them involved in playing the respective gender role. Such learning can fix their behaviour just on the lines of stereotypes prevailing in the society for the male and female genders.

Social and Cultural Influences on Gender Role

What happens in the neighbourhood community and society of children casts a quite deep impression on their tender minds from a quite early age. They pick up all social habits and culturally associated ways of living and behaving from the characteristics and activities of the people surrounding them. Thus, the role a girl or boy child is found to play by classifying and associating her or him with a particular gender is a typical learned behaviour and way of living resulted through the impacts and influences of the society and culture in which one lives. In Haryana, for example, you may very often observe a young lady carrying luggage on her head or shoulder while male counterpart accompanying her to walk comfortably with no luggage. Such behaviour fits well into the gender roles expected from them, their society and culture. In a sharp contrast, such behaviour or gender role played by a husband along with his accompanied wife in Uttar Pradesh or various other parts of the country may become a thing of hard condemnation.

Apart from this, the gender roles are many times very much influenced by the social and cultural norms of a particular society. In female dominated communities of various regions of our country, females may be found to perform all such activities and engage in all such behaviour that are typically considered as the birth right of males in the male dominated or governed communities. It is nothing but a true impact or influence left over the prevailing social and cultural norms in particular community.

School and Educational Influences on Gender Role

What the children experience in their schools and avail in terms of their education in various institutions (formal or informal) cast a decisive impact and influence in shaping them to play their gender roles. A good school with a progressive and open environment may work well for doing away with the prevailing gender stereotypes coming in the way of wholesome development and progress of the male and female children. It may help the children to grow and develop according to their own nature and abilities with no obstruction imposed through the prevailing stereotypes. Boys can perform all arts and things of aesthetic expression traditionally thought as an exclusive field of the girls and girls on the other hand can perform all the adventuresome and difficult functions and practice profession traditionally considered as the male dominated areas. Such ill conceived boundaries and limitation imposed on the boys and girls by the gender stereotypes are now seemingly getting vanished through the positive impact or influence of proper schooling and educative experiences. The development in science and technology, the impact of globalization, urbanization and multi-culturism have also provided a good support bringing new definitions for the gender roles played by boys and girls by removing all stereotypes and rigid boundaries lying around them. Truly it has resulted through the knowledge and skills developed and attitudinal changes brought out in the society through the influences of good schooling and education available to the children of the country.

7

Childhood in the Context of Poverty, Globalization and Adult Culture

Introduction

Today we are passing through the era of 21st century. In this modern age we are witnessing a tremendous change in the pattern of growth and development of the children and subsequent resultant changes in their behaviour and personality. The developments in the modern age have affected the development of the children in a variety of ways. However, the increasing gulf between the haves and haves not, rich and poor, educated and uneducated and cultural differences, etc. have resulted in a wide range of diversity and differences among the growing ups. Globalization and rapid industrialization have also affected the learning and development in its own ways. Similarly, the changes brought out in adult culture has influenced the development and behaviour of the developing children. The question arises how these factors have affected the development of the children? In this chapter here we would like to look at the childhood in the context of poverty, globalization and adult culture. However, let us first see what do we mean by childhood.

What is Childhood?

Childhood in its simple meaning stands for the state of being a child, the time of being a child. The UN convention on the Rights of the Child (United Nation, 1989) defines "Child" as all those under the age of 18 years — every human being below the age of 18 years or the age specified by the law of a country to be declared as adult. According to the law of our country, we treat a person below the age of 18 years as a child and the state of his / her being the childhood.

Childhood in the Context of Poverty

Poverty is a great sin and poverty ridden children are the worst sufferers in terms of various types of deprivations and disadvantages suffered by them on one or the other accounts. The story of their sufferings and deprivations in this connection starts well from the time of their conception in the womb of their mothers and then gets continued throughout their developmental period affecting their growth and development, education and progress as well as interests and welfare in a variety of ways mentioned below:

1. The poverty ridden children may inherit many of the hereditary diseases and ailments, inabilities and incapacities, weaknesses and limitations through the defective genes and chromosomes transmitted to them by their immediate parents who are unfortunate enough to get inflicted by them on account of their poverty ridden defective environment and humiliating conditions of living and working. This defective inheritance may prove them quite costly in terms of the poor base and weak structure for starting their journey of development and progress in their life.

2. In the womb of the mother these poverty ridden children do not get needed nourishment and care for their proper growth and development. The mothers are helpless in supplying them due nourishment as they themselves may be found in passing through the state of starvation, malnutrition, unhygienic living, physical ailments and mental agony or stress.

3. At the time of birth also there may arise a number of problems and adversity to these new born children. There may be no proper facilities available for the delivery of these poverty ridden children. The environmental and sanitary conditions are very poor and unhygienic and thus there are many chances of picking up a number of abnormalities and defects by these children at the time of their birth

4. Many of the times the birth of these children is not welcome on the part of their parents or other family members as they may think it as an extra burden on their poverty. They may thus have to bear the blunt of the negligence, indifference, apathy, antagonistic attitudes and ill feelings of their dears and nears with no fault on their part.

5. After birth on wards these children are deprived with what is needed to them in terms of their proper nourishment, care and satisfaction of their basic needs, availability of essential material facilities, education and progress in their developmental period. The poverty and poor socio economic status of their parents and family may be found to stand firmly well against their progress and development in many ways and consequently they may have to face the blunt of so many disadvantages, discriminations, prejudices, stereotypes, marginalization and deprivations of one or the other kind resulting in various negative outcomes to them as summarized below.

- On account of the poor and pathetic conditions the children of the poor families cannot dream of the balanced diet and nutritious food, clean water, hygienic living conditions and other physical and material facilities essential for their adequate physical development and healthy disease free living.
- The poverty ridden children being victims of malnutrition and unhealthy as well as unhygienic living conditions right from their conception do not have natural growth of their sensory nerves and brain cells. As a result there is every possibility of retardation in terms of their intellectual functioning.

• The poverty ridden children do not get proper opportunity for their language development. Generally their parents and family members are uneducated and illiterate. They have neither the time for a proper dialogue with their children (on account of their struggling for earning livelihood) nor have the proper vocabulary and command over the language. In their poverty ridden homes and neighbourhood there are no newspapers, magazines, books and library facilities, radio, television or internet services available for them to provide adequate experience for the development of expressive and communicative skills.

• The deprivation suffered by the poverty ridden children may cast quite an adverse and retrogressive impact upon the development of essential cognitive abilities, and attainment of essential social and emotional maturity and getting desired academic progress in their learning pursuits. One's thinking, feelings and actions are always influenced by what is going on with him as a living and social being. One's mental and emotional state at a particular time thus proves a great determinant of his mental, emotional, social and academic functioning. The disadvantaged poor children often remains tensed, worried and emotionally maladjusted on account of the paucity of resources and humiliation suffered in meeting their one or the other developmental and educational needs and it may cast a quite adverse effect on their mental, social, emotional and academic development and progress.

• The overall development, adjustment and progress of the poverty ridden children may also suffer on account of the denial of proper educational facilities to them. Their parents do not send them schools on account of taking their help in their bread earning pursuits, domestic assignments or getting engaged them in child labour. In case they intend to send them schools, then it becomes an uphill task for them to afford the expenses even for the state running institutions. The schooling of their children in the reputed good schools is entirely out of the question for the poverty ridden parents. In case they get admission in some schools anyhow, they have to suffer from maladjustment on one or the other grounds. More often, here they are ridiculed, humiliated, discriminated, marginalized and victimized on account of the poverty or socio-economic status of their families. It gets them emotionally and mentally disturbed resulting in their under-achievement and backwardness in curricular and co-curricular pursuits.

• The hardships faced, discrimination and marginalization suffered and obstacles faced in the developmental path cast a quite negative effect on the proper development of self-confidence, self-efficacy and self-esteem among the poverty ridden children. More often these children are found to suffer from the feelings of insecurity, lack of self-confidence, guilty consciousness and inferiority complexes causing great harm to their adequate adjustment, development and progress in life.

In this way, it may be properly visualized that a child's poverty and low socio-economic status may prove quite costly to him or her in terms of his or her adjustment, development and progress in school, society and life. Such children, therefore needs adequate help, assistance and guidance for dealing with their problems and progressing to their maximum on the part of the government, non-government organizations, school authorities and teachers. The suggestion like below may prove fruitful in this direction:

1. There should be well planned scheme on the part of government and non-government organizations for providing financial assistance and incentives to the poverty ridden children for their schooling.
2. The schooling should be free to the poverty ridden children. The community and government should take care of their dress and other reading material needed by them for their education.
3. There should be a fixed proportion of seats reserved for the poverty ridden children in all types of schools (Government, Aided and Private or Public schools.).
4. There should be proper arrangement of midday meal program especially suited to the poverty ridden children.
5. Care should be taken for paying attention up on the living conditions of the poverty ridden families. They should be helped in improving their sanitary conditions, and feeding them in a proper way. They should also be helped in having their *pakka* houses, electricity supply, kitchen gas and clean water to drink with a sufficient subsidy and concessional rates.
6. There should be free and concessional provision of essential medical facilities to the poverty ridden families and children
7. The community services, games and entertainment facilities should be suitably available to the poverty ridden children with no cost.
8. They should be given all incentives to take part in co-curricular activities and programs helpful in the wholesome development of their personality
9. They should be helped in knowing and learning that poverty does not come in the progress and development of a person if he tries to proceed on his path with a firm determination. There should be arrangement of such motivational lectures, dialogues and workshops in the schools as well as in community centres.
10. Whenever, a poverty ridden child is found to excel in one or the other field, he should be duly encouraged for his or her efforts and attempts should be made to produce him or her as a living example to others.

Childhood in the Context of Globalization

Globalization, a quite distinguished feature of modern era, has been responsible for influencing the development and behaviour of children in a variety of ways. Let us discuss it. However, before engaging into such a discussion let us first try to know about the meaning and concept of globalization.

Globalization: Meaning and Concept

Globalization in its simple meaning stands for a sort of integrated and global view of the things and practices going on all over the globe in our world of living and behaving. It reflects a feeling that all what exists on the globe in the form of the contributions of the nature or human beings may influence the life and work of all who belongs to this globe. For its understanding and comprehension well, the term globalization has been defined in a variety of ways by many scholars and writers. Let us reproduce a few here in drawing conclusion about the meaning and concept of the term globalization.

Martin Albrow and Elizabeth King (1990: 8): Globalization represents all those processes by which the peoples of the world are incorporated into a single world society.

Anthony Giddens (1990): Globalization can be defined as the intensification of worldwide social relations which link distant localities in such a way that local happenings are shaped by events occurring many miles away and vice versa.

Thomas Larson (2001: 9): Globalization is the process of world shrinkage, of distances getting shorter, things moving closer. It pertains to the increasing ease with which somebody on one side of the world can interact, to mutual benefit, with somebody on the other side of the world.

Lechner and Boli (2012): Globalization means more people across large distances becoming connected in more and different ways.

Brine (1999): Globalization as a cultural process has been seen as an extension of mass media and the consequent universalization of western mores and culture.

Gibson-Graham (1996): Gobalization is a set of processes by which the world is rapidly being integrated into one economic space via increased international trade, the internationalization of production and financial markets, and the internationalization of a commodity culture promoted by an increasingly networked global telecommunication system.

A close analysis of the definition given above may help us to reveal the things like below about the meaning, nature and significance of globalization:

- Globalization stands for a process resulting into a number of productive outcomes influencing and affecting our living and behaving at the individual, group, community, national and international level in varieties of ways.
- It has helped in shrinking the boundaries and providing maximum opportunities as well as facilities for the mutual interaction and

cooperation among the individuals, communities, and nations all over the globe by removing the barriers of space, distance and time.

- It is associated with the evolution and emergence of the faith in industrialization commercialization, barrier free trading, banking and business promotion all over the globe between and among the people and countries.
- It has provided scope and facilities for visiting places and seeking employment for the people belonging to one area of the globe to other areas of globes
- It has resulted in the interactions and assimilation of different cultures on account of knowledge explosion, and migration of the people belonging to different cultures from one area of the globe to another.
- It has helped in the establishment and maintenance of cross border economic, political and socio-cultural relations between the people, communication and nations of the world.
- It aims for sharing the knowledge and understanding, inventions and discoveries ideologies and values, fashions and arts, means and programs of health, education and entertainment among the people and communities of the world.
- It owns its existence on the development and technological progress visible in the field of transportation, information and communication techniques, computer applications, space science and satellites technology.
- It has resulted in laying emphasis on material value and styles dominated by western philosophy and way of life.
- It has resulted in turning the people of the world into a single world society and feeling the jerk of the things and events happening in any corner of the globe.

In view of the above meaning and features of globalization we can refer globalization as a process of interlinking and affecting the life and working of the individuals and institutions of the world community, in a variety of means and ways such as economically, educationally, politically and socio-culturally by breaking the barriers of space and time.

Impact of Globalization on the development of children and adolescents

The changes affected on the economic, political, educational and socio-cultural fabrics of the global community on account of the above discussed globalization process may be seen to cast quite mentionable impact on the development of the children and adolescents all over the world. As happens with the outcomes of any efforts of introducing change or bringing modernization, there is always a mix trend of positive and negative influences. The same is also true with the impact of globalization on the development of our children. We can summarize these impacts in the ways given ahead.

A. Positive and favourable impacts

Globalization may be credited to offer a number of benefits, right opportunities and assistance contributing towards the proper progress and wellbeing of the children in the following way:

1. Globalization has resulted in the great exposure of the children to the world of multiculturalism. They have now more opportunities and facilities to get acquainted with the living and behaving of the people belonging to different cultures, religious faiths and ideologies. It has helped the children to develop respect and tolerance about the people and communities belonging to different religious faiths, cultures and ideologies.

2. Exposure to outside world coupled with the knowledge explosion and scientific progress is helping our children and adolescents in getting rid as well as protecting themselves from a number of social evils and disparities prevalent in our society in the name of superstitions, stereotypes, prejudices, marginalization and deprivation.

3. The opportunities in abundance available to the children on account of the impact of globalization for acquiring knowledge and skills of various sort are helping the children in widening their mental horizon, seek proper development of their intellectual capacities and learning appropriate skills for their adjustment and progress in life.

4. Globalization has been able to remove any type of hesitation and fear about going abroad. It has been responsible in developing right attitude in the children to utilize educational, business and employment opportunities available in different parts of the globe. The adolescents have started to plan their careers and choose subjects or courses that can help them in getting benefitted from the impacts of globalization.

5. Globalization has been responsible for the establishment and running a number of world and regional bodies like UNESCO, UNICEF and WHO for rendering necessary assistance to the developing children, in their educational and cultural development, maintenance of health and hygiene and protection from the diseases. These organizations have been doing commendable job in the task of helping the children all over the globe in their proper development and progress. The efforts in the direction of the removal of the deadly diseases like polio and measles, TB etc., previously affecting the health and wellbeing of the children in a quite adverse way, may be cited as a glaring impact of global cooperation made possible through globalization. Similarly, we may witness a lot of cooperation and coordination among the communities and nations of the world on a global and regional basis for providing, assistance and help to the children in their educational and career building through the provision of scholarships; students and teachers exchange programs; and organization of educational seminars, workshops and conferences, etc.

B. Negative and unfavourable impacts

Besides, the positive and favourable impacts pointed out above, globalization may also be found to exercise a quite negative and adverse effects on the development of children in the manner given below:

1. On account of providing a huge or say unlimited exposure to the children to the outside world through its development in transport, ICT, electronic, mobile and computer technology, globalization has resulted in shaping and moulding the life, working and behaviour of the children in a specific mode dominated by western culture, ideals and values of life. Every culture or mode of life, adopted by the communities and races, has its strengths and weaknesses. Where its strengths or positively provides inspiration and brings improvement in the life of the followers, the negativity and weaknesses takes them away from their right path. In imitation, as we know, it is the negative that attracts more and is picked up easily for one's living and behaving. Here our children and adolescents have also been attracted by the negativity and weaknesses present in the western culture. It has been responsible in making many of our children and adolescents to get imbibed with the habits, attitudes, interests, values and life style affecting their development in an adverse way. The same is the case with the children who have been influenced and mesmerized with the ideas and doctrines spread over on the globe by many vested interests, religious extremists and terrorist organizations and taken a wrong course for their living and behaving.

2. Globalization is associated with the emergence of heavy industrialization, urbanization, and centralization of marketing, trading and commerce. It has resulted in the huge increase in the number of migration of the people from one region to another region or one part of the globe to another for want of earning their livelihood or seeking better opportunities for living and earning. In some cases, where the migrants have been fortunate enough to get better facilities, the cause of the development of their children in a better way has been satisfactorily served. But for a quite huge number of them their migration is proving quite detrimental to the development and wellbeing of their children. Many of them have to leave their families and children to their place of origin for taking time to get settled in their new employment or business. In the absence of father, the children do not get sufficient attention and care as needed for their adequate development. The case becomes more typical when mothers have also to serve or devote time in looking after the family occupation or source of earning.

3. Globalization associated with the ideas or approaches of capitalism, materialism and a blind race of getting prosperous by hook and crook has been responsible for the loss of moral values all over the globe. The same has affected the ways of living and behaving of the world community and it has adversely affected the rearing and parenting styles, caring and education

of the children responsible for the loss of moral, social and cultural values among the children. The relations between the parents and children, teachers and students and children as friends and peers have been centered round the narrow materialistic interests and self-defined goals and the same has been responsible for many drawbacks in the proper growth and development of the children.

In this way, globalization may be seen to influence the growth and development of the children in both aspect of its positivity and negativity inherent in its nature and processing. However, globalization as a whole in its functioning and objectives stands for the unity, cohesiveness, progress and wellbeing of the world community and as such it may be viewed and employed as a means of bringing lot of improvement and hope in the activities and programs related to the development and wellbeing of the children and adolescents.

Childhood in the Context of Adult Culture

Culture of a society or community, referred to as adult culture from the angle of children, may be defined as a way of living and believing on the part of the adults of that society or community. A child from his or her earlier age learns and acquires the way of living and behaving of the adult members of the society through the deliberate attempts made by the adults on this account or picks them up through observation and initiation in a quite spontaneous way. What ever the mode may be his or her way of living and behaving are very much influenced by the cultural modes of the adults including parents, family members and community people. Adult culture may differ from community to community and region to region throughout the globe in terms of the philosophy of life or life style, ideals and values, thinking and behaving, mores and traditions, habits and temperament as well as goals and ambitions of life. All these things related to the adult culture of a society cost a strong impact or influence over the growth and development of the children and it is why adult culture is said to be a quite effective and dominant factor in shaping the minds and personality of the developing children particularly in the period of their childhood. Wide diversities and differences may be witnessed between the diverse adult cultures available in a region such as rural and urban cultures, eastern and western cultures, tribals and non tribals cultures, Punjabi, Haryanavi, Rajasthani, Gujarati, Bengali and South Indian cultures. The adult cultures prevailing in the Muslim countries and the communities following Islamic religion may differ a lot from the adult cultures prevailing in the regions and communities following other religions, like Christianity, Buddha, Hinduism, etc. Similarly, a lot of differences may be found among the adult cultures prevailing in the different regions of the globe covering Europe, Africa and Asian countries. At present, the technologically advanced communities of the world may be seen to exhibit different ways of living and behaving in comparison to those who have been left behind in such race. There is also a wide gap between the educationally enriched communities and educationally backward or illiterate communities in terms of the quality and kind of adult culture. Similarly, the cultures of the communities adopting joint family or nuclear family systems, unprogressive or progressive life styles, orthodox or productive new ideas may differ a lot in terms of its outputs and consequences for the growth and development of children. In nut shell we can say that "what the culture so the nature of the childhood". Many times influences of the cultures are said to have great weight and force in comparison to what is resulted through the mechanism of heredity characteristics. What we get in terms of the personality development and behaviour of the developing children is mostly controlled and shaped by the impact and influences of adult culture.

As an instance we may cite the following in the supporting our derived conclusion on the influence of adult culture. In a society or community where adult culture is characterized with a number of negative things, undesirable and anti-social behaviour, disputes and fighting loss of moral values and unhealthy habits of living, the children pick up and imbibe in their behaviour and living all such negativity. Their childhood drifts into wrong direction and they pickup ugly path for their living and behaving. The criminals, anti-social personalities, alcoholics and drug addicts, failures and beggars are said to be the product of such negatively characterized adult culture. In a positively characterized healthy culture of a society or community, the childhood gets nourished and developed in a quite positive and desirable ways by laying emphasis over social and moral values and right way of living and behaving.

In this way, we may witness a wide range of similarities and diversities between the childhoods of the developing children as a result of the impact or influences left over them by the adult cultures of the communities in which they live and grow. Let us think more about such similarities and diversities giving birth to multiple childhoods in our country's social life.

Similarities and Diversities within the Stage of Childhood

Childhood is defined as the stage and state of being a child. At this stage children are found to demonstrate a typical behaviour named as childish behaviour, quite distinct and different from the behaviour shown by them as grownup and mature individual in their thoughts, feelings and actions. All individuals in their childhood are found to demonstrate some generalized tendencies and common characteristics in their child like behaviour. Such similarities found in the behaviours of individuals in their childhood may be summarized as below:

- They are found to show a lot of dependency on their parents, guardians and others who provide support in the task of their upbringing nourishment, development and the satisfaction of basic needs.

- They are generally taken as the individuals of pure heart, quite honest in their behaviour with others.
- The period of their childhood in more often taken as synonymous with innocence, freedom, joy, play and like. The children at this stage are found to remain away from social evils and relatively enjoy a carefree life spared from the regions, responsibilities and obligations of adult life.
- They may demonstrate a lot of immaturity in their ways of thinking and performing the day to day tasks. Actually they are in the process of the development of the abilities and capacities in the physical, mental, social, emotional and moral dimensions of their personality and consequently they may be found to demonstrate a lot of incapacity and immaturity in their thinking, feeling and actions in comparison to the adults.
- Children are quite curious by nature. They have a genuine love for creativity and constructiveness, are interested in doing the things by themselves for their learning.
- All children are found to be struggling for the satisfaction of their common basic needs classified as physical or physiological needs, and socio-psychological needs. In addition to these common needs, they may also be found to have their specific or special needs depending upon their own individualities, specialities and differential abilities.

In this way individuals in their childhood may be found to possess a number of common characteristics and demonstrate a lot of similarities in their cognitive, conative and affective behaviour. However, it does not mean that they do not have their own uniqueness and individualities. Actually as may be witnessed at home, neighbourhood, community and school situations, there lies wide diversity among the children in terms of so many wide and varied aspects. It is more clearly visible and loudly pronounced in an inclusive class, where the differences and diversities among the learners of the same class and age group may pose a great challenge for the teachers in the matter of providing quality education to all with no discrimination of any kind. The learners of the inclusive class may present a variety of multiplicity of childhood instead of a childhood characterized by the common features, behavioural characteristics and needs. We may classify this diversity or multiplicity of childhood as childhood lived and experienced on the part of:

(i) Children with disabilities and impairments of various nature, such as hearing, visual, locomotor, mental, emotional, learning, etc.

(ii) Non disabled normal children possessing differences and divergence in terms of the possession of differences in their physical, mental, emotional, social, moral and aesthetic abilities, interests, attitudes, habits, levels of motivation, goals and ambitions, possessing self confidence, persistence and other desirable or undesirable personality traits, learning styles and problems, etc.

(iii) Marginalized and deprived children suffering discrimination on diverse grounds such as caste, colour, race locale, language gender, socio-economic status, rural and tribal areas, minority communities, etc.

(iv) Problem children suffering from various types of social and behavioural problems, delinquent and anti-social behaviour, drug addicts and alcoholics, backward and slow learners, etc.

(v) Children suffering from various types of health problems and issues.

(vi) Children from the privileged sections of the society belonging to higher caste, higher socio-economic status, getting full facilities for their upbringing, education and development.

(vii) Creative and talented children having higher achievement motivation.

It may be observed in the cases of the above cited children, that all of them exhibit a quite wide variety of diversities and differences from each other in relation to the nature of childhood enjoyed and lived by each of them. It is why we are forced to witness the presence of multiple childhoods in inclusive setting of the schools. Now the question here may arise that what are the underlying causes or factors responsible for the birth and perpetuation of such multiple childhoods. Factors leading to the formation of multiple childhoods (characterized with diverse level of abilities and disability) among the developing children may be summarized as below:

- Deprivation and marginalization suffered by children at their home, neighbourhood, society, and school on one or the other accounts such as poverty, gender discrimination, caste, colour, regionalism, language, belongingness to rural or tribal areas, etc. may provide a quite bleak picture of the childhood before the developing children against the bright picture portrayed by the facilities and advantages received by the children representing mainstream belonging to privileged segments of the society.
- The various types of impairments disabilities and handicap suffered by the developing children in various areas of their growth and development against the normality and non-disability observed in the developing children.
- The limits imposed on the developing children by their hereditary endowment on the growth, development and progress of the children against the right push up provided by the genes and chromosomes of the parents for touching the sky in their lives.
- The proper or improper ways and styles adopted by the parents and family member for rearing and nourishing the children in their childhood.
- The degree of satisfaction or dissatisfaction availed by the developing children in the satisfaction of their physical, biological and socio-psychological needs.
- The type of proper and improper schooling and educational opportunities available for the developing children for their development and progress.

- The presence or absence of stressful situation in the period of childhood of the developing children in the form of separation or loss of parents, denial of child rights, victim of child abuse and cruelty, etc.
- The presence or absence of the severe health issues and problems, accidents and heart breaker incidents faced by the children in their childhood.

The factors or elements cited above may provide sufficient ground for shaping and providing the childhood of an individual, a particular shape. Since the nature of these factors or elements are not uniform and similar to all children, we may witness the huge diversity in the status and condition of childhood for the population of children belonging to a particular society or inclusive school giving birth to the concept of multiple childhood.

8

Socialisation — Concept and Agencies

What is Socialization?

Man is said to be a social animal meaning thereby that he ought to be social while living in and adjusting to the society. Society is as essential as food to him and consequently he has to maintain social relationships and try to adjust with others. But this does not mean that he is born with such social behaviour and social qualities. Actually the child is very much selfish and unsocial at the time of his birth and earlier years of life. His basic animal nature is then gradually changed into man-like social nature through a process of learning *i.e.,* reconstruction of experience's. The forces and elements present in one's environment make him to think, feel and act according to the norms, ideals and aspirations of the society. The processes and the acts through which his basic animal like selfish nature is changed into man like social nature are referred to as processes of socialisation. In this way socialisation may be defined as a process which brings desirable changes in the behaviour of an individual as to convert his unsocial nature into the social one in order to make him adjusted in the society to which he belongs.

Various thinkers have tried to define the term socialisation (or social development) in a variety of ways. Let us have look into a few definitions.

Sorenson (1948, p. 50): consider socialisation as "an increasing ability to get along well with oneself and others."

Hurlock (1959, p. 257): Socialisation (or social development) means the attaining of maturity in social relationships.

Garrett (1968, p. 555): Socialisation is the process whereby the biological individual is converted into a human person.

Let us try to analyse above definitions. The first definition given by Sorenson emphasizes that socialisation of the individual results in the increased improvement and development of his social abilities or skills. Such improvement and enhancement further helps him in bringing improvement in his capacity of maintaining social relationships which ultimately result in his proper adjustment to his self and others.

The second definition given by Hurlock carries a wide meaning by emphasizing that socialisation makes an individual socially mature. As a result he can demonstrate a quite desirable and proper behaviour with regard to the maintenance of desirable social relationships and adjustment to socio-cultural environment.

The third definition given by Garrett is based upon the distinction between the term 'individual' and 'person'. We cannot name each and everybody as person. The person always possesses same personality.

The personality is the product of social interaction between him and his socio-cultural environment. Socialisation as a process of social interaction helps the individual to attach the status of person by imbibing essential personality traits.

In the light of the views expressed in the above quoted definitions we can come to the conclusion that *socialisation is essentially a process or combination of processes that helps an individual to imbibe such essential behavioural characteristics and social virtues which results into the:* (i) *attainment of social maturity,* (ii) *conversion of his animal nature into humanistic social nature* and (iii) *enabling him to live in harmony with his self and other members of the society.*

Agencies of Socialisation — Meaning and Types

Now the next question arises as to what brings the socialisation *i.e.,* desirable changes in the social behaviour of the individual. Essentially there must be the elements or factors present in one's socio-cultural environment. We may name them as parents, family, neighbourhood, playing mates, friends, school, social and religious institutions, the regional and political organisations community, clubs, means of transport, communications and entertainments, fairs and excursions, libraries, newspapers, magazines and printed literature, etc.

The socialising agencies mentioned above as part of one's socio-cultural environment cast a very deepening impact on the ways of behaving and working of the individuals to the extent that he becomes almost a slave in the hands of these so powerful environmental forces. It is in this reference that the famous behaviour psychologist J.B. Watson had to comment in the following words.

> *"Give me a dozen healthy infants, well informed and my own specific world to bring them up in and I will guarantee to take anyone at random and train him to become any type of specialist, I might select — doctor, lawyer, artist, merchant chief and yes, even beggarman and thief"* (Watson, 1930).

The above saying may seem a bit of an exaggeration. However, one thing is definite that agencies of socialisation play quite a leading and assertive role in developing our actualities and potentialities, shaping and moulding our behaviour in many of its ways and means. As an illustration of the impact of the socio-cultural forces of our environment on the development of one's personality and behaviour we would like to concentrate on the roles of the most important agencies of socialization namely, family, school and peers.

Role of Different Agencies in Child Development

Role of Family

The home and family is the birth place and starting phase of one's development. All the earlier lessons regarding the shaping of behaviour and development of personality are well learned on the part of developing children in the company and direction of their parents, caretakers, siblings and other members of the family. How well a child grow and develop in form of his physical, motor, mental / cognitive, emotional, social or moral development depends upon the type of favourable or unfavourable environment available for his living and developing at his home. The things and factors like below present in one's home and family environment may play a quite decisive role in setting the course of child's cognitive, affective and conative development.

- The healthy or unhealthy living conditions, food habits, availability of nutritious and balanced diet, play and healthy entertainment facilities at home.
- Type of bond and relationship existing between parents.
- The attitude and behaviour of the parents and members of the family towards the child showing over-affection, partiality, neglect, hatred, prejudices, over-anxiety and over-security, strictness or carelessness etc.
- The size of the family and birth order of the child.
- Relationships among the members of the family.
- Socio-economic status and position of the family in the society.
- The traditions, cultural values and ideals of the family.
- The education level of the parents, their interest and attention in bringing up of the children and their abilities and capacity for this purpose.
- The organised or broken homes.
- The individual behaviour, habits, temperament and other personality characteristics of the parents and other members of the family.
- The attitudes and ideals of the parents and members of the family towards social norms, ethical, moral and human values.
- The changes introduced in the set up and status of the family on account of the extreme variations of the conditions like sudden losses in terms of human lives, natural calamities, economic disasters, etc. or gain in positive side like increase in wealth, social status and power equations, etc.

All of the above things and situations prevalent in the home and family environment cast a considerable impact in influencing and providing a definite direction to the growth and development of the child including his personality make-up and behavioural traits.

In the homes, where the children get a desirable stimulating and enriched environment for the development of their linguistic ability, communication skills, creative potential and mental faculties they may be found proceeding well on the path of their proper language and cognitive development in comparison to those who are deprived with such facilities and congenial home conditions. Similarly, the children who are privileged to have conditions at their home quite congenial to their physical or motor development may be found to go far ahead in terms of the acquisition of motor skills and physical development in comparison to the children being deprived of such congenial conditions. Actually every child learns and acts what is observed and imitated by him through the behaviour of his parents, elders, siblings and other members of the family. Therefore, all what is there in child's behaviour and development with respect to his habits, temperament, emotional expressions, social traits, morality, etc. are mostly learned and reflected in his behaviour through the impact or influence of the home and family environment. The satisfaction of basic needs — physical and socio-psychological — is very much essential for the proper cognitive, conative and affective development and adjustment of a child. As far as the home and family environment remains congenial and helpful for the child in the realization of his desired needs, the child may remain on a proper track, of his adequate adjustment and development but as soon as things drift on the other side, the child begins to feel despair and frustration, become maladjusted to his self and the environment and consequently may lag behind in his cognitive, conative affective development or may learn maladapted or socially undesirable behaviour in the chain of his doomed future. In this way, the uncongenial or defective home and family environment may prove not only a great obstacle in the proper development of children but it may also provide all what is needed for the full growth and nourishment of unsocial or immoral behaviour. The development, proper or improper and good or bad behaviour, thus may have its origin as well as its further stimulation and reinforcement from what is available to it from the family and home environment.

Apart from what has been said above about the role of family in the development of the children, one specific thing that influences the development of children in a variety of ways is the nature of the parenting style or child rearing practice adopted by the parents for the rearing of their children.

Let us discuss it in detail.

Meaning of the Term Parenting Styles or Child Rearing Practices

The term child rearing practices in its word meaning stands for the practices adopted for rearing or bringing up the children by their parents. In its technical language, in psychology it is termed as parenting styles or practices of child rearing. The practices or styles adopted by the parents in rearing their children are quite unique in their nature and are largely determined by the factors like (i) influence of one's own parents and culture i.e. they learn (copy or select) rearing practices from their own parents and culture in which they grow and develop, (ii) temperaments of the children, (iii) their own temperaments, (iv) the circumstances and environment in which they have to rear their children.

The Types of Parenting Styles or Child Rearing Practices

The parents may be found to adopt one or the other type of rearing practices or parenting styles for rearing or bringing up their children to help and guide them in the needed tasks of their growth and development, adjustment and progress in their life. In view of Diana Baumrind (1967), the famous sociologist cum psychologist known for putting up an effective theory of parenting style, there are four basic elements — responsiveness v/s unresponsiveness and demanding v/s undemanding — that may be seen involved in shaping one or the other practice or style adopted by the parents in rearing their children. These basic elements in their respective combination may give birth to four types of rearing practices or parenting styles such as: (i) Responsiveness and demanding, (ii) Unresponsiveness and demanding, (iii) Responsiveness and undemanding, and (iv) Unresponsiveness and undemanding.

Based on these combination, Maccoby and Martin (1983) have emphasized that there are the following four major practices or styles adopted by parents for rearing their children.

1. Authoritative parenting style or child rearing practice
2. Authoritarian parenting style or child rearing practice
3. Indulgent child parenting style or child rearing practice
4. Neglectful parenting style or child rearing practice

Let us discuss these practices along with the influences they may carry on the developing children.

Authoritative Parenting Style or Child Rearing Practice

In such practice or style there is proper positive integration of the elements responsiveness and demanding turning it to be a responsible and balanced parenting in true sense. The main characteristics or features of such integration may be outlined as below.

(a) The element of responsiveness: The parents exhibit responsiveness in rearing their children in terms of the following:

- They try to understand the feelings of their children and teach them how to regulate them.
- They help them in solving their problems by providing appropriate outlets and opportunities for doing so.
- They have desired interaction with their children by, having the communication channel open for verbal dialogues. Moreover in such communication they remain reasonably warm and caring.
- They do not believe in dictatorship and strict control and thus allow their children to have freedom of exploration and make their own decisions based upon their own reasoning.

- Their approach in the rearing of their children remains mainly a child-centered approach instead of the parent centered approach. They care for nurturing the needs, expectations, wishes and aspirations of their children instead of making to fulfill their needs, expectations and desires.

(b) The element of demanding: On the other hand, parents remain quite watchful of the interests and welfare of their children by putting the demands like below:

- They set limits and expectations before their children for their growth and development in various dimensions of their personality.
- For the achievement of these limits and expectations, they set clear standards, and milestones of the progress before their children and monitor their progress regularly for keeping them necessarily attentive and alert towards the realization of their goals.
- They expect and demand the maturity in the behaviour of their children in accordance with their age and stages of development.
- However in meeting these demands, they remain quite reasonable and democrats. That is why the authoritative rearing practice or style is known as the assertive democratic practice (assertive as well as democratic in its nature). It can be demonstrated in their parenting behaviour in the manner given below.
- They are attentive to their children's concern and typically adopt a practice of forgive and teach instead of punishing or pushing the child on his failure to reach the set limits and expectations.
- In case whenever they punish their children, they resort to it with great concern and positive outlook *i.e.* not punishing the child but his undesirable behaviour and lack of attention. Moreover, they are quite homogeneous, impartial and fair in their punishments whether one is a girl or boy child. The punishment mode is never harsh and arbitrary and the reason or motive of punishing the children is also made quite clear to them.

Influence on the Development

This type of authoritative rearing practice or parenting style is supposed to carry a number of positive and desirable effects on the proper development and progress of the developing children. On the following grounds:

- It provides due encouragement for the children to grow and develop their capacities by providing them proper freedom and opportunities but in doing so it does not allow them to go out of track and still places needed limits and controls at their actions. Therefore, there are little chances for the developing children to get lost or de-railed in their developmental path.
- The children rearing so are found to be quite self-satisfied in terms of the fulfillment of their basic needs — physical, social and emotional. They know the ways of channelizing their instincts and emotions and

developing their basic potentialities by their own independent efforts.

- They are found to be quite sincere to their duties and remain disciplined in life by observing self-restraint and are law-avoiding by nature. They are observed to feel obliged to their parents in providing them all what is needed for their proper growth and development with a proper check on their independent activities.

In this way this type of rearing practice, is expected to result in children having a higher self-esteem, seeking in dependent self-growth with higher achievement motivation. It can help maximum in all round expected development of the children in all the dimensions of their personality with no ill effects or painful memories in their mind and it is why this type of rearing practice or parenting styles is considered as the most recommend style of parenting by child rearing experts.

Authoritarian Parenting Style or Child Rearing Practice

In adopting such rearing practice, the parents are observed to be more demanding and less or least responsive to their children's needs, capacities, desires and ambitions. They do not give opportunities to the children for the expression of their needs, desires or ambitions but impose their own will and expectations by enforcing strict disciplines, code of ethics and their own authority. Some of the distinguished features and characteristics of such rearing practice or parenting style may be outlined as below.

- It is absolutely a totalitarian or authoritarian style of parenting and rearing one's children in contrast to the previously mentioned authoritative or assertive democratic style of parenting.
- It is a rigidly controlled strict disciplinary style in contrast to the authoritative balanced style and totally loose, unbridled or uncaring parenting styles.
- It is characterized by high expectations of conformity and compliance to the rules and directions framed by the parents and allows a little or no scope for open dialogue between the parents and children.
- It represents a quite rigid, non-flexible, restrictive and punitive style where the parents expect from their children to follow their direction without raising any question and seeking reason behind the orders issued, rules prescribed or boundaries fixed for their movements.
- The parents are all set to see that children are observing the rules and respecting their work and efforts directed towards goals and limits decided for them by their parents with the least care of their potential capabilities desires and ambitions.
- Here the parents are too selfish to think always about their own ambitions and self-interests to be served through the outcomes or accomplishment of their children with the least care whether they are willing or capable of coming to their expectations or not. They wish and push their children forcefully to achieve all what has been denied to them in the past *i.e.* the parents not fulfilling their own desire of

becoming doctors / engineers / IAS officers may adopt an authoritarian parenting style for enforcing strict, restrictive and punitive style to their one or the other children to develop and progress on the lines and limits of their own dreams.

- The parents adopting this style are seen to shut their eyes and ears to the needs and desires of their children. They are not at all responsive and sensitive to their children's feelings rather they cause the repression of their wishes and inner feelings by enforcing their authority rules and strict discipline. They always make the children to follow instead of giving any space for choosing them their own path or course of self-development.

Influence on the Development

Authoritarian child rearing practice or style of parenting is said to influence the development of the children in some of the following ways.

- They may become handicapped in taking their own decisions in solving their problems or planning and executing the tasks of their life as they have been reared in the circumstances where their work had been merely to follow and not to take initiative / decision by their own.
- Their intellectual, emotional and social development suffer a great set back on account of being denied the needed essential opportunities and independent facilities for doing so in their early life by their authoritarian parents.
- Their instinctive and emotional energy does not find the suitable expression and outlet for the desired channelization, sublimation or catharsis in the environment surcharged with authoritarian code of conduct prescribed by their parents. As expected, the repressed wishes, unfulfilled desires and the uneasineness felt by the children in the slave like conditions prevailed in the authoritarian rearing, may force the children to develop serious behavioural and conduct problems. If the demands and descriptions are pushed too forcefully upon the children, it may either make them to seek withdrawal from the positive work and efforts for progress or burst into social deviant, rebellion or delinquents.
- Such type of parenting does not help the children to acquire needed social skills and competencies for leading their life in a proper way. They can't learn and live with democratic principles and ways of life. The qualities of democratic living and good citizenship can hardly be developed among the children brought up in such authoritarian parenting style.

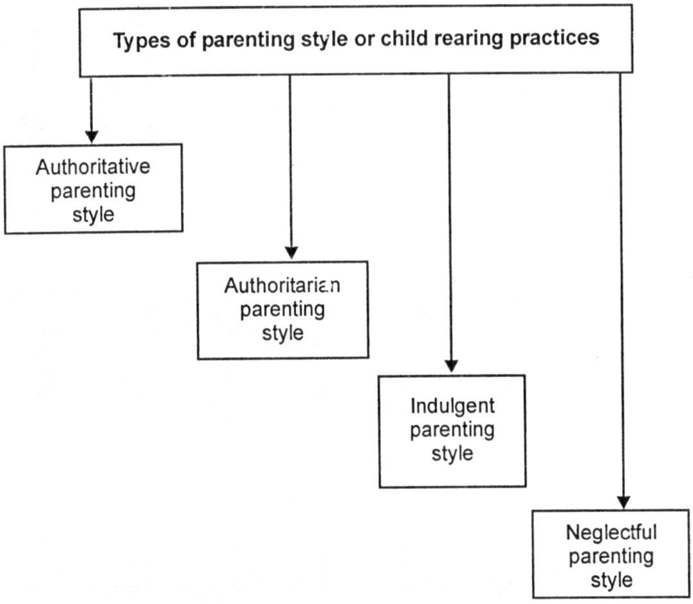

Fig. 8.1: Parenting Styles or Child Rearing Practices

Indulgent Parenting style or Child Rearing Practice

This type of child rearing practice or parenting style is employed by the parents who are responsive but not demanding. In this way indulgent child rearing practice or parenting may be termed as a style of parenting in which parents may be found to be highly responsive, indulged or involved with the care and look after of their children by giving them over protection, warmth and affection at the cost of caring for placing any demand, expectations or control on them. The main features or characteristics of this style of parenting may be outlined as below.

- The parents are too much attached and involved with their children. They show a great concern and responsiveness to the needs and desires of their children by blindly accepting them genuine and worthwhile for the joy and happiness of their children.
- The indulgent parents are observed to offer and offer every facilities demanded by the children time to time without placing any demand from their side, expecting them to behave in a certain way or regulate and control them in term of showing the desired behaviour appropriate to their age and stage of development.
- Indulgent child rearing practice is termed as most permissive, non-directive or lenient in the sense that here the parents are too lenient and non-directive as to remain always playing on the terms of their children. They are unable to frame any rules or principles to be followed by their children for their good behaviour or learning

desirable habits for their needed progress and development.

- The indulgent parents, although quite high on responsiveness, warmth and affection are found quite low in terms of their accountability towards their children for their adequate age related progress and development. The child rearing practice adopted by them is termed as free ranger parenting where a ranger or care taker allows all freedom without taking notice that such unbridled freedom may prove harmful and dangerous to their normal growth and progress.

Influence on the Development

Indulgent child rearing practice or parenting style may influence the development of the growing children in the ways outlined below.

- The children brought up in this environment never learn to control their own behaviour and always expect to get their way.
- They grow as more impulsive, unreasonable and immature children and may be observed to demonstrate socially irresponsible deviant and morally deficient behaviour in their teen and adult life in the shape of drug addiction heavy drinking, delinquency or other anti-social behaviour.
- Brought up in excessive care and look after, they are hardly to learn independent ways of leading their own life. They depend on others to solve their problems and arrange for the needs of their life.
- The children reared in this set up may have all possibilities of de-figuring or spoiling their future prospectus. Most of them are seen to be turned as "Spoiled brats" or "Spoiled sweet" children proving a red signal for the welfare of their self and the society.

Neglectful Child Rearing Practice or Parenting Style

This type of child rearing practice or style is employed by the parents who are quite careless, negligent and irresponsible in exercising their roles as a parents towards their children. They may be found as quite uninvolved, detached, dismissive or hands-off in exercising their parental duties in the desired way. In going through their own easy and convenient style, they make themselves neither demanding nor responsible to the needs and desires of their children. The main features and characteristics of this style of parenting may be outlined as below.

- Parents adopting this rearing practice do not show any indulgence or involvement in their children's life. They generally remain disengaged, indifferent or neglectful to the needs and desires of their children.
- They remain undemanding and do not convey any expectation as a parent from their children. They do not frame any rules or regulation for their children to behave in a certain way and set no limits, targets or boundaries for their expected development and progress.
- They are quite low in warmth and are generally not expected to show

their parental love and affection towards their growing children. Either they do not intend to devote their time for doing so or may feel it useless or harmful to the independent growth of their children.

- Neglectful child rearing practice in characterized with the absence of necessary emotional touch, intimacy, interaction and verbal communication between the parents and the children. There is no place of children's opinions, emotional feelings, desires and wishes in the parent-child relationship as parents are in no mood or time to attend to them. Inspite of getting support for the satisfaction of their basic needs like food, housing, clothes or pocket money, the children are hardly to get necessary emotional support, attention and care from their parents.
- They can't open their heart before their parents and get support / guidance for their needed development and progress.
- Neglectful parents do not earn any respect or liking from their children. Children soon may take note of their parent's indifference or negligence towards them. They may understand that other things in their parent's life are more important to them than they are. It may add to an increased distance and wide gulf in their relationship to their parents. While living under one roof, parents and their children live their life in their own ways.

Influence on the Development

Neglectful child rearing practice or parenting style may influence the development of growing children in the ways outlined below.

- This type of set up is unable to fulfill the children's social and psychological needs. As a result, they may remain emotionally starved and socially undeveloped throughout their life.
- They may be grasped with the feelings of insecurity or unsafety as an outcome of the neglectful or indifferent attitude shown by their parents in their upbringing and look after. It may create quite undesirable complexes in their minds many times coupled with the feelings of anxiety, depression or rebellion attitude on the part of the growing children.
- The neglectful rearing environment may provide the children defective model of social relationships and emotional bonds among the members of the family. It may take roots in their behaviour for being practice in the future life.
- The unbridled freedom, coupled with emotional insecurity and lack of support may push the children to adopt withdrawal or rebellion behaviour in their life style. As a result they may be found to suffer from shyness, social and emotional incompetencies delinquent and anti-social behaviour in their adolescence and adult life.

With the mention of these four child rearing practices or parenting styles, it should not be understood that parents generally stick to one or the other of these four styles in words and deeds. In their practical approach, they try to pick up their own style in its mixed aspect depending upon so many factors like the way of their own rearing, their own views and considerations about good parenting, the child's temperament and ways of behaving, prevailing environmental situations and cultural contexts, giving weightage to their own needs and desires or ready to strive for their children's future success. Whatever parental style or rearing practice, they may adopt in a particular situation, it is absolutely true that it is going to cast a great impact on the nature of the development of their children. Where the positive factors or conditions inherent in one's rearing practice positively favours the direction and magnitude of their children development, the negative one's bring quite adverse and negative effects to their adequate development and future progress. The rearing conditions where parents themselves are involved in bigger conflicts, show down and mutual distrust, show partiality and favour to one child at the cost of other, engage in over protecting and appearing the child in any way, provide the child very harsh and cruel treatment through verbal abusing or corporal punishment or deprive him with the needed love, sympathy, support, praise, attention or encouragement, may prove quite detrimental to the normal development and progress of the children. In most cases, it may prove a great cause for arresting their normal development and turning them into a quite maladjusted personality harmful to their self and the society.

Role of Peers in Child Development

Who are Peers?

The term peers is used for the children and youths of the same age having similar levels of ability, reasoning and socio-emotional skills for their needed interaction, interplay and cooperation in the existing environment. The children begin to establish relationship bonds with the peers right from the period of infancy. The peer relations are formed by the growing children with the children of their own age and rank either being reared along with them simultaneously at their home and family environment or outside it in the neighbourhood, community surroundings, school and college campuses etc. with the sole objectives:

- —spending as much time as possible in each other's company.
- —enjoying a lot of freedom in opening their self to each other.
- —getting companions for playing, exchanging views and developing friendship bonds.
- —enjoying company and sharing learning with each other without feeling any pressure of big or small in status, rank and abilities.

Development of Peer Relationships

Making friends and developing peer relationships is not so easy task for any age group of the developing children as may be thought otherwise by we elders. It is difficult even for kids and toddlers seek entry into play groups and there are many chances of facing peer group rejection. Surely there exists sharp individual differences, among the children in the matter of making friends and developing peer relationships. Some children know how to successfully enter the group and others do not. It depends upon so many factors inherent in the very nature or temperament of the children *e.g.* social vs shy nature, adjusting vs aggressive temperament, cooperative vs quarrelling or selfish tendency, etc.

Moreover the task, however, does not end with a simple entry into a play group or getting opportunity to have dialogue and interaction with the peer group. There are many challenges before the growing children right from the pre-school era in the matter of developing peer relationships e.g. making a new friend, maintaining existing friendships, fitting into peer groups, seeking peer group acceptance, eliminating the chances of peer group rejection, avoiding bullies, etc. The growing children should be helped in facing the challenges and difficulties coming in the way of developing the needed peer relationships. For this purpose, let us first analyse the things and factors that may be held responsible for the acquisition of necessary "social competence" on the part of growing children helpful in winning friends and developing peer relationships.

It has been established through the ongoing researches in the field of behavioural sciences that in addition to certain inborn tendencies, body structure and health conditions, many things regarding one's social competence to earn friendship and peer relations are well learned through the early experiences gained by the children in their rearing and sibling interactions well within their home and family set up. For example, if the home environment and parent's behaviour teach their children empathy, cooperation, mutual love and respect, trust and faith, democratic and socialized norms of behaviour, then they are more likely to take along with them all these virtues quite helpful for winning friends and establishing proper peer relationships. But, however, in case the things go wrong with them in their rearing and sibling interactions, then it will certainly effect their social competency in the negative way resulting into a lot of problems or obstacles for them in the establishment and maintenance of peer group relations. Certainly who will like to have friendly relations and peer group ties with the children who are unsocial, study, aggressive, extremely shy or timid, selfish, revengeful, quarrelsome, bickering and problem creator to their own and others.

Issues Involved in Peer Relationships

Development and maintenance of proper peer relationships among the growing up typically involves a number of issues like below.

(a) Friendship and Gender
(b) Competition and Cooperation
(c) Competition and Conflicts

(d) Aggression and Aggressive Behaviour

(e) Bullying

The last two involves the behavioural problems suffered by the children in their relationship with peers. We will be taking these issues separately after discussing the first three issues generally appearing in the mutual relationship of the peers.

(a) Friendship and Gender: The task of forming or making relationship with peers as such above, rests on the quality, characteristics or ability of the children to win friends. The children who are physically and mentally healthy, emotionally stable and socially competent may be found to achieve more success in winning friends and establishing effective peer relationships. In the earlier year of childhood, there is no consideration of gender, socio-economic status and other physical or material incentives in the minds of children for seeking and maintaining friendship with each other. During this period the girls and boys may be seen to engage in play activities and useful friendly exchanges with no consideration or discrimination of any sort among themselves. As they grow up in age, there comes a consideration of mutual likings and disliking, tastes and interests much dominated by their respective genders. It is why girls and boys are seen to pay more weightage to their respective genders in establishing and maintaining friendships among them. This trend is continued up to the period of early adolescence after which the preference may switch over to opposite gender. There is also a lot of difference between the friendship bonds visible in childhood and adolescence. As the children matures in terms of their physical, mental, social and emotional development, the areas of their interests and activities are widened and they get more intensely and deeply involved in their friendly relationships. The friendship ties become more intimate and emotional in the period of adolescence for both boys and girls and that is why the friendship earned in adolescence may be seen too lasting for them sometime as life partners or most reliable friends.

(b) Competition and Cooperation: Competition as you know, always takes place between the equals and therefore, peers are very much targeted with the urge and opportunities of getting involved in competitive pursuits. Their competitive ventures begin well right from the infancy, *i.e.,* the period of peer relationship initiation. They may be found to compete in racing their toys cars, flying their toy aeroplanes and showing their collections of dolls, and toys. As they grow up in age the areas and scope of their competitive ventures get widened. In schools they have competition with their peers not only in excelling academic areas but also in various co-curricular areas including games and sports, hobbies and project activities. In childhood, the children may also has competition in raising themselves in the eyes of their parents, elders and teachers. In adolescence, however, they care more for peer group and thus they get engaged more in competitive activities raising their status among peers. Girls have competition with the fellow girls in

looking more attractive in the eyes of the boys and boys have competition with their fellow boys in looking more masculine in the eyes of the girls. This is the age linked phenomenon and there is no harm in having such competitive spirit. However, it may take an ugly turn if competition is turned into unhealthy rivalry. When one tries to take lead by causing harm and loss to the competitive peers or use foul and unfair means for putting him or her ahead to cthers, then it becomes a thing of concern for the elders and teachers. It should be checked and the growing children must be directed and guided to get engaged in healthy competitive tasks by setting aside the unhealthy and improper rivalries. They must be taught to compete and go ahead by utilizing and maximising their own abilities and capacities rather than thinking ill of others or causing obstacles in their path.

Peer relationship may be seen to take a quite positive and healthy lead if the efforts of growing up are drifted towards cooperating and helping in place of competing and pulling each other. The emphasis should therefore, be laid over the group activities, cooperative learning and group games so that children may work for the welfare and progress of their peers and group members. They must learn to help and cooperate with their peers and team mates for developing individual competencies and achieve group goals rather than concentrating only on individual welfare and progress.

(c) Competition and Conflicts: In peer relationships cooperation and trust play a quite significant and positive role for turning them into a thing of mutual benefit and advantages to the involved peers. Competition of any sort may place the peers standing against each other. It may bring bitterness in their otherwise cordial relationships giving birth to conflicts of one or the other nature. Therefore, it is essential that as far as possible we must try to lay emphasis on cooperation rather than competition in our teaching learning endeavour. If there is any competition then it should be internalized, meaning thereby that a child should be persuaded or motivated to excel him self or herself in his or her achievements and performances rather than defeating or excelling others in the pursuit of his or her goals. In one's struggling for improving his performance or developing arises among peers then it should be resolved then and there by clarifying the situation and seeking necessary negotiations. The solution lies in believing the philosophy of "be prosperous and let others be prosperous" by contributing towards the welfare and progress of each other in one's living and working relationship.

Influence of Peer Relationships on Development

Peer relationships are found to carry a lot of significance in one's life circling and affecting the course of one's entire development in all the dimensions of his personality.

It is bound to happen because peers in one's life right from the stage of infancy are those companions who are most liked and tied with deep emotional bonds. They provide true company as playmates or classmates and are supposed to carry the bond of friendship for mutual sharing of the joy and happiness of the life. On account of their equal status or rank in terms of age, abilities and skills, they are more believed and understood than the teachers and elders in the matter of learning and acquiring one or the other concepts, habits, interests, attitudes, skills and other things related to children's all round growth and development.

The task of learning and acquisition of new things becomes relatively simpler, easier and graspable to the peers in the company of each other. They feel no hesitation or fear in revealing their weaknesses or shortcomings to each other.

Actually the peers are the only one who can play the natural role of proper teachers to teach what they know to their fellow peers by sitting at the same platform and interacting with each other on the similar maturity level. That is why, in many situations, tutoring and assistance given by the fellow peers in a formal way may prove quite advantageous to the learning and development of the growing children. Besides such formal assistance and deliberate attempts, peer relationships have been found exercising great impact on the overall growth and development of the children in their very informal, spontaneous and non-deliberate ways. A glimpse of such peer influences-deliberate or spontaneous provided below may be quite enough to show a significant relation between peer relationships and children development:

1. Right from the period of infancy, the company and play activities enjoyed with peers provide the child enormous opportunities for his adequate physical, motor, cognitive, social, aesthetic and moral development. Therefore, it is not surprising to see the infants and younger one's to pick up speed in learning age related motor, social cognitive and emotional skills particularly when they enjoy adequate opportunities to learn so in the competition and cooperation with their peers.

2. The task of acquiring needed pro-social skills such as verbal communication and interaction, helping, sharing and cooperating with each other etc. can be properly learned and practised through peer group interactions and relationships.

3. The task of developing peer relationships, as discussed earlier, is linked with a lot of challenges to the developing children in connection with the matters like winning friendships, getting entry into a pre-existing peer group, acceptance or rejection on the part of the peer group, facing bullies or fitting into the norms and culture of the group. It is here, they get a lot of opportunities to learn and imbibe valuable lessons for the development of a few important social and life-supporting skills such as assertiveness, conflict management, competition and cooperation, earning respect and recognition, exercising desirable control over emotions, particularly involving aggression and withdrawal tendencies.

4. The peer relationships may prove quite advantageous to the progress and development of the children by helping them in their adequate

adjustment to their self and the environment. Firstly, it is for the reason that peer relations may provide a proper catharsis channel or safety valve, for the pent up emotions and feelings of the children. They can open their hearts and minds to those peers who are quite close to them in peer relationships. In this way, they can discuss their problems, difficulties and events involving joy and sorrows of their lives. Proper outlet and a desirable channel got through the peer relations may then help the children received from so many conflicts, tensions and troubles resulting in their proper adjustment to the self. Besides this, secondly, the company and support received through the peer relations, may help them in learning desirable skills and pick up necessary habits for meeting the adjustment demands of their home, school and community environment.

5. The peer relationships are quite effective and important to the developing children in the acquisition and learning of the essential communication skills, development of the linguistic abilities and experiment with social roles. The children who are not so fortunate to enjoy the privilege of proper peer relationships are most likely to suffer adversely in this matter.

6. It has been well experienced and also established through on going researches in the field of behavioural sciences that the children in their developing age (from infancy to adolescence) are quite fond of their peer relationships. Whether it may be the period of childhood (referred to as gang age on account of making gang with the peers for sharing the life's activities) or adolescence (the period of too much involvement and intimacy with the peers), they wish to spend as much time as possible with their peers. They speak the language of their peers, patronize the peer group life style, behaves or most likely to be fashioned or modelled on the ideals of their peer relations. As a result, their development may take a positive or negative direction depending upon the type of influences — positive or negative casted on them by their peer relations. They are moulded as their peers. It is why the peer influence may be found to exert both the positive or negative influences on the needed development and adjustment of the growing children. In the bad company of their peers, there are all possibilities for the children to pick up unhealthy and undesirable habits, anti-social behaviour and all what is harmful and devastating to their development, progress and well being in their life.

In this way, it can be well concluded that peer relationships carry a lot of meaning, weightage and significance in the children's life. They fashion, mould and shape the development, progress and adjustment of the developing children through their unmatchable impact over the path of their progress and ways of behaving and developing in the various dimensions of their personality.

Aggression and Aggressive Behaviour among Children

What is aggression or aggressive behaviour among children?

Many times you must have come across with the people who try to demonstrate their dominance or assertion over other people bringing some sort of aggressiveness in their behaviour. Their behaviour may be seen to the coloured at this stage with the intensity of emotion of anger, aggression and blind self assertion, it may be their typical style of getting their way often putting down and thus seek their adjustment or fulfilment of their motive. Upto this point such behaviour may not cause much harm. Because the victims of such aggression may find their own ways to deal with such excessive tone of assertiveness or aggression of cite aggressor. However, it becomes a problem in a situation when the individual begins to lose control over his emotions to the extent of causing harm to himself and others.

The children showing the problematic aggressive behaviour may get engaged in the behavioural activities like below:

- Pushing, kicking, biting, beating and hitting hard and victims especially the younger and weaker ones.
- Trying to throw and damage the articles, objects and immovable property.
- Using inappropriate language, expression and bad names in the communication with others.
- Forcing or thrusting their views or desires through their own ways like bullying, blackmailing, intimidation and manipulation.
- Providing a frightening or interning experience to others while letting them wondering what instigated such behaviour or what he or she has done to prompt the aggression.
- Screaming and rolling on the ground in a threatening way.
- Beating the self, including hitting the head with hand surfaces or objects.
- Disobeying and misbehaving with the elders in a quite unsocial and uncivilized ways.
- Demonstrating a reactive behaviour characterised with, the feeling of insecurity and disturbed state of mind.
- Boosting braveness but proving their timidity before the stronger and more powerful children or adults.

Probable Causes of Aggressiveness

The causes like below may be found to act behind the aggressive behaviour of the children:

1. Aggression is more likely to arise when a child is feeling hungry, thirsty, tired or sick. Children who want or need attention may also act aggressively to get it.

2. Children occasionally resort to aggression as a means of asserting themselves. You may notice a three years old who topples over a

playmate's block tower. While this act may appear to an adult to be a sort of hostile takeover, it's more likely to be a declaration of independence, assertiveness or an attempt to initiate play. Nonetheless, children need to learn more appropriate vehicles of expression.

3. Children who witness violent behaviour — either on television, in movies or first hand — are likely to imitate aggressive actions in their interactions with peers, teachers and family members. Likewise, children who are witnesses to or victims of abuse or violence at home or in school are likely to respond with temper tantrum in their play or any social situation.

4. Children who have not learned self-control often act aggressively. When the adults in their lives set clear and consistent limits, young children will eventually learn to set limits on their own behaviour. However, when children have limited or inconsistent guidance from parents and care takers, they have difficulty in recognizing and monitoring their aggressive behaviours.

5. Children who have not learned more appropriate problem-solving techniques often resort to violence as a means to resolve conflict. When children become frustrated because their playmate don't share a favourite toy, a parent is busy talking on the phone or a sibling has got favour and recognition, they often respond with aggressive behaviour. Children need guidance in finding other strategies for solving these types of problems and venting their frustration.

6. Angry defiance may be associated with feelings of dependency and angry outburst may be associated with sadness and depression. In childhood, anger and sadness are very close to one another and it is important to remember that much of an adult experiences as sadness is expressed by a child as aggression.

7. The uncongenial home and family environment may prove a germinating soil as well as nourishing agent for the aggressive behaviour of the child. When the child is unable to satisfy his basic physiological and socio-psychological needs, he begin to drift towards maladaptive styles of his behaviour including temper tantrum. In the environment, where child feels, that he is unnecessary ridiculed, rebuffed and punished and is subjected to partial, prejudiced, cruel and unjustified behaviour at the hands of the elders he resorts to angry and aggressive behaviour for his self defence to cover the feelings of insecurity or to take revenge.

8. Many times, the aggressive mode of the child's behaviour in the form of temper tantrums get linked with the reinforcement received by him through the satisfaction of his desires or needs through his temper outbursts. Once he realises his objectives through such means, he is habituated to repeat it whenever he needs so in future.

9. According to Adler, the famous psychologist belonging to analytical School of Psychology, the need to dominate or self assertion is the prime

motive or spring board of human behaviour. In some of the children, it is found in excess which may compel them for resorting to temper outbursts or uncontrolled rage in order to make others fearful and accept their dominance.

10. In some cases, biological factors may also play a decisive or side role for inciting or paving the way for sudden emotional outbursts and aggressive behaviour. The malfunctioning of the glands and nervous system may well trigger off such situations in some or the other cases.

How to deal with the aggressive behaviour problem of the children?

Handling children's aggression can be puzzling, draining and distressing for adults. In fact, one of the major problems in dealing with anger in children is the angry feelings that are often stirred up in us. It has been said that we as parents, teachers, counsellors and administrators need to remind ourselves that we were not always taught how to deal with anger as a fact of life during our own childhood. We were led to believe that to be angry was to be bad and we were often made to feel guilty for expressing anger.

It will be easier to deal with children's aggression if we get rid of this notion. Our goal is not to repress or destroy angry feelings in children — or in ourselves — but rather to accept the feelings and to help channel and direct them to constructive ends.

Parents and teachers must allow children to feel all their feelings. Adult skills can then be directed toward showing children acceptable ways of expressing their feelings.

Strong feelings cannot be denied and angry outbursts should not always be viewed as a sign of serious problems; they should be recognized and treated with respect.

Although like other behavioural problems, the aggression is to be handled as an individual case in itself. In general, the following points may prove quite helpful to the parents, teachers and elders in dealing with aggression of their children:

1. Try to anticipate a melt-down. Being aware of when your child is feeling hungry, tired, sick or frustrated is your first line of defense against aggressive behaviour. If you know when aggressive behaviour is likely to strike, you can head it off with a diversion — food, a new activity or a break in the action.

2. Encourage your child to use words for describing his feelings. When your child seems out of control, help him talk about how he is feeling and let him know that you understand his feelings. 'I can see that you're feeling really angry right now because you want to stay at the playground. But it's time to go home now.' Let your child know that it's okay to express his feelings in words. Help him to generate a list of words — angry, mad, sad, upset grumpy, etc., for describing his feelings.

3. Introduce acceptable strategies for dealing with aggression. With younger children, it's sometimes helpful to offer an invigorating physical

activity such as bouncing on a trampoline, running around outside of the house three times or stamping, their feet on the driveway to help them blow off steam.

With older children (six and up), discuss appropriate times and places for handling anger. Teach children to count backward from 10 before acting out. If your child is on the verge of a breakdown in the middle of the shopping mall, remind her that a public place is not the appropriate spot, acknowledge her feelings and let her know that you'll discuss the situation with her as soon as you get home.

Follow through with your commitment and be sure to give her plenty of time to vent her frustration. Children of all ages often find drawing a picture about a difficult moment or writing an apology letter to be a helpful cooling off technique.

4. Set clear limits about aggressive behaviour. Make sure your children understand the consequence for inappropriate actions and be consistent in following up on them. When your child initiates a loud tantrum during a play date, remove her from the situation immediately. Tell her, 'It's not okay for you to behave that way. When you kick and scream, then we have to go home.' Once you've established a rule, don't open it up to negotiation.

5. Help your child develop appropriate problem-solving strategies. With very young children, you'll have to initiate the technique. For example, with a two year old who's having difficulty sharing a favourite plaything set a timer so that each child has equal time.

Encourage older children to work independently to develop solutions. Intervene only when necessary and limit your involvement. When siblings are arguing over the last cookie, state the problem and ask for solutions — 'So, there's only one cookie left. What could you do so that all three of you could have a snack?' Then step back and let them negotiate with one another.

6. Pay close attention to television viewing, video game playing and on-line surfing. Set limits on the amount and type of television programming your children watch. Watch television along with your children and encourage discussion about program content.

Don't be afraid to shut off an inappropriate program, prohibit violent computer games and closely monitor time on-line.

7. Choose books and movies that promote themes of kindness and assistance in finding appropriate books for children of all ages. Reading aloud to children of all ages is a great way to promote conversations about values and appropriate behaviour. A family movie might provides an opportunity for similar conversations.

8. Make a consistent effort to recognize kind behaviours. Let children know that you value their kindness by pointing it out as often as possible. For example: 'I noticed that you shared the last bit of Cheetos with your sister this morning. That was very thoughtful.' Making it clear that you

expect good things and acknowledging positive acts will send a clear, motivational message to children.

9. Hold male and female children to the same standards. Many parents are tempted to follow the old adage 'Boys will be boys' when it comes to managing aggressive behaviour. It's essential that both boys and girls learn to express their aggression appropriately. Make it clear that physical aggression will not be tolerated. At the same time, make sure that children of both genders are given ample opportunity to express their feelings.

10. Be a supportive role model. Above all, act kindly and compassionately toward your children and other family members as well as friends and strangers. Always use polite language toward your children and be sure to apologize for any unkind action. Avoid using sarcasm with children. Never respond to inappropriate behaviour with violent language or actions.

11. Ease tension through humour. Kidding the child out of aggression outburst offers the child an opportunity to "save face". However, it is important to distinguish between face-saving humour and sarcasm, teasing, or ridicule.

12. Manipulate the surroundings. Aggressive behaviour is mere likely to happen or reinforced by placing children in tough, tempting situations. We should try to plan the surroundings so that certain things are less apt to happen. Stop a "problem" activity and substitute, temporarily, a more desirable one. Sometimes rules and regulations, as well as physical space, may be too confining. Hence, if you know what situations trigger temper tantrums in your child, try to avoid them.

13. Use closeness and touching. Move physically closer to the child to curb his or her angry impulse. Young children are often calmed by having an adult come close by and express interest in the child's activities. Children naturally try to involve adults in what they are doing and the adult is often annoyed at being bothered. Very young children (and children who are emotionally deprived) seem to need much more adult involvement in their interests. A child about to use a toy or tool in a destructive way is sometimes easily stopped by an adult who expresses interest in having it shown to him. An outburst from an older child struggling with a difficult reading selection can be prevented by a caring adult who moves near the child to say, 'Show me which words are giving you trouble.'

14. Use a time-out-briefly isolating the child immediately after the aggressive behaviour occurs. Rather than scolding or physically punishing the child, place him in a quiet room or on a chair in the corner for a short period of time (many experts recommend one minute per year in age) in order to cool off.

15. Try not to use physical punishment. It may stop aggression temporarily, but there is evidence that in the long run such punishment may actually increase aggressive behaviour, probably because it conveys the idea that hitting is okay.

16. Reinforce the non-aggressive and good behaviour of the child immediately as and when it happens with your problem child.

17. Reduce the time your child spends with playmates who engage in aggressive behaviour.

A Five-step Programme to Reduce Aggression

1. Make a colourful chart with a space for each day of the week. If the child is quite young, divide each day into smaller intervals to accommodate a shorter attention span. Hang the chart on the wall.

2. For each time the child does not display aggression, give the child a sticker and help him place it on the chart. Say, "Good, you didn't hit" (or bite or kick, etc.).

3. Supplement the sticker with a snack or treat or a few minutes of special attention.

4. After the child has gone a whole week without aggression (or a shorter time for a younger child), show him the stickers on the chart and say, 'You haven't hit (or kicked, bitten, fought, etc.) for a whole week. Now, you've earned a special reward.' This reward can be an outing with a parent, an extra period of time alone with mother, or anything you know your child would like. It should be unusual enough to motivate the child strongly.

5. When the child in aggressive, say, "no-hitting". At the end of the day of interval, show the child the chart and say 'you didn't get a sticker this time because you hit'.

Bullying among Children

What is Bullying?

In its word meaning, bullying may be taken as a behaviour characterized well with the behaviour of a bull full of harassing and intimidating others especially the cow like creatures of its own species. In the school context, it may be defined as an ongoing misuse of power and unwanted aggressive behaviour repeatedly demonstrated by a child (called bully) through his words and deeds to another child (called bullied) with the intention of causing him or her physical, and / or psychological harm. It has real or perceived power imbalance in the sense that the bully seems to enjoy more physical strength, is relatively older and stronger in power and position than the bullied and is often assisted and encouraged by the members of his group. Bullying can involve an individual or a group misusing their power over one or more person. It can happen in person or online, and may be obvious or hidden.

Types of Bullying

Bullying can happen anywhere at school, travelling to and from school, in sporting teams, or in a work place and activities going in and outside the school. In its occurrence, bullying behaviour may take a variety of forms like below:

1. *Physical*: In this type of bullying a child is harmed physically, or economically through the bullying acts such as:

- slapping, hitting, pinching, punching, biting, kicking, pushing and shoving
- locking in a confined space
- making things to get one in trouble
- excluding from a group
- unwelcome touching
- taking things, snatching or damaging belongings
- extortion

2. *Verbal*: In this type of bullying a child's feelings are hurt through the bullying acts like

- name-calling
- threatening and intimidating
- unwelcome teasing
- taunting
- spreading rumours, gossiping
- racist or racial comments

3. *Written or on line bullying*: In this type of bullying a child is threatened, harassed or intimidated by the bullying acts like

- threatening notes and letters
- making silent or abusive phone calls
- sending insulting or threatening text messages
- publishing someone's personal or embarrassing information online
- creating hate sites or starting social exclusion campaigns on social networking sites

Why do the bullies engage in bullying?

- they think it's fun, or that it makes them popular or cool
- they want to impress or entertain their friends
- they feel more powerful or important, or they want to get their own way all the time
- they think that they will win or get what they want
- they feel insecure or lack confidence or are trying to fit in with a group
- they are fearful of other children's differences
- they are jealous of another child
- they are unhappy
- they do not even realize that they are hurting the other person
- they enjoy feeling power over someone because sometimes they are being bullied by someone else
- they are copying what they have seen others do before, or what has been done to them

Role of bystanders and spectators in one's bullying behaviour

Most of the time bullying takes place with bystanders present. Bystanders are those who witness or know bullying is occurring. The way bystanders act has a major impact on bullying. Bystanders who are passive (take no action) or behave in ways that give silent approval (watching, nodding, walking away) encourage the behaviour to continue.

Why don't bystanders step in?

- for fear of their own safety (now and later) or position in the group
- they think that someone else will help
- they are worried about making things worse
- they don't know what to do
- they think their actions won't make a difference
- they think it's none of their business
- they think the student being bullied deserved it
- they think it's fun to watch

The Impact of Bullying

Bullying has a negative impact on everyone involved; the target, the bully and the bystanders.

The Impact over students who *are bullied:* Students being bullied are more likely to:

- feel disconnected from school and not like school
- have lower academic outcomes, including lower attendance and completion rates
- lack quality friendships at school
- display high levels of emotion that indicate vulnerability and low levels of resilience
- be less well accepted by peers, avoid conflict and be socially withdrawn
- have low self-esteem
- have depression, anxiety, feelings of loneliness and isolation
- have nightmares
- feel wary or suspicious of others
- have an increased risk of depression and substance abuse
- in extreme cases, have a higher risk of suicide, however, the reasons why a person may be at risk of suicide are extremely complicated

Impact on bullies: Students who frequently bully others are more likely to:

- feel disconnected from school and dislike school
- start doing poorly in school in matter of participation and achievements
- come home with torn clothes, unexplained bruises, new clothes or other items, or money not accounted for
- talk about responding to others in a way that may result in the school taking disciplinary action

- demonstrate bullying behaviour to their siblings, neighbourhood and disrespect to their family members
- get into fights, vandalize property and leave school early
- be associated with an increased likelihood of theft, violent behaviour, delinquent acts and binge drinking

Impact on bystanders: Students who witness bullying may:

- be reluctant to attend school
- feel fearful or powerless to act and guilty for not acting
- have increased mental health problems, including depression and anxiety
- have increased use of tobacco, alcohol, or other drugs

Impact on schools: When bullying continues and a school does not take action, the entire school climate and culture can be negatively affected. This affects student learning and engagement, staff retention and satisfaction and parental confidence in the school, which can lead to:

- the school developing an environment of fear and disrespect
- students experiencing difficulty in learning
- students feeling insecure
- students disliking school
- students perceiving that teachers and staff have little control and don't care about them

Remedial Measures for Controlling the Menace of Bullying

Bullying is a great menace and major problem in many of the schools. It affects badly the welfare and progress of the all connected and affected through this menace, *i.e.,* the bullies, the bullied, the onlookers as well as the peace and progress of a school, family and society. The question arises how to get rid or put a reasonable restraint over the menace of bullying. The problem needs a collaborative efforts from the part of all who are connected and affected through its consequences. Therefore we will be considering the role and contributions of each of the stake holders on this issue one by one. But let us first try to know why do some children turn to bullying? How and why do they pick up bullying behaviour?

How do the children imbibe the skill and habit of bullying?

Bullying is learned behaviour like other sorts of behaviour and habits acquired by the child in course of his upbringing and schooling. It is fashioned, designed and imbibed through the principles of classical and operant conditioning as well as social learning theory propagated by Albert Bandura. Let us see how do the children imbibe the skill and habit of bullying?

1. The children may learn bullying through the direct experiences as well as indirect experiences. They may observe and witness the bullying behaviour of their elders at their home, neighbourhood, school, and other places of the social interaction and find it rewarding to those who resort to it

as a habit of getting their way out. The bully may be his father, the elder sibling, or school mate, or even a character of the movie or TV serial. Look at men who beat or intimidate their wives and scream at their kids. They've never learned to be effective spouses or parents. Instead, they're really bullies. And the other people in those families live in fear — fear that they're going to be yelled at, called names, or hit. Nothing has to be worked out, because the bully always gets his way. The chain of command has been established by force, and the whole mindset becomes, "If you'd only do what I say, there'd be peace around here." So the bully's attitude is, "Give me my way or face my aggression and be ready to face the consequences." When a child witnesses such behaviour of his elders, he may consciously and unconsciously adopt them as his role models, imitates their bullying acts and learns to imbibe the acts of bullying in his behaviour after finding them as an easy way out for enjoying power, status and getting always his own ways without really trying to become capable of something worthwhile in his life.

2. The maladjustment felt by the children at their home, school and social company may also result in making them a bully. They are educationally and academically failed as well as emotionally and social starved souls in themselves who are grasped with the feelings of inferiority and fear of failing and social dejection. Their so picked up bullying behaviour then works for them on temporary basis a saviour of their lost honour and prestige before their peers. The varied reasons for their maladjustment and resorting to bullying behaviour may be summarized further as below:

- Some bully because they feel insecure. Picking on someone who seems emotionally or physically weaker provides a feeling of being more important, popular, or in control.
- In other cases, kids bully because they simply don't know that it's unacceptable to pick on kids who are different because of size, looks, race, or religion.
- In some cases bullying is a part of an ongoing pattern of defiant or aggressive behaviour.
- Some kids who bully at school and in settings with their peers are copying behaviour that they see at home. Kids who are exposed to aggressive and unkind interactions in the family often learn to treat others the same way. And kids who are on the receiving end of taunting learn that bullying can translate into control over children they perceive as weak.

3. In some cases the bullying behaviour of the children may be the consequences of their learning helplessness, undiagnosed or diagnosed learning disability or educationally and academically failure faced in the stream of our educational system. In such situations they may not get opportunities for learning the needed academic, social, emotional and

problem solving skills for managing their strong emotions like anger, frustrations, or insecurity and getting along well with their colleagues and expectations of their teachers and parents. As an easy way out then they try to practice the bullying-behaviour and after finding them satisfying and rewarding imbibe them as a way of their usual behaving. Bullying behaviour may be satisfying to them as they don't have to learn problem solving, because they just threaten the other kids. They don't have to learn how to work things out because they just push their classmates or call them names. They don't have to learn how to get along with other people — they just control them. The way they're solving problems is through brute force and intimidation. So by the time that child reaches the adolescence, bullying is pretty ingrained — it has become their natural response to any situation where they feel socially awkward, insecure, frightened, bored or embarrassed.

Suggestions for Rectifying and Dealing with the Bullying Behaviour

As already emphasized earlier, the problem needs to be solved with the cooperation of all who are connected and affected with the menace of bullying. Let us see what can be done by each of the stake holder.

Role of parents and school authorities

Parents and school authorities are required to engage in the activities like below for preventing as well as dealing with the incidence of bullying:

1. Producing own examples of good behaviour is the best thing that we elders can do for the welfare of our children. It is therefore needed on the part of parents, teachers and other members of the family not to indulge in unwanted aggressive and bullying behaviour among themselves and especially with the children.
2. As far as possible the children should be saved with any kind of emotional starvation and social isolation or getting maladjusted in any way at home or school. If noticed so, then suitable remedial steps should be taken without blaming and pushing them into acts of resentment and revolt.
3. It is advantageous to make the children well aware about what a bully is and then set a standard that clearly warns them not to indulge in such behaviour in any way anywhere home or school. It may help the children to remain conscious and alert to identify and stop the bullying behaviour, both in themselves and others.
4. There should be norms and rules for dealing with the cases of misbehaviour, indiscipline and bullying on the part of children at home and school and these should be strictly enforced. If anybody breaks the rule and indulges in bullying acts, he should be held accountable, and it's very important that we let him deal with the natural consequences and not try to shield or get him escaped under one or the other excuses.
5. It is good on the part of the parents and school authorities to be vigilant and watchful for any undesirable activities, ragging and bullying

going at home and school campus. The school may have CCTV camera fitted for noticing any unwanted activity going around the campus. Moreover, in your interactions whenever you notice any observable signs and symptoms of a bully or bullied in the child's behaviour, then necessary steps should be taken for probing further into the nature and causes of his or her peculiar behaviour for arriving at necessary conclusion.

6. The bullies should be taught to learn how to solve social problems and deal with their emotions without acting out behaviourally. As a result, attempts should be made to make them learn: (i) how to resolve conflicts and manage their impulses and emotions, (ii) how to share and make compromises and do sacrifices for the sake of unity, cooperation and getting along with others, (iii) how to stand with goodness and deal with injustice. A lot of benefit may be derived by making attempts for devising means for helping the bullying to find socially desirable ways and outlets for letting out their unwanted aggression and overfilled impulses instead of resorting to short cuts of intimidating and harming the kids less powerful and junior to them.

7. The parents and school authorities should also give necessary education and training to the children for facing the problem and menace of bullying to them as well as others. They should be made to learn the important things to be done on their part when they are made victims of bullying or they happen to watch some body being bullied.

Role of the child who is bullied

It is your duty to teach and train your children / students to do all what is necessary on their part for saving themselves from the sufferings at the hands of bullies. They can remind the children, the things like below:

- Remember that it is you who has to take initiative in getting rid of your problem. If you are being bullied at school, tell a friend, tell a teacher and tell your parents. It won't stop unless you do. It can be hard to do this so if you don't feel you can do it in person it might be easier to write a note to your parents explaining how you feel, or perhaps confide in someone outside the immediate family, like a grandparent, aunt, uncle or cousin and ask them to help you tell your parents what's going on.
- Your tutor needs to know what is going on so try to find a time to tell him or her when it won't be noticeable. You could stay behind on the pretext of needing help with some work. Don't be tempted to respond to any bullying or hit back because you could get hurt or get into trouble.
- In your first attempt, if the person you told cannot help you or does not do anything, find someone else! Never keep being bullied a secret!
- Try not to let the bully see you are upset. (Bullies are looking for signs that you are upset and they may do it more).

- Avoid areas where the bully feels comfortable picking on you (for example, place where teachers cannot see you — such as corners of the playground, lonely corridors and behind large furniture in the classroom.
- Try to surround yourself with friends and people who will stand up for you.

Role of bystanders and spectators in checking one's bullying behaviour

- Get friends together and TALK to the bully. Let the bullies in your school know that bullying is not accepted in your school.
- Don't cheer the bully on or stand around to watch. (The bully might like the attention, and pick on the kid even more).
- If you see someone being bullied, find someone to help stop it. (Get another friend, a teacher, a playground safety, a principal).
- Be nice to, include, and get to know the people, who are being bullied: You may find they are similar to you.
- Try to make friends with the bully too — show them other ways to interact with others. (They don't need to bully others to be accepted or cool).

Role of School in Child Development

The other most important social agency to influence the development and behaviour of the children after the home and family is the school. It is the centre of learning for the child and therefore the learning experiences — formal or informal — he gets inside the school, control and shape his behaviour. There is no exaggeration in saying that a man can be identified and known through the names of the institutions from where he gets his education. It is also true that every institution or school has its own impression or reputation for being relatively good and bad. These are labelled so on account of what is being done there through their curricular and co-curricular experiences and the ways of administration for the growth and development of the personality of their students making them to — acquire the desirable played by the parents and members of the family in the home and family set-up.

Apart from the human factors, the nature and quality of the material resources, psychological, social and cultural environment of the school also work as a great deciding factor in influencing and controlling the developmental direction and behaviour of the students. Some of the things, situations and factors inherent in the overall environment of the school which work as the determinants of the students' cognitive, affective and conative behavioural development may be named as below:

- The educational and professional qualification of the teachers, their teaching experience, personality and behavioural make-up.
- The sweetness or bitterness in the relationships among the teachers and other employees.

- The mental and physical health of the teachers.
- The sincerity and devotion of the teachers towards their duties and profession.
- The abilities and competencies of the head of the institution, his personality and behavioural traits, his relationship with the fellow teachers, students, employees of the institution and parents of the students.
- The nature of the relationship between the teachers and students.
- The nature of the relationship existing among the students of a particular class or the school in general.
- The nature of the discipline and administrative arrangements prevalent in the school.
- The nature of the organisation of the academic programmes and the educational standards maintained by the school.
- The provision for co-curricular activities and the nature of their organisation.
- The examination results of the school.
- The place, status, name and fame of the school with respect to the achievements in games and other co-curricular activities.
- The nature of the facilities available in the school for the organisation of various co-curricular activities, hobbies and other talents development progammes.
- The nature of the facilities regarding library, reading room, museum, laboratories, work places, etc. available in the school.
- The nature of the arrangement for mid-day meal, canteen, common-room, drinking water, laboratories, etc.
- The appropriateness or inappropriateness of the things and situations related to the physical environment of the school like adequacy of the school building, sanitation, pollution free environment, seating arrangement, proper ventilation and lighting, etc.
- The provision and adequate arrangement for the education and adjustment of the gifted, the creative, the backward, the problematic and the handicapped children with their special problems.
- The nature of the provision and arrangement for guidance and counselling services to the students.
- The adequate arrangement with regard to the evaluation of the progress of the children in quite an objective and impartial way.

Besides the things pointed out above, we may include many other things, attributes or factors related with the physical, educational, administrative, social or cultural environment of the school in this list which may directly or indirectly influence and control the cognitive affective and conative development of the children including their learning potential and ways of behaving. In fact, what we appreciate in our children with regard to their good habits, temperament, desirable personality traits and ways of behaving, to a large extent, is the sole product of the school environment. The children learn and grow in the way they are shaped and moulded by the presence and interaction of the various things, situations and factors present in their school environment. A single factor, incident or accident may make and mar the whole life of an innocent child. A sympathetic, affectionate and inspiring behaviour of a teacher may bring in the child the needed enthusiasm, motivation, confidence and will power to develop in a desired way. On the other hand, the partiality shown and injustice done to the child may vitiate his mind to such an extent that he may be forced to adopt reactive and maladapted behaviour patterns first by developing hatredness towards the teacher and his subject and then by isolating himself completely from the class and the school for playing truancy and engaging in other deviant behaviour.

In this way what goes inside the school and how the children react to the school environment, may definitely work as a potent determinant of their present and future development with respect to their cognitive, affective and conative behaviour.

Apart from the things said above about the role of school in the development of growing children, a few specific things like below are said to influence their development in a big way. We may name them as: (a) Peer influences, (b) Relationship with teachers, (c) Teachers' expectations and school achievement, and (d) Overage learner.

Let us discuss their nature and impact over the development of children one by one.

(a) Peer Influences

The peers available in the school to the developing children in the shape of classmates and school mates and the type of relationships existing among the peers exercise a great influence in the adjustment, education, development and progress of the developing children studying in a school. In brief we can summarize the nature and impacts of peer influences in the following way:

1. Peer influences exercise big impact in the acquisition of desirable and undesirable behaviour on the part of developing children in the form of the acquisition of habits, interests, attitudes, learning styles, ways of working and behaving, cooperating and competing with each other, and engaging in the activities helpful or damaging to their progress and wellbeing.

2. On positive side, the impact of peer influences may take a quite favourable turn to the developing children in the shape of: (i) inspiring and motivating each other, (ii) helping one another in their respective advancement with the true spirit of cooperation and collaboration, (iii) working as a role model for learning and acquiring many things concerning the curricular and co-curricular areas, and (iv) imbibing a number of useful traits, habits, skills, interests, attitudes and ways of behaving helpful in their wholesome personality development.

In this concern, we should not forget that it has been strongly emphasized by the humanists like Bandura and constructivist like Vygotsky and Bruner (and also confirmed through working experience in a number of situations) that a child learns and understands in a quite amazing manner in the company of an able peer even much better than the class and subject teacher or instructor.

3. On negative side, we may see that a bad company of the peers comprising the incapable and inefficient, careless and aimless, failures and frustrated, timid and cowardice, spoiled and delinquents, problematic and maladjusted, truant and backbenchers, bullies and aggressive, rule breaker and bad reputed may push the developing children consciously and unconsciously into the behaviour and action patterns of their companion peers.

4. In the era of preadolescence and adolescence, the effect or influence of the peer behaviour on the developing children is so intense and deep that they may be found to ignore the advice and warnings of their dearest and respected elders or teachers for the sake of maintaining their ego and showing their loyalty towards their peer groups. They want to think, feel and act as their companions in peer group think, feel and do.

(b) Relationships with Teachers

Teachers stand to be a quite potent factor in helping the developing children in their desired learning in the schools. The task of desired modification of the behaviour and wholesome development of their personality can only be performed with the active involvement and conscious efforts of the teachers in this connection. A teacher has to understand a student well in terms of his abilities, capacities, strengths and limitations for setting his learning path and guiding him on his learning path for the realization of the set goals. For this purpose he needs to be in a constant touch with his student and it can only be possible if the relationships between the teacher and student are mutually satisfying, cordial and respectful. The continuity of a teaching-learning act also can only be ensured on the effective lines if there is no hurdle in the communication and exchange of opinion between teacher and a student. Such effective communication can also be properly possible with the help of mutually satisfying cordial relationship between the teacher and a student. In schools it is the learners whose interests are specifically watched by all. In fact all what stands in the schools in terms of men-material facilities and their organization is essentially meant for looking after the interests of the students and it can be effectively materialized with the active and satisfying relationships between teachers and students.

In case we try to visualize the significance of such healthy relationships from the view point of the students we may see that it is most essential for them to have quite satisfactory, cordial and trustworthy relationships with their teachers. The importance of having such healthy relationships can be realized on the grounds mentioned below:

1. Teachers are found to take much interest in classroom teaching and working with their students for guiding their learning path in cases where they find that their students pay due respect and listen to their advice and instructions in a proper way. In the absence of such satisfactory relationship with their students they lose interest and begin to observe mere formalities with no real intention and absorption in their teaching and guiding assignments and its affects the learning outcomes of the students in a quite adverse way.

2. In the cases when a teacher is found to make negative opinion about a child related to some or the other negligence on the part of student regarding his learning or about his misconduct and improper behaviour on one or the other account, the same may be continued for a long in the absence of a proper dialogue between them. The things can come on the right lines only when a satisfactory relationship exists between them for doing so at the right time in a right way. In its absence a vicious circle may start. The teacher may think that the student is wrong, he is careless and not serious at all about his learning or he is problematic, mischievous and spoiled and so he ignores or dislike him or punishes him in his own way. The child feels that it is not proper on the part of the teacher to behave with him in such a way; he is jealous of him or is prejudiced on account of his belongingness to a different caste / gender / religion / region, etc. He shows his displeasure in one way or the other and his disrespectful or reactionary behaviour may further antagonize the teacher for taking further action against him and thus the gulf between the teacher and student gets widened and widened. The ultimate sufferer is student as he begins to lose his emotional balance and is distracted from his real goals.

3. In an environment where there prevails a proper goodwill, mutual love and respect, and faith and trust in the intention and working of each other, teachers and students both find great opportunity for enjoying their efforts of teaching and learning. Students have the feeling that they are with their teachers for telling them about their fallacy, guiding them at the time of needs, praising them at the time of their right step and warning them about the inherent dangers and the same helps them much in their desired progress and career building. Nobody can match the magic of the teachers in guiding and enlightening the path of the students in the situations where a bond of the desired satisfactory relationships exist between the teacher and students. In its absence, neither a teacher can teach well nor their students can learn well, in the manner they are supposed to learn, for their proper development and wellbeing.

([illegible]) Teachers' Expectations and School Achievement

Teachers who try to know their students in a proper way are always in a position to have prediction about the success or failures of their students in one or the other ventures of their learning pursuits. Based upon their knowing about their students they may have certain expectations of one or the other nature from their students in relation to their progress and wellbeing. These expectations may range from a quite high level to a quite discouraging level of achievements expected from the students in one or the other learning pursuit at one or the other learning situation. These expectations made about their students by their teachers carry a wide significance in relation to the development and wellbeing of the developing children on account of their capability of exercising positive as well as negative influences on the achievements of the children in the way discussed and outlined below.

Positive impacts and outcomes

1. Expectations and aspirations of the teachers about their students are the first step for initiating and igniting the flame of determination and will power to do and perform one or the other tasks on the part of the students in such an effective way as to turn their efforts into the real stories of their success much in line with the expectations and aspirations of their teachers.

2. It can be properly seen that the students who are high in the eyes of their teachers receives much attention, care and guidance on the part of their students in comparison to others. They are the favourable ones and thus receive more time to perform experiments in the laboratories, much time and facilities for carrying out their practice work and are helped more in learning the things in a more effective way and in a large amount with the expectations that they are going to bring name and fame to the teachers and the institution. Such special individual attention and extra facilities provided to them may help these students in excelling others in terms of their achievements and performances.

3. The expectations of the teachers from the students in a positive note may instill the favoured students with a new sense of motivation and expectation from their self. They are seen to have more self-confidence, self-efficacy and self-esteem in comparison to those who are estimated as incapable or inefficient in the eyes of the teachers and are thus consequently seen to surpass others in terms of good performances and high achievements.

Negative impacts and outcomes

1. A quite high expectation of the teacher from a developing child much above his underlying capacities and abilities may frustrate the teacher and students both in terms of the actual achievements and performances resulted through their efforts. It may adversely affect the self-confidence, self-esteem and self-efficacy of the developing children for their further learning and achievements.

2. The children with low expectations from their teachers begin to underestimate and see themselves through the eyes and expectations of their teachers in spite of the presence of required abilities and capacities for doing and performing in a better way than the teacher's expectations. It

proves quite damaging to their progress and achievements in tune with their actual potential.

3. The mind-set of the teacher about the low expectation or discouraging outcomes from a student may naturally drift the teacher to pay less attention and ignore him at the time of usual classroom teaching and working in the laboratories. He may not encourage him to take initiative for the creative and constructive activities or engaging in useful projects and practice work with the assumption that it will not serve any useful purpose in developing their achievement and performance level. A negative attitude of the teacher and painting a student as a student of no hope or less expectation may thus push the student towards under-achievements and failures with no fault of him.

(d) Overage Learner

In reference to a particular class or grade of the school, the term overage learners is referred to the learners who are much more in age then the average age ought to be for studying in that very class or grade. Let us make it clear by a simple analogy. A child is entitled to gets entry into class I of an elementary school at the age of completion of five years. Accordingly, at the time of his studying in class VII he should be running in the age period of 11-12 years (in case he regularly passes out every class in one year). The average age of the children thus studying in class VII should also lie approximately between 11 and 12 years. Now if the age of a child studying in class VII is considerably much more than the age period of 11-12 years, let we say 14 years or more, he is designated as overage learner — a learner who has passed the average age of studying in that class. In this way, an overage child is generally older and more mature than other children studying with him in a class.

In case if it is pointed out that how does one turn into an overage learner the reasons for becoming an overage learner may be traced out in:

(i) One's getting entry in to class I of an elementary school relatively at a quite increased age.
(ii) His inability to pass out one or the other classes or grades in the prescribed time of one year
(iii) His leaving out the school in between for one or more years for one or the other reasons.

Now the next question arises then after all what is the hitch of his being overage? Does it affect him or his classmates in any way and if so how? Let us think about it:

1. An overage learner may face difficulty in getting him adjusted with the physical environment available in the classroom, laboratories and workshop planned and organized for the average age learners. For example there may be small size chairs, desks and working tables, appliances and work instrument especially suited for younger and small children and certainly in this situation he may feel a lot of difficulty in getting him adjusted along with his classmates.

2. An overage child may face problems in terms of his academic adjustment while studying along with the children of the younger age in a particular class or grade. As we know, the teaching — learning task in any teaching — learning situation is always planned, organized and executed in view of the average age of the students studying in that class. Since the method of teaching-learning and execution of work activities does not match with his age and maturity level, the overage children has to face a lot of maladjustment on this account.

3. An overage child may also face a number of problems in relation to his socio-psychological adjustment and development such as:

(i) He has difficulty in establishing friendship and having useful interactions with his classmates on account of age difference and maturity level.

(ii) He faces rejection on the part of his classmates in play activities and games on account of his being much older than them.

(iii) He also faces much difficulty in getting along with his classmates in a number of co-curricular activities.

(iv) He feels a sort of guilt on account of his being overage. The same is also constantly reminded to him by his teachers and classmates on one or the other grounds.

(v) He feels a sort of restlessness, anxiety and stress on account of lagging behind in the level of education and development needed for his age.

4. The academic difficulties suffered by the overage children coupled with his socio-psychological maladjustment may push him towards problematic and delinquent behaviour such as playing truancy, bullying, becoming drug addict, or falling in the company and entrap of socially undesirable and culprits.

Social, Economic and Cultural Differences in Socialization and its Implication for Inclusion

The process of socialization helps the children in having proper interaction with the people and events going on in one's society or community including their schools. However, it is not also unusual to witness considerable social, economic and cultural differences among the children coming in the way of their proper social interaction, mutual cooperation and collaboration with each other. It may also result in creating differentiation in the attitudes of teachers and bias towards one type of children against the other. Let us try to know and understand the nature of such differences existing among the diverse learners of the inclusive class.

Social Differences: As the children grow and develop socially they begin to notice that how they are different from other children in terms of their social status. On the other hand, in case when we look at the learners of an inclusive class from the angle of their social status, we may come to the conclusion that there exist considerable differences among them on this account. We know that in our society, the social status of a family and members belonging to that family is decided on the basis of the caste, colour, creed, race, religion, language, nationality and belongingness to the local area, etc. The differences in social status on these accounts may result into creating a number of problems for the adjustment and education of the children specially for the marginalised, discriminated and excluded from the mainstream on account of their lower social status. The children belonging to lower castes, tribal belts minority groups, migrants and other nationalities may be looked down, segregated and socially excluded on the part of the children belonging to mainstream. The attitudes of the teachers towards them may also remain more or less unfavourable antagonistic and partial. Therefore, proper attempts need to be made to bring desirable attitudinal changes towards the marginalized and excluded children on account of their social differences from the mainstream children.

***Economic Differences*:** Socialization, the process of making interactions with others may prove an effective media to acquaint and expose the existing differences among children in terms of the economic status of their families. In this respect we may find that there are children in an inclusive class who belong to poverty ridden and starving families in sharp contrast to those who are lucky enough to belong with the rich, prosperous and well to do families. As a result while children belonging to the poverty ridden families are found to pass through all types of hardship in struggling for the satisfaction of their basic needs, particularly the physiological needs and economic demands of their schooling, the children from rich and well to do families enjoy an anxiety free smooth selling for the satisfaction of their all such needs. Poverty ridden children and their families experience all types of economic deprivation, marginalization, humiliation and discrimination at the hands of the privileged ones. The children are forced to suffer from malnutrition, unhealthy living condition and worst conditions for their upbringing, schooling and development. They are ridiculed and worked down by their well to do peers and neglected and ill treated by the mainstream of the society. Many times, these children have to spend their time in joining their parents for their bread earning and they may get little time for their study. They may be forced to turn in to backward and slow learners, besides being irregular in their attendance. It may earn bad reputation for them in the eyes of their teachers and they are met with the indifference on the part of the teachers for them. They need careful handling on the part of the teachers and school authorities in terms of their needed adjustment and proper education in the inclusive set up of school. In its absence, there lie greater chances after getting them turned either into a failure or frustrated personality, or become a permanent nuissance to the society. They need to be properly accommodated and adjusted in the school environment especially in their interaction and relationship with their peer and teachers. Their difficulties and hardship arising on account of economic reasons should be properly attended by the school authorities government, NGO's and the well to do persons of the society through their welfare schemes assistance and donations. They must be taught to regain their lost confidence and work for utilizing their inner potential. The rich and privileged peer should also be taught to learn realising life and treat their poverty ridden peers on equal terms by respecting their individualities goodness and potential.

Cultural Differences: As a result of socialization and getting opportunities for the interaction with others, children may begin to experience the one or the other cultural differences lying between and among them. They may find that their families and communities differ from other families and communities in terms of the modes of their living and behaving. It is reflected through their dresses, food habits, traditions and rituals, language and communication means, marriages and child rearing practices, ways of thinking and feeling, values and ideals and goals of life, etc. These cultural differences may alienate, marginalize and segregate minority communities adopting somewhat different culture from the majority or mainstream society. Their marginalization or alienation gets transferred to their children who are forced to bear the consequences of such marginalization or alienation.

However, cultural diversity or multiculturism found in a society is a quite distinctive and productive characteristic of a healthy democratic society believing in the equity, equality, liberty and dignity of human values of its members. An inclusive class tied with the claim of providing quality education to all its learners with no discrimination of any kind is supposed to accept and include all the learners by ignoring all the differences and diversities found in them. The multi-culturism characterized with a high degree of cultural differences among the learners is thus fully accepted and respected in an inclusive class. It is taken as a boon and not an obstacle or a matter of concern for the learners of an inclusive class. They can learn a number of good things from everybody's culture and can seek unity in diversity for their individual and social progress.

9

Counselling of Children in Specific Stressful Conditions

Introduction

Childhood as we all know is much remembered for the spontaneity of life, freedom to do and speak with no responsibilities on the shoulders. It is referred to as the most valuable and golden period of life where the child is found to lead an anxiety free royal life. However, whatever fine image we have built up for the childhood, it is not so universal and bed of roses for everyone at everytime. There are situations and circumstances where children may be found to bear the consequences of a lot of stress and adverse life conditions. In these adverse conditions many of the children may have to pass through a period of utter sadness, isolation, exploitation, oppression, cruelty and abuse of one or the other nature. At this time what is needed to them utmost is the availability of some type of proper guidance and counselling accompanied with the measures to physically help them in their adjustment and living. In this chapter here we would like to focus upon discussion on the three more specific stressful conditions faced by many of the children in their life named as: (i) Separation of parents, (ii) Loss of parents in armed conflicts etc., and (iii) Victims or survivours of child abuse. Let us discuss them in reference to their nature, problems and its solution in the form of providing some appropriate counselling to the children.

Separation of Parents

This social problem is increasing day by day on account of various socio-psychological, economical and global cultural changes introduced in the structure and functioning of the family system. However, the most damaging effect of the separation or divorce among the married couple reflects in the problems faced by their children on this account. These problems in general may be of the following nature.

- Their parents may engage in legal disputes to take their custody and these children may be forced to watch the ugly scenes of disputes, quarrelling and fighting among their parents.
- The children may be forced to make their choices for remaining with their mother or fathers. It may put a child in a severe psychological conflict unable to decide what would be better for him or her.

- While forced to live with a single parent, mother or father, the child is deprived of most of the privileges, socio-psychological advantages and needs satisfaction as enjoyed in the company of both. He or she may show a great hunger or need for having his / her mother or father in case he or she lives with a single parent.
- Many times, the divorced couple may make their child an orphan child as none of them opts for his / her brought up for one or the other reason such as getting re-married.
- The separation or divorce of the parents may cause a great psychological damage resulting in intense grief, lack of security and fear, anger and frustration, depression, etc. to the suffering child. It may completely ruin his or her childhood and bring a shock wave to his / her mental health and overall well being.
- These children may suffer from social exclusion and negative comments over the status of separation or divorce of their parents. Deprivation of any one of the parents costs them dearly in terms of their adjustment, development, brought up and wellbeing.

Counselling of Children Facing Separation or Divorce of Parents

The children facing one or the other types of problems enumerated above are in a great need of being counselled at the hands of the trained professionals and counsellors. As far as the meaning and purpose of the counselling to problem ridden child is concerned we can define it as a process carried out under the leadership of a counsellor to express care, understanding and concern towards the problems of the child on one hand and to make him understand his problems and develop the means to deal with them on the other. The purposes or goals of the process of counselling to a child thus may be laid down as below:

- To help the child by creating an environment of trust expressing his / her emotions and feelings freely in a particular situation about his / her felt difficulty or problems arising out of parental separation or divorce.
- To offer proper opportunity to the suffering child for a direct and open relationship with the counsellor and create a proper environment for a useful dialogue between the child and counsellor with a hope of the evolution of appropriate solutions of the child's problems.
- To help the child in understanding his problem / problems in a proper way resulted through the separation of his parents in the light of the circumstances being faced by him at the present moment.
- To help the child in developing means and measures for dealing with the problems or difficulties resulted through the separation of his parents.
- To help the child in building his self-confidence and self-esteem by bringing out the feelings of shame or low self esteem resulted through

the separation of his parents and face the reality of life in a proper way.

Methods or Modes of Counselling

Methods or modes of counselling of the children victim of separation or divorce of their parents may be broadly classified as group counselling and individual counselling.

Group counselling: In group counselling a group of children suffering on account of separation or divorce of their parents is subjected to counselling on the part of the counsellors. In the group these children find valuable opportunities for getting along with the peers passing through the similar problems. They can easily open up to each other for the expression of their feelings and emotions and understand each other's problems for facing the reality lying before them. In the group, these children may be made to learn how to deal with the hardships faced by them through group discussion, role playing and showing them videos or films related to dealing with crises.

Individual counselling: Here counselling is provided to the suffering children on individual basis. The counsellor tries to have support with the child for letting him / her express his / her feelings emotions and difficulties before him. The child is then gradually made to face the realities of his/her faced problems and learn to cope with them satisfactorily.

In addition to the counselling provided to the suffering children, efforts can also be made to provide needed counselling to the parents of the children. They must be made to realize that the innocent child should not suffer at a heavy price of their discord, separation or divorce. When a single parent, mother or father, feels a need of taking his a her child to a counsellor, he or she also shows a necessity for undergoing counselling for bringing needed behavioural changes for meeting the interests and welfare of their children.

Loss of Parents in Armed Conflicts etc.

There may happen a number of instances in the case of growing up children when they are found to suffer with the loss of their parents on one account or the other. These may be accidental death of their parents on account of meeting with some at the time of their road, train or air journey, trapped into fire, drawn into river, etc. In addition to such accidental deaths, there may be instances where they may lose their parents on account of som armed conflicts such as terrorist, jehadis and naxalites attacks, robbery, attack of the enemy nation, armed turmoil in the region between the rival groups, mutual clashes and armed conflicts among the families and members of the communities for settling personal scores or getting victims of the caste and religion wars. The loss of parents on account of the latter reason i.e. armed conflicts proves more costly and damaging to the suffering children than the loss of parents on account of the former reason i.e. accidental death as it provides more psychological setback to these children in the manner given below:

- It becomes quite difficult for these children to forget the horrified experiences available to them at the time of loss of their parents on account of armed conflicts.
- They can feel guilty of not saving or protecting their parents by being killed in the armed conflict.
- They may develop a strong feeling of taking revenge from those who are responsible for killing their parents in the armed conflicts and thus may indulge in the acts of continuing rivalry and conflicts with the opposite camp.
- The experiences encountered on their part at the time of killing their parents may result in spoiling their mental health. They may fall victim of utter depression, fear anxiety, low selfesteem, phobia and other neurotic / psychotic symptoms.

What may happen in real sense with the children losing parents in armed conflicts can now be properly witnessed in the stories and live scenes of the war torned or terrorism ridden countries and regions of the globe. Whether it may be Syriya, Iraq, Afganistan or naxalites and terrorists ridden parts of our country, the miseries and agonies of the children losing their parents in armed conflicts are quite touchy and multi-dimensional. They are not only struggling for their day to day living but are also facing a number of problems for their adjustment to their self and environment. Such children need properly planned and organized counselling services for coping with the stress caused on account of the loss of their parents in such a way.

Counselling of the Children Losing Parents in Armed Conflicts etc.

Both group counselling and individual counselling may be carried out for helping the suffering children to cope with the stress experienced by them on account of the loss of parents in armed conflicts etc. Through such counselling, we may help them:

(i) to express their feelings, resentment and anger, fear and phobias related to their experience encountered at the time of loss of their parents in armed conflicts, etc.

(ii) to help them in coming out of the shocks and horrified experience by resorting to the therapies and techniques helpful in

- deconditioning of the fears and phobias related to horrified experience.
- Providing them incidences for modelling of their behaviour and imbibe moral courage as well as self confidences for dealing with the odds of their present circumstances with the help of stories and books, multimedia presentations, discussions and social interactions.

- Providing them mental peace and measures to seek adjustment with the self and environment by learning relaxation and conflict resolution techniques.
- actualizing their potentialities for becoming self-reliant and brave enough for finding out the solution of their difficulties and problems.

(iii) to help them in channelizing their resentment and anger towards the constructive activities helpful to them and the society.

(iv) to help them in working as models for the others in coming out of similar difficulties faced on account of the loss of their parents.

Survivors of Child Abuse

Many of the children in the society world wide may be found to pass through the horrified experiences of child abuse in one situation or the other. These children known as the survivors of child abuse grow up with the ill consequences and pains of the abuse lasting along the rest of their life. Let us see what we mean by the term child abuse, its nature, types and consequence along with its prevention and cure.

What is Child Abuse?

Ill treatment and harm caused to the children on the part of adult members of the society in a physical, verbal or emotional form resulting into their pain and suffering in one or the other ways and affecting their life in a quite negative and adverse way is commonly known by the term child abuse.

Types of Child Abuse

Child abuse may be categorized into four distinct types depending upon the nature of the harm or maltreatment caused to children by the adult members of the society discussed as below:

1. *Physical abuse*: In such type of abuse, the child is subjected to maltreatment and assault on the part of adults in the physical form resulting into physical harm and agony accompanied with mental or psychological shock to the victim. The fact that a particular child has been subjected to physical assault and abuse is surfaced through the physical indicators like below:

(i) Unexplained bruises and welts on the body parts suggesting the use of instruments like belt buckle, electric cord, hunters, sharp edged objects, etc.

(ii) Unexplained burns in the shape of cigarette burns, utensils or kitchen appliances burns, rope burns on the body parts.

(iii) Infected burns or wounds indicating delay in treatment.

In addition to such physical indicators, the survivors of physical abuse can also be identified through the behavioural indicator like below:

(i) In appropriate or excessive fear of some particular adult such as caretaker, parent, teacher or a near relative.

(ii) Unusual shyness, withdrawal, depression, sadness and socially cut off behaviour.

(iii) Anti-social behaviour such as drug addiction, truancy, running away from home, aggression and bullying, etc.

2. Emotional / Psychological abuse: In such type of abuse the child is subjected to maltreatment and misbehaviour on the part of adults in an emotional or psychological form inflicting mental / psychological pains, agonies and wounds on the mind and heart of the suffering child.

In their actual happening, the emotional or psychological abuse may include a chronic pattern of criticism, coercion, humiliation, accusation or threat to one's physical and social safety.

In general, survivals or victims of such abuse may be found to exhibit the following types of physical and behavioural symptoms or signs like below:

- Exhibiting a number of maladaptive behaviour or disorders like eating disorders, including obesity or anorexia, speech disorders (suffering, stammering), anxiety or nervous disorders (rashes, facial ties, stomach aches), habit disorders (biting, rocking, head banging), aggression and cruelty (hurting others including animals), age in-appropriate behaviour (bedwetting, wetting, soiling), mood disorders etc.
- Showing developmental delays in acquiring norms in terms of their physical, mental, social and emotional maturity.
- Exhibiting socially and emotionally deviant behaviour.

3. Neglect abuse: In such type of abuse, the child is subjected to maltreatment and ill behaviour on the part of caring adults in the form of neglecting and showing indifference to the satisfaction of his or her basic needs—physical and socio-psychological. In such a situation parents and members of the family may be found to show negligence / indifference for maintaining proper hygienic conditions, providing food and eatables at the needed time in an appropriate way, caring for the proper clothing, living, vaccination and immunization at the proper time, caring for their schooling and proper education, socialization and culturalization and emotional channelization in a proper way.

The negligence and indifference shown towards the developing children on the part of parents family members, teachers, and care givers may prove quite costly to the developing children. They may be deprived with the satisfaction of their basic needs — physical and socio-psychological and it can result in their under development and maladjustment with their self and environment making them hopeless and failures at one or the other situations in their life.

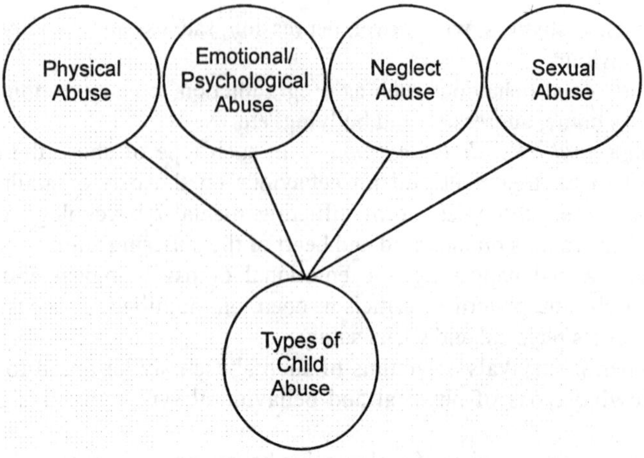

Fig. 9.1: Types of Child Abuse

4. Sexual Abuse: In such type of abuse, the child is subjected to maltreatment or assaults on the part of sex offenders (adults as well as peers) in the form of undesirable and unwanted sex behaviour and harm or pain causing sexual activities against the wishes and welfare of the victim. The range of sexual abuse committed to children is quite wide. The behaviour and activities like passing remarks or uttering indecent words, touching body parts especially the nipples, lips, buttocks, genitals of the female child with a motivated ill intention, engaging in oral and physical sex with the children (male or female) causing harms to their genitals and body parts in the form of rape and coercion, etc. all fall in the domain of sexual abuse. Moreover, the range of people who may be found to commit such sexual abuses is also quite wide. Any person of any age, background and relationship having a developed sexual libido and more powerful than the victim can be found to commit sexual abuses to the developing children.

The after effects and consequences of the sexual abuse are quite better to the survivor or victims. In addition to suffering from physical damage, pain and agony, the victims are subjected to quite horrified experiences, distressing memories, anxiety, blocks to establish normal social relationship, intimacy and trust in their future life. The wounds inflicted in emotional and psychological forms are quite harder to be healed than the physical / bodily injuries inflicted on the sexually abused children.

Identification of the Victims or Survivors of Sexual Abuse

In general, the children subjected to sexual abuse may be found to exhibit the symptoms and activities like below in their physical examination, and day to day behaviour.

- Torn clothes and stained or bloody underclothes.
- Bruises and scratches on the body parts

- Bleeding from external genitals, vagina or anal region.
- Detection of the attempts for sexual inter course through a medical examination or pregnancy report.
- Improper changes in behaviour such as extreme withdrawal from the social company, demonstration of anxiety, fear and phobias, disturbed sleep patterns including recurrent nightmares, distrust even in the intimate people, etc.
- Somatic complaints such as difficulty in walking or sitting, pain and irritation of the genitals.
- Disclosing the incidence of sexual abuse to their intimate parents and other well wisher.
- Sudden decline in the quality of their functioning at home and the school such as forgetting the things and events, committing mistakes in doing routine work, fall in their school attendance and performance level, etc.

In this way, we may find the children suffering from one or the other types of child abuse narrated above. In addition, it can also be properly seen that a particular child may also be found to be the victim of more than one type of child abuse. For example, a victim of sexual abuse may also be found to experience physical abuse and emotional abuse at his / her home and school. Similarly, a child experiencing physical abuse at his / her home may also be subjected to emotional abuse and neglect abuse from one or the other corners. No matter, whether child is subjected to one or the other types of abuses singally or in combination, it is quite certain that all types of abuse carry a long lasting influence and impact over the present and future life of the victimised children in physical, mental, social, emotional, moral and wholesome development and progress form.

How to Deal with the Problem of Child Abuse

The problem of child abuse is universal. It can happen with any developing child in any family and community all across the globe. As a parent, close family member, neighbour, acquaintance, friend, teacher or even stranger we can either play a substantial role in preventing or engaging in child abuse only because the child trusts us or he or she is more vulnerable for becoming victim to one or the other type of abuses on our part. It is also quite difficult to detect the cases of child abuse that are taking place in quite silent and methodological ways at home, social places and the school by even the intimate one's unless they are reported by the children themselves or come into the notice of some one who dares to help the victim. However, the methods and strategies used for dealing with the problem of child abuse can be broadly categorized under three heads, namely

(A) Educating Stakeholders,
(B) Creating awareness about the Child Rights,
(C) Counselling the survivors of child abuse.

(A) Educating the Stakeholders

The real issue and the thing that is coming in the way of preventing the problem of child abuse is lack of information and proper education in this matter to the many stakeholders such as parents, members of the community, teachers, media personnel and law enforcing agencies. This shortcoming needs to be properly handled by taking case of the availability of needed information and education to all the stakeholders in the manner given below:

1. Educating the parents and elders: Parents as well as elders in the family are the real well wisher of their children. However, in search of the well being of their children they are many times misguided to resort to hard punitive measures like neglect or physical abusing of their loving children. Therefore, there is a need to teach alternative method of disciplining the child in place of physical abusing. They should also be warned not to resort neglecting or depriving their children with the satisfaction of their basic needs — physical and socio-psychological as it may lead to the path of maladjustment and inadequate development harmful to them and the society. Emotionally, the children should not be felt starved and essential measures to be taken by the parents for the preservation and promotion of their mental health. Parents and elders need also to be educated properly for preventing the cases of sexual abuse. They must have a proper rapport with their developing children and try to get skilled in noting down any unwanted sudden changes in the behaviour of their children. By winning their confidence and trust, they should try to go in the deep of the crisis of physical, emotional and sexual abuse perplexing the mind and heart of their children. The physical symptoms regarding child abuse should be well noted and cared by them for helping the children to disclose any incidence of abuse inflicted on them. In addition, the parents should also be helped in seeking remedy to the victimized child through a number of available legal provisions, community help centres and counselling services.

2. Educating the teachers: Like parents and elders, teachers also need to be properly educated with the dealing of the issue of child abuse by learning and equipping them with the things like below:

- Awareness about the rights of the child including the legal provisions available for the enforcement of these rights.
- Knowledge and skill related to the warning sign for child abuse.
- The enforcement of constructive and self-imposed discipline in place of adopting hard punitive measures in the form of physical abusing or neglecting.
- The ways and means of securing cooperation of the parents, community people, NGO's and Government agencies for the protection of child rights and prevention of child abuse.
- The means and ways of establishing rapport and winning the confidence and trust of the children for knowing about their problems

related to abusing or maltreatment by the elders or peers.

- Providing needed guidance and counselling for the children for the purpose of getting them aware of their rights, need and means of preventing abuses and maltreatment to them by the elders.

3. *Educating the children:* It is also essential for the children to acquire needed information, knowledge and skills for getting them properly equipped for protecting themselves from the possible maltreatment and abusing on the part of their elders and peers. For this purpose the children should be helped by the parents, family members, NGOs, teachers and government agencies working for the education and welfare of the children to acquire knowledge and skills related to the following.

- Awareness about their rights known as Right of the children and agencies (Government as well as non government) helpful in securing these rights to them.
- Way and means of securing needed help at the time of distress while subjected to physical or sexual abuse on the part of elders and peers.
- Awareness of the type of touch, physical contact and behaviour shown towards them by the elders and peer that could be signalled as sexual abuse.
- Ability to make use of self-defence methods or techniques for protecting themselves from the physical and sexual abuse.
- Providing cooperation to the parents, teachers, guidance personnel and government agencies for the prevention as well as follow up actions related to child abuse.

B. Creating Awareness about the Child Rights

A proper awareness of the 'Child Rights' on the part of various stakeholders like parents, family members, care takers, community people, teachers and children themselves may help much in the prevention of child abuse and follow up of the abuse survivors.

For this purpose, let us first know about the meaning and nature of these rights.

What are Child Rights?

By the term Child Rights we mean a category of those human rights that are universally available to all children i.e. human beings below the age of 18. World wide universally, the Child Rights as a part of human Rights have been defined by the United Nations and United Nations Convention on the Rights of the Child (UNCRC). According to the UNCRC, (United Nations, 1889), Child Rights (as a part of human Rights) may be considered as those minimum entitlements and freedom that should be afforded to all persons below the age of 18 regardless of race, colour, gender, religion, opinions, wealth, birth status, disability or other characteristics and therefore apply universally to all children everywhere on the globe.

Types of Child Rights

By laying down Rights for the children on the lines of establishing Human Rights for the human beings, UNCRC has tried to ensure children their required freedom and civil rights, appropriate family environment, necessary health care and welfare, education, leisure and cultural activities as well as special protection measures. For ensuring these to the children, the UNCRC has tried to classify the Rights given to children with the four major types detailed as below:

1. *Right to Survival:* A child's right to survival begins within the womb of the mother well before his or her actual birth. The right of survival ensured to the children includes the following: (i) Right to be born, (ii) Right to minimum standards of food, shelter and clothing, (iii) Right to live with dignity, and (iv) Right to health care, to safe drinking water, nutritious food, a clear and safe environment and information to help them stay healthy.

2. *Right to Protection:* By providing his right to the children UNCRC tries to ensure the measure to be taken for the prevention of or responding to the incidence of child abuse, exploitation, violence and neglect of children. Accordingly, Right to Protection tries to ensure for the children: (i) Right to be protected from all sorts of violence, (ii) Right to be protected from neglect, (iii) Right to be protected from physical and sexual abuse and (iv) Right to be protected from the dangerous drugs.

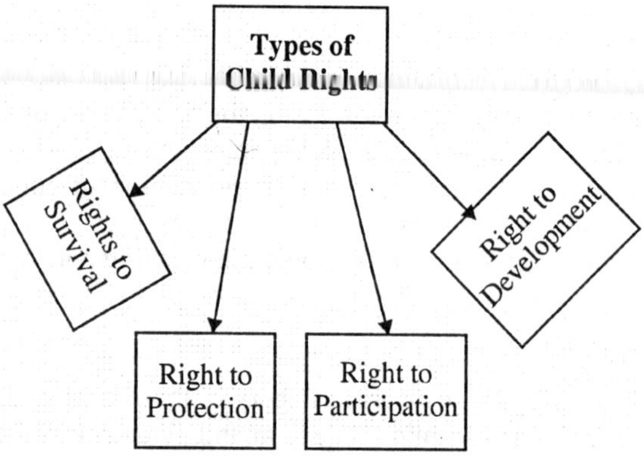

Fig. 9.2: Types of Child Rights

3. Right to Participation: The child as a human being has the right to participate and involve him or her freely to interact in the social situation. Accordingly, the right to participation given to the children includes the following:

(i) Right to freedom of opinion, (ii) Right to freedom of expression, (iii) Right to freedom of association, (iv) Right to information, and (v) Right to participate in any decision making that involves him / her directly or indirectly.

4. Right to Development: By laying down the right to the children, UNCRC has tried to ensure ways and means for the proper wholesome development to the developing children. Accordingly, the Right to Development given to the children includes the following:

(i) Right to education, (ii) Right to learn, (iii) Right to relax and play, and (iv) Right to all form of development — Social emotional, mental and physical.

Although all the above mentioned rights offered to the developing children cater to the satisfaction of their physical and socio-psychological needs, education and adjustment, leading to their proper progress and wholesome development, the Right to Protection is directly concerned to take care of the essential measures for the needed prevention and cure of one or the other types of child abuse inflicted on the children such as physical abuse, emotional or psychological abuse, neglect abuse and sexual abuse.

Right to protection ensures for the children the appropriate measures to be taken for the prevention of or responding to the incidences of all types of child abuse. In practice with regards to the prevention and responding to the cases of child abuse, it asks to employ ways and means for:

(i) Providing sensitization and awareness to the problem of child abuse in relation to the nature of its occurrence, its prevention and cure for the stakeholders — parents, teachers, community people and children themselves.
(ii) Establishing appropriate laws and policies, mechanisms and systems for the prevention as well as responding to the cases of child abuse and taking care for their proper monitoring and implementation.
(iii) Providing necessary access, assistance and relief for the victims of child abuse as promptly as possible.
(iv) Seeking cooperation and assistance from all the stakeholders, support groups, non-government organization and Government agencies to provide a proper safety network against the problem of child abuse and take proper measures for the cure and rehabilitation to the victims in case they fell through the holes in the security system.

Legal Provisions in our country for the Protection of Child Rights and Child Abuse

In our country, apart from the provision laid down in constitution, we have established the "National Commission for Protection of Child Rights" as a statutory body under the administrative control of the ministry of women and Child Development, Government of India. It works for ensuring the implementation of all laws, policies, programmes and administrative mechanisms as enshrined in the Constitution of India and also the UN Convention on the Rights of the Child.

In addition to deal with the protection of child rights, the commission enjoys the privilege of being armed with "The Protection of Children from

Sexual Offences (POCSO) Act, 2012" specifically for helping children with sexual abuse.

The Act defines a child as any person below eighteen years of age, and regards the best interests and well-being of the child as being of paramount importance at every stage, to ensure the healthy physical, emotional, intellectual and social development of the child. It defined different forms of sexual abuse, including penetrative and non-penetrative assault, as well as sexual harassment and pornography, and deems a sexual assault to be "aggravated" under certain circumstances, such as when the abused child is mentally ill or when the abuse is committed by a person in a position of trust or authority vis-à-vis the child, like a family member, police officer, teacher, or doctor. People who traffic children for sexual purposes are also punishable under the provisions relating to abetment in the Act. The Act prescribes maximum term of rigorous imprisonment for life, and fine.

C. Counselling of the Survivors of Child Abuse

Consequences of the child abuse are quite alarming and damaging to the victims of child abuse. They have to pass through a quite difficult period of the dreadful memories and horrified painful experiences after falling victims of the physical and sexual abuse. The other types of abuse, emotional and neglect, are also quite powerful to act adversely on their mental health. Thus in all cases of abuse, the victims need the services of a good counsellor for helping them to come out from their inappropriate and damaging mental state.

Both individual and group therapies may be employed by the counsellors for helping the abuse survivors depending upon the nature of their problem and the victims themselves. For example, in the cases where survivors need social support for coming out of their mental state and getting rid of the feelings of insecurity and vulnerability, the group therapy may work well for them. But for those who fear the vulnerability and exposure, they may experience in a group setting, the individual therapy (working one-on-one with a therapist) can be more advantageous. What ever mode one-on-one or group setting may be employed by the counsellor for helping the abuse survivors, it is bound to aim for the realization of the following objectives:

1. To provide opportunities and environment for the victim to narrate and tell about his / her dreadful experiences related to one or the other types of abuse, open up his / her heart and mind to express his / her bottled emotion, feelings, anxieties, fears, phobias, and thinking on the various aspects of his / her problem.

2. To help the victim in understanding the true nature of his / her problem and feel necessity of finding and its situations with the search and adoption of some suitable means and alternatives.

3. To help the victims for coming out with the feelings of guilt and shame, self condemnation and self destruction and regain their self-confidence and feelings of self respect and self-esteem.

4. To help them in giving up their inappropriate fears, anxieties, phobias and feelings of insecurity associated with the horrified experiences of their abusing with the application of suitable means and ways like aversive therapy, de-conditioning, group support, narrative therapy, modelling, meditation and relaxation techniques, art and creative therapy, etc.

5. To help them in regaining their trust in the social relationships, company of others, elders and peers, and the environment conditions available to them at present for their proper adjustment and productivity at work.

10

Protection of Child Rights

Introduction

On the line and pattern of Human Rights being prescribed for humans to live with dignity as human being, Child Rights have also been prescribed and laid down on global basis by the world authorities like UNO and UNICEF. We have already initiated some useful discussion in the previous chapter regarding the meaning, nature and broad classification of Child Rights. The question here may further arise that what should be done for helping the children in availing the benefits of these rights. In other words, what should be done for the protection of the Rights prescribed or laid down for the children by the global or regional authorities and agencies. In this chapter, we would like to discuss the role played by such various organizations and agencies for securing the protection of Child Rights in an appropriate way.

Role and Contribution of UNICEF

United Nations International Children Emergency Fund (UNICEF) having its head quarter in New York (USA) is one of the important UN agency dedicated to helping the world realize the rights of the children.

It lays emphasis on developing community-level services to promote the health and overall well being of children with the help of funds at its disposal created through the contribution from governments and private donors. According to its mission statement, "UNICEF is mandated by the United Nations General Assembly to advocate for the protection of children's rights, to help meet their basic needs, and to expand their opportunities to reach their full potential."

Though UNICEF headquarter is in New York, the organization has its wide extension throughout the globe with its regional offices in the member countries. UNICEF's work can be grouped into five main strategic areas. They are all inter-related as progress in one leads to progress in the others. These are:

A. Young Child Survival and Development
B. Basic Education and Gender Equality
C. HIV / AIDS and Children
D. Child Protection
E. Policy Analysis, Advocacy and Partnerships for Children Rights

In this way, UNICEF may be found to work in all areas concerning the welfare of the children such as reducing gender bias to girl child, providing care for the children and people affected with HIV / AIDS, immunization of children, including helping in their proper nutrition and health maintenance, child protection in times of conflict and peace, assistance in time of disaster, and aim at improving the life of every child on the globe.

With regard to the protection of the Child Rights as defined by the United Nations and the United Nations conventions on the Rights of the Child (UNCRC), UNICEF is functioning at its all fronts by providing its multi dimensional services for the protection of all the civil, political, social, economic and cultural rights of every child, classified as: (i) Right to survival, (ii) Right to Protection, (iii) Right to Participation, and (iv) Right to Development.

For providing shield and protection to these rights, UNICEF is actively engaged to provide its services and help (in the form of financial and technical support) to the children of the countries of the world in the areas like below:

- Anenatal care of pregnant women and neonatal care in the first four weeks after birth.
- Providing vaccination services in developing countries for protecting children from various diseases.
- Providing support to local programmes relating to nutritional diet to the poverty ridden children and access to basic water and sanitation facilities.
- Promoting, funding and facilitating universal primary education and gender equality in developing countries.
- Support programs helping the prevention of mother-to-child transmission of HIV / AIDS, supporting children orphaned by HIV / AIDS and educating the adolescents about the spread of these diseases.
- Providing support for creating needed protective environments to help prevent and respond to violence, exploitation abuse and discrimination, and for children made vulnerable by emergencies like separation of parents, survivors of child abuse and loss of parents in armed conflicts, etc.
- Strengthening national and local policies aimed to protect Child Rights to survive, protect, participate and develop in a proper way.

Role and Contribution of WHO

World Health Organization (WHO) is a specialized agency of United Nations (UN), working in the field of health. According to its mission statement "WHO is mandated by United Nations General Assembly to support and improve Public Health System around the world by promoting health development, fostering health security, strengthening health systems, engaging in research, mediating partnerships, and bring about reforms in health systems."

For the improvement of the health systems WHO also set out norms and standard of health and health services for being followed by respective stakeholders — the governments of the member nations. The WHO in this way in responsible for providing leadership on global health matters (including the health and well-being of the developing children) by working in collaboration with its member nations usually through the Ministries of Health.

It has its headquarters in Geneva (Switzerland). The WHO country office for India is headquartered in Delhi. In collaboration with Ministry of Health, Government of India, WHO is engaged in carrying out the following six core functions:

(i) Providing leadership on matters critical to health and engaging in partnership where joint action in needed;
(ii) Shaping the research agenda and stimulating the generation, translation and dissemination of valuable knowledge;
(iii) Setting norms and standards and promoting and monitoring their implementation;
(iv) Articulating ethical and evidence based policy option;
(v) Providing technical support, catalysing change, and building sustainable institutional capacity, and
(vi) Monitoring the health situation and assessing health trends.

As a leading partner in securing good health to the world citizens, WHO is contributing substantially towards the child and adolescent health and development along with looking into the issues of their environmental health. Since one's health is a basic parameter of attaining success in developing one's full capacity and potential, it can help in ensuring a maximum number of things related to protection of human and Child Rights. WHO in collaboration with governments of the member states is constantly engaged in the activities related to the protection of the child right to life, survival, maximum development, access to health and access to health services in a quite standardized form.

Role and Contribution of National Commission for Protection of Child Right

The National Commission for Protection of Child Rights (NCPCR) is a statutory body working under the administration control of the Ministry of Women and Child Development, Government of India. It was set up in March 2007 under the Commission for Protection of Child Rights (CPCR) Act, 2005, an Act of Parliament. The Commission's Mandate is to ensure that all laws, policies, programs, and administrative mechanisms are in consonance with the Child Rights perspective as enshrined in the constitution of India and also the UN convention on the Rights of the Child.

Composition

Besides the Chairperson, it has six members from the fields of child health, education, childcare and development; Juvenile justice; children with disabilities; elimination of child labour; child psychology or sociology and laws relating to children.

Tasks and Activities undertaken by NCPCR

In order to attain the commission's mandate of ensuring that each and every child has an access to all entitlements and enjoys all his / her rights, the commission is engaged in carrying out the following activities.

- The first is to build public awareness and create a moral force in the country to stand by children and protect their rights. A national conscience has to be generated that captures the imagination of each citizen to take pride in the nation because it takes care of all its children.
- Armed with this kind of a mood the Commission's task is to look at the gaps in the policy framework and the legal framework and make recommendations to see that rights-based perspective is adhered to by the Government, while it makes its policies.
- Thirdly, the task of the Commission is to take up specific complaints that come up before it for redressal of grievances and also take up *suo moto* cases, summon the violators of child rights, get them presented before the Commission and recommend to the Government or the Judiciary, action based on an inquiry.
- Finally, the role of the Commission is in arming itself with proper research and documentation. The legitimacy and credibility to what the Commission says and does is based on solid research and data. Though everyone in the country knows that the predicament of the majority of children in our country is vulnerable and that children are not treated well, this has to be substantiated by information; it cannot just be an emotional argument..

The above tasks are to be rendered in a manner that the child is regarded as an individual with a character and mind of her own, not to be patronized in a relationship of benefactor and beneficiary. There is no favour to the child, it is the duty of the State to fulfill its obligations and the duty of society to create the environment where the child is in the centre of all decisions pertaining to the child. The Commission is of the opinion that in addressing the child, there is a focus on rendering dignity to the child, who is at the moment most vulnerable in society.

Role and Contribution of National Human Rights Commission

The National Human Rights Commission (NHRC) is an autonomous statutory body established in 1993 according to the provisions of the Protection of Human Rights Act, passed by the Parliament of India in 1993.

Composition

It consists of a chairperson and six other members in the manner like below:

- A chairperson should be the retired Chief Justice of India.
- One member who is, or has been, a judge of the Supreme Court of India.
- One member who is, or has been, the Chief Justice of a High Court.
- Two members to be appointed from among persons having knowledge of, or practical experience in, matters relating to human rights.
- One member who is the chairperson of National Commission for SC.
- One member who is the chairperson of National Commission for ST.

Functions and Activities carried out by NHRC

Under the provision of the Protection of Human Rights Act, 1993 NHRC is required to carryout the following functions.

- proactively or reactively inquire into violations of human rights or negligence in the prevention of such violation by a public servant
- by leave of the court, to intervene in court proceeding relating to human rights
- to visit any jail or other institution under the control of the State Government, where persons are detained or lodged for purposes of treatment, reformation or protection, for the study of the living conditions of the inmates and make recommendations
- review the safeguards provided by or under the Constitution or any law for the time beings in force for the protection of human rights and recommend measures for their effective implementation
- review the factors, including acts of terrorism that inhibit the enjoyment of human rights and recommend appropriate remedial measures
- to study treaties and other international instruments on human rights and make recommendations for their effective implementation
- undertake and promote research in the field of human rights
- engage in human rights education among various sections of society and promote awareness of the safeguards available for the protection of these rights through publications, the media, seminars and other available means
- encourage the efforts of NGOs and institutions working in the field of human rights
- such other function as it may consider it necessary for the protection of human rights
- requisitioning any public record or copy thereof from any court or office

In this way, National Human Rights Commission is responsible for the protection and promotion of human rights defined by the Act as "rights relating to life, liberty, equality and dignity of the individual guaranteed by the Constitution or embodied in the international covenants".

When any individual or institution finds that there is violation of human rights in its case, then a petition can be made directly to the commission in this concern by him / her or any NGO. After receiving such petition, NHRC is required to investigate the violation of human rights or the failures of the state or other to prevent a human rights violation.

The commission can visit state institution and other places to examine the condition prevalent there for knowing about the violation of human rights. It can also examine any law or constitutional provision, for ensuring the safeguards of human rights besides creating awareness among the people about their rights as human being.

Role and Contribution of Child Helplines

Child helplines can play a quite effective role in safeguarding the Child Rights especially in terms of their protection from child abuse and accidents and incidences of life.

What is a Child Helpline?

A child helpline is an emergency phone service responded by a friendly 'didi' or a sympathetic 'bhaiya' for helping the vulnerable children 24 hours of the day, 365 days of the year. It aims to respond to calls from children (or a concerned peer or adult) in distress offering immediate assistance and linking them to long term rehabilitation.

Child helpline exists as a uniform toll free number in a country. In our country it exists in the name of Childline 1098 Service. Immediate help is available to the child in distress by dialing this toll free number 1098 from any place in the country. The helpline known as Childline 1098 in our country works as a 24-hour free emergency phone outreach service for children in need of care and protection. It is supported by the ministry of Women and Child Development, Government of India; and run through the cooperation received from various sectors like Department of Telecommunication, Street and Community Youth, NGOs, academic institutions, the corporate sector, police system, health care, judiciary, transport, labour, media, elected representatives, individual concerned and all of us. Some NGO's are providing quite commendable services on the account. For example, Childline India Foundation is providing toll free 1098 telephone service to the children in distress. Its head office is in Worli, Mumbai and regional offices are in New Delhi, Kolkata and Chennai.

The Field of its Operation

The child helpline working in our country (1098 Tele Helpline) although stands for the welfare and protection of the rights of all children in general, yet its main attention is focussed on helping children in distress, especially the more vulnerable sections, which include:

- Street children and youth living alone on the streets.
- Child labourers working in the unorganised and organized sectors.
- Domestic help, especially girl domestics.
- Children affected by physical / sexual / emotional abuse in family, schools or institutions.
- Children who need emotional support and guidance.
- Children of commercial sex workers.
- Child victims of the flesh trade.
- Victims of child trafficking.
- Children abandoned by parents or guardians.
- Missing children.
- Run away children.
- Children who are victims of substance abuse.
- Differently-abled children.
- Children in conflict with the law.
- Children in institutions.
- Mentally challenged children.
- HIV / AIDS infected children.
- Children affected by conflict and disaster.
- Child political refugees.
- Children whose families are in crises.

Objectives Served by the Child Helpline

- To reach out to every child in need of care and protection by responding to emergencies on 1098.
- Awareness about CHILDLINE 1098 amongst every Indian child.
- To provide a platform of networking amongst organisations and to provide linkages to support systems that facilitate the rehabilitation of children in need of care and protection.
- To work together with the Allied Systems (Police, Health Care, Juvenile Justice, Transport, Legal, Education, Communication, Media, Political and the Community) to create child friendly systems.
- To advocate services for children that are inaccessible or non existent.
- To create a body of NGOs and Government organisations working within the national framework and policy for children.
- To be a nodal child protection agency in the country, providing child protection services to children in need of care and protection.
- To contribute and work towards strengthening and participating in a global movement that addresses issues related to child protection and ensures that children's voices are heard.

Functioning of Child Helpline

A child helpline net work may be found to be functioning in the ways as laid down below:

1. A call is received on the helpline toll free number 1098 at the help centre established for the purpose.

2. The staff working at the centre may respond in two ways:
   (i) It provides needed guidance and institutions for helping the child or well wishers of the child (who has dialled 1098) for coming out from his / her problem.
   (ii) It directs the call for the required intervention to the local intervention unit working in the neighbourhood of the child in distress.
3. The neighbourhood intervention unit then may get engaged in the help rendering tasks depending upon the nature of the emerging or distress reported through call. It may be ranged as below:
   - Filing FIR and take the help of police personal if needed.
   - Providing immediate assistance in the form of food and water, medicines and doctors, temporary shelters, clothes and transport, etc.
   - Taking the help of experts and specialists for deciding what actions or help should be rendered to the child in distress.
   - Linking the child in distress for getting benefited from the help and services of counsellors, health personnel and medical help centres, shelter homes, legal advisors, and other individuals / institutions for providing help and assistance to come out from the period of his or her distress.

Role and Contribution of NGOs

What are NGO's?

Non government organizations (NGOs) are the organizations that are created by the community people for being operated independently and differently from governmental organizations for rendering help and assistance to needy people and performing other works related to the service to humanity. These are essentially not a part of the government. In the cases in which NGOs are totally or partially funded by governments, they maintain their non-governmental status by excluding government representatives from membership in the body of organization or administration. NGOs are referred to as not-for-profit bodies which means they do not have any commercial interest. NGOs are run on donations made by individuals, corporate and institutions. They engage in fundraising activities to raise money for carrying out the work they do. Ever since the time of providing a framework of goals for the vital activities of NGOs by the UN convention on the Rights of the Child (CRC), NGOs have played a crucial role in protection of Human Rights including the Child Rights in the developed and developing countries of the world.

The convention on the Rights of the Child (CRC) has issued guidelines for the NGOs to work on the two lines simultaneously:

- to remind government of their obligation through approach to ministries, elected officials and the media, and
- to undertake their own operational efforts.

NGOs Operating at the International Level

Globally, Non-governmental Organisations (NGOs) are playing a quite significant role in championing the cause of Human Rights including the protection of Child Rights. For coordinating the functioning and operation of NGOs world wide, there has been an attempt to establish a coordinating agency in the name of the NGO Group. It is a global network of a number of national and international NGOs committed to ensuring that all children fully enjoy their rights as defined by Convention on the Rights of the Child. The NGO Group provides a coordinated platform for NGO action and plays a central role in key child rights developments at the international level. The NGO Group works through its secretariat and thematic working groups to fulfil its mission to facilitate the promotion, implementation and monitoring of the Convention on the Rights of the Child (CRC).

Practically in a global scenario, there are a number of NGOs working on the international level for carrying out the mission of NGO Group of helping in the task of children's Right protection. A few of these NGOs operating at the international level may be mentioned as below.

Amnesty International

Amnesty International is a worldwide movement of people who campaign for internationally recognized human rights for all. With more than seven million members and subscribers in more than 150 countries, they conduct research and generate action to prevent and end grave abuses of human, rights and to demand justice for those whose rights have been violated. It has its headquarters in London, United Kingdom with the motto "It is better to light a candle than to curse the darkness". In India, it has its regional office in Bangaluru (Karnataka)

Children's Defense Fund (CDF)

The CDF is a child advocacy organization that works to ensure a level playing field for all children. CDF champions policies and programs that lift children out of poverty, protect them from abuse and neglect and ensure their right to equal care and education. Its headquarters are in Washington, D.C., USA.

Human Rights Action Center

The Human Rights Action Center is a non-profit organization based in Washington, DC, headed by Jack Healey, world-renowned human rights activist and pioneer. The Center works on issues of the Universal Declaration of Human Rights and uses the arts and technologies to innovate, create and develop new strategies to stop human rights abuses. They also support growing human rights groups all over the world.

Human Rights Watch

Human Rights Watch is dedicated to protecting the human rights of people around the world. They investigate and expose human rights violations, hold abusers accountable, and challenge governments and those who hold power to end abusive practices and respect international human rights. It has its headquarters in New York, USA.

Human Rights Without Frontiers: (HRWF)

HRWF focuses on monitoring, research and analysis in the field of human rights, as well as promotion of democracy and the rule of law on the national and international level. It has its headquarters in Etterbeck, Belgium and affiliation with European Union Agency for Fundamental Rights.

NGOs working at the National Level

There are a number of NGOs working in our country for the protection of human rights including child rights. The significant ones, in this regard are mentioned as below:

1. Sammaan Foundation (established January 25, 2007): Originally established to link the poor to the mainstream through education, training and financial support, the current project of this NGO involves the rickshaw pullers to help them earn a better livelihood. This NGO also has notable contribution in areas like children education, health services and welfare of women.

2. Goonj: A recipient of the "NGO of the Year" award in 2007 at the India NGO Awards, this NGO aims at solving the clothing problems of the downtrodden. Goonj also provides relief during Rahat floods in West Bengal, Assam and Bihar.

3. Akshaya Trust: The sole aim of this NGO is to restore human dignity. Operating in Madurai. This NGO offers rehabilitation, healthy food and care to the street destitute.

4. Smile Foundation: The main aim of this NGO is the rehabilitation of the underprivileged by providing them education and healthcare services, thereby converting them into productive assets. It is run by a group of corporate professionals.

5. Udaan Welfare Foundation: The main aim of this NGO is to help the destitute, the main area of stress being women, children and senior citizens and also environmental welfare. One of their main projects is a cancer chemotherapy centre.

6. Pratham: The main aim of this NGO is to provide education to the children living in the huge slums of Mumbai and even providing education to those people who are unable to go to school. Their projects have increased enrolment of children in schools thus promising them a better tomorrow.

7. Lepra society: This NGO aims at prevention and control of diseases like AIDS, leprosy and tuberculosis in poor communities.

8. Deepalaya: This NGO aims at providing education to the children living in the slums of Delhi. Their projects also include providing healthcare, education, vocational training to the downtrodden and the physically disabled. They have contributed towards significant rural development in Haryana and Uttarakhand.

9. Uday Foundation: A New Delhi-based NGO, the Uday Foundation provides support to the parents and families of children suffering from congenital disorders and other syndromes. Their projects also include research to open new horizons of healthcare technologies. They also have health projects for common people. Their special stress is in the area of protecting child rights.

10. Helpage India: Established in 1978, the sole aim of this NGO is to provide resources to the elderly people of our country. Their objective is to make aware the senior citizens of their rights and protect the rights of the senior citizens of our country so that they can also play a key role in our society. They also work with the government (both local and national level) to implement policies that will be beneficial to the senior citizens of our country.

11

Child Obesity — Causes and Remedies

What is Obesity?

Obesity is regarded as one of solid cause for giving birth to a number of ailments and diseases among the children. As a matter of definition, children obesity may be regarded as the condition or state of their body in which there is so much excess in the amount of fats in the body on account of which not only their health is affected in an adverse way but also it may prove a great obstacle and hurdle to their development and progress by affecting their daily routine and working in a negative way.

Identification and Diagnosis of Obesity among Children

We can easily identify and consider a child suffering from obesity by looking at his / her body structure and ways / styles of performing their day to day tasks. The body structure of these children in quite bulky and out of proportion. Too much excess of the fats are easily reflected through the outward appearance of their body and the mode of performing day to day task and physical activities. They feel a lot of difficulty in running, racing and performing the physical tasks with a fast speed. By nature they have great attraction for not doing any physical activity or hardwork and love to sleep and rest most of the time. They are in the habit of eating all times and have taste and liking for the food stuff linked with the accumulation of fats in their body.

Apart from such informal observation, a formal and scientific procedure may be employed for the identification of the obesity among children in the ways detailed below.

1. The usual way to determine the status of one's obesity is to find out the BMI or Body Mass Index. After attaining the age of two year, every child is entitled for the computation of his / her BMI. For determining one's BMI, we have to take two measures in the measurement of the height and the other is the measurement of weight. After that BMI may be computed with the help of the following formula.

$$\text{BMI of the child} = \frac{\text{The body mass or weight of the child } (w)}{\text{The square of the height of the child } (H^2)}$$

BMI of the Child: The Body Mass of the child (W) BMI is universally expressed in units of kg / m^2 resulting from mass or weight in kilogram. and height in meters. How much BMI will term the child an over weight or obese may be ascertained with the help of charts available for this purpose. These charts have been prepared by using the needed statistical methods separately for the regions and countries of the world. In principle the value of BMI, more than the average (with respect to his or her own groups) is taken as the indicator of the state of obesity. However, for the interpretation of BMI scores in the case of children (aged 2 to 20), instead of comparison against fixed thresholds for underweight and overweight, the BMI is compared against the percentile for children of the same sex and age. Here a BMI less than 5th percentile is considered underweight and above the 95th percentile is considered obese. Children with a BMI between the 85th and 95th percentiles are considered to be overweight.

2. In addition to BMI, WHtR (Waist-to-Height Ratio) and WHR (Waist-Hip Ratio) are also used as the indicators of obesity among children and adults. We may compute one's WHtR and WHR in the following ways:

$$\text{(i) Waist-to-Height Ratio (WHtR)} = \frac{\text{Circumference of the Child's Waist}}{\text{Height of the Child}}$$

Here, the computation of Waist-to-Height Ratio index provides a measure of the distribution of body fat. A WHtR of over 0.5 is referred to as critical for the people under 40. Hence the values more than 0.5 of WHtR may be regarded as the indicators of increased obesity among the children.

$$\text{(ii) Waist to Hip Ratio (WHR)} = \frac{\text{Circumference of the Child's Waist}}{\text{Circumference of the Child's hips}}$$

The computation of WHR helps in assessing the presence of obesity among children. According to WHO standard of a Waist Hip Ratio above 0.90 for males and above 0.85 for females indicates the presence of obesity among males and females respectively.

The above mentioned measures in the form of the computation of BMG, WHtR and WHR may prove a good indicator for ascertaining the presence of obesity among the children but however, they, in combination or alone, can't guarantee for the same. The wise thing in this regard now is to go for medical testing and examinations like medical examination of adipose tissues and skin fold held responsible for the obesity among children.

Ill Effects of Obesity

The presence of obesity among children may prove harmful and dangerous to them in the ways discussed ahead.

1. Ill effects on their health: The children's obesity is responsible for making them victim of a number of ailments and diseases at present or push them towards the same in future by making them sufficiently vernerable. As a result, obese children are usually found to be grappled with the following types of health problems and ailments.

- Cardiovascular diseases
- High blood presence
- Types 2 diabetes
- Strokes
- Cancer growth of many types
- Asthma and respiratory disorders
- Sleep disorders
- Bone and joint problems
- Early puberty or menstruation
- Skin diseases and problem such as heat rash, fungal infection and acne.

2. ***Ill effects on the composition of somatic structure***: The somatic composition or outward appearance of the body is badly effected by the presence of obesity among the children. There is lack of symmetry and right amount of proportions visible in the parts of the body. They look awkward and ugly in terms of the physical appearance of their body mainly on account of excessive fats deposit, exposition of their stomach in a quite awkward way and improper body proportion. All these things may make them different in their bodily appearance and composition from the normal healthy population of the children giving birth to so many problems of the adjustment to their self and the environment.

3. ***Ill effects on physical activity and day to day functioning:*** Obesity affects the physical efficiency, the attitude and habit of being physically alert and active, the interest and inclination towards engaging in physical activities in a quite adverse way. Obese children experience difficulties in the alteration of their physical postures and functioning their body parts in a speedy way. As a result, they are quite hesitant to take part in the physical activities or performing day-to-day tasks that need alertness, speed and promptness in their execution. They prefer to do activities or play games that can be performed and played while sitting at one place in a comfortable way. They do not include running, racing, doing physical exercises, playing major outdoor games and performing physical labour based activities in their daily routine at their home and school. In this way, obesity makes them to pick up a life style of leading an inactive, lazy, restfully comfortable life with no physical activity and games for getting entrapped to become more and more fatty and obese at the cost of their health and wellbeing.

4. ***Ill effects related to psychological wellbeing:*** From psychological angle also children obesity proves harmful and dangerous to them in many ways detailed below:

(i) While compairing their body structure and functioning with other non-obese children, they may develop feelings of inferiority and dissatisfaction in relation to their body image and appearances.

(ii) The obesity of children may make them handicap or incapable of taking part in a number of social, cultural, sports and educational activities that are undertaken by their normal peers in an appropriate way. It may make them to feel uncomfortable by instilling in them the feelings of inferiority, guilt and frustration. On account of their such non-participation they may also become victim of the social isolation resulting into more psychological disadvantages and mental problems to them.

(iii) Their body composition and inactivity may make them the object of being ridiculed and teased on the part of their peers, teachers and other members of the community. Such attitude shown and behaviour demonstrated towards them may make them feel psychologically insecure; it may further result in lowering down their self-esteem and self-confidence and cause a number of problems related to their maladjustment and mental health.

Causes related to Obesity

The probable causes or factors responsible for obesity among children may be described as below:

1. Genetic Factors: The obesity may be found to be travelling from generation to generation. The family members of the obese children like parents, sisters and brothers may also usually found to be quite fatty and obese. It may happen on account of the life style, food habits and working pattern going on in the family. However, much of the research work done in this concern has revealed that the chromosomes and genes transferred to the children from their immediate parents are very much responsible for causing obesity among children. They may inherit a particular type of body composition, physical structure and its functioning for causing and perpetuating the things responsible for the their obesity.

2. Improper Dietary Habits: A quite solid reason and factor working behind the obesity of children may be cited in the name of improper dietary and food habits among the developing children. The things in this concern may be detailed as under:

(i) From the very early young age, children may now a days be found to consume food material that is very much associated with the increasing cases of obesity among them. As an example we may name them as a variety of fast food and junk food, chocolate, cold drinks, ice cream, pizza, burger etc.

(ii) Many children fall victims of obesity on account of consuming food in a quite excess amount or due to their habit of consuming always one or the other types of food stuff.

(iii) The habit of consuming food while watching T.V. or working on laptop / mobiles had made the children eating and drinking for too long without taking note of the food consumption on their part. It has resulted in the increasing cases of obesity.

(iv) The habits of consuming tea, coffee, cold drinks from a quite early age has also been found a quite contributing factor for the obesity among children.

(v) The eating habits of family members, the prevalent practices of consuming food in the community, and the industrial and commercial organization engaged in advertising their food stuff responsible for the obesity, have all joined hands for creating a quite improper environment and role model being picked up by the children in the name of modernization. It has provided a single solid reason for the spread of the virus of obesity among children.

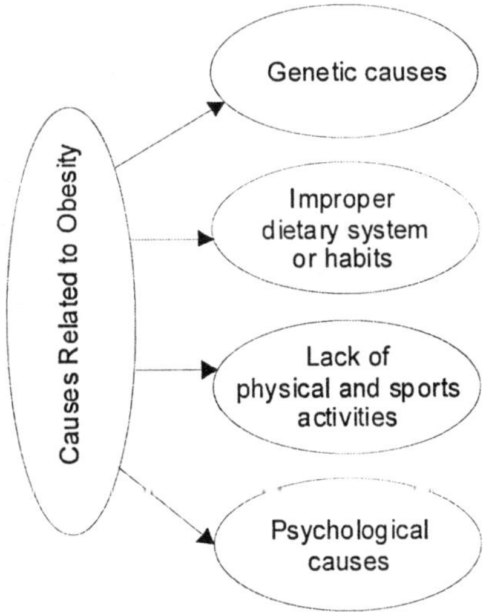

Fig. 11.1: Causes Related to Obesity

3. Lack of Physical and Sport Activities: Besides picking up the improper unhealthy habits, the children of now a days are moving far from engaging in the practices of physical labour and participating in the physical activities, games and sports, their home and school. It has been responsible in a big way for their obesity. We can name the things like below responsible for their inactivity and lack of physical and sport activities.

(i) Children imitate their elders. The habit of walking and using stairs is almost gone and we are now adapt to make use of vehicles and lifts. All these things are now getting transferred to our children.

(ii) In the rich families, the dependence on servants has ended the habit of doing our work with our own hands. Besides this the modern age has also uttered good bye to do the work with the hands on account of getting accustomed to the use of machines and appliances. It has snatched the opportunities of getting engaged in the physical labour and doing day to day work with their hands on the part of our children.

(iii) Our children have been forced to get continuously engaged in their study in school and at home on account of being given a lot of home work and project assignment as well as loaded with the pressure of excelling others in the blind race of securing good position in the class. Their over engagement in the study is thus leaving no time to them for their participation in physical activities and sports.

(iv) After devoting time to studies, whatever time is left for them now getting reserved for seeing movies and T.V. programs, working on computers and making use of smart phones. It has resulted in the complete avoidance of taking part in the physical activities, games and sports both at home and the school.

(v) Schools are not properly caring for the organization of physical activities, sports and games for the benefit of the students. In many of the schools there in no space and arrangement for the organization of these activities. In case if they are organized in someway, the student do not seem to take interest in participating in these activities. In such circumstances, the children have been found to take no advantage from the opportunities otherwise available to them is school or in neighbourhood community centres.

Psychological causes: In many of the situation, there may exist a variety of psychological factors working behind the obesity of children. It has been well established through the ongoing researches in this field that the children who remain stressed, anxious and restless suffer from lack of confidence and lost in depressive and tensed state may pick up the habit of eating in excess or consuming one thing or the other without the need of doing so and it may result in the causation of obesity among them.

Prevention and Treatment of Obesity

The causes lying behind the obesity among children may themselves suggest the ways and means of its prevention. In case we remain cautions and take suitable measures for not allowing the things and factors germinating and perpetuating obesity among children, then we may get considerable success in checking out the menace of obesity. However, nothing can be done by us for restraining the influence of the genetic factor in developing obese. It is beyond our control. But apart from the limitation much can be done by us for the prevention of obesity among children in the ways discussed below:

A. Exercising control over psychological factors: The psychological factors compelling the children to consume excess food and pickup the habit of always eating something or the other for getting relief from the stressful state may be kept in proper control by resorting to suitable psychological measures. They may be provided appropriate counselling and therapies like individual and group counselling behavioural therapy, deconditioning and relaxation therapies, etc. for getting rid of their anxiety, stress, depression, inferiority and guilt feelings and lack of self-esteem and self confidence, etc.

B. The improper life style and dietary habits is considered a quite significant factor contributing towards the obesity of children. In case proper care is taken on the part of the parents, family members and community people, teachers and school authorities for getting the children pick up a proper healthy style of living and eating, then much can be done in the prevention as well as treatment of the obesity among children. The things like below may help much to them in this direction.

1. The parents and other elder members of the family including elder sisters and brothers should try to present themselves as a model for the development of healthy eating habits among children. The family members thus should try to adopt such an appropriate routine as well as healthy eating habits that may help the children in picking up the right healthy food habits in their daily routine.

The things like below may be well emphasized for this purpose.

(i) The children should take their meals in a proper schedule, in the right proportion well in tune with their developmental needs.

(ii) They should avoid to consume food frequently without the need of doing so.

(iii) They should try to imbibe the habit of consuming the healthy well balanced diet in place of tempting to stuff their stomach with the harmful eatables like fast and junk food, cold drinks, tea and coffee, etc.

(iv) The children should be made to take their meals at the dining table along with other family members instead of consuming food while watching TV or working on laptops or smart phones.

2. In addition to helping the children in picking up appropriate healthy eating habits, the family members should also try to provide themselves as a model of healthy and active life style by getting engaged in physical activities and manual labour in their day to day functioning such as walking on foot instead of using vehicles, using stairs instead of the lift, doing their personal work and house hold activities by themselves instead of depending on the servants.

3. The children should be helped in imbibing and integrating the things like manual labour, physical activities and exercises in their daily routine by developing the healthy habits like below:

(i) Children should be made to perform their personal work by themselves and also help the family members in doing their personal work and fulfilling house hold duties.

(ii) Children should pick up the habit of walking on foot instead of using vehicles for a short walking distance. They should also be made to use cycles instead of machine operated vehicles like scooter, motorcycle, etc.

(iii) They should be made to pick up the habit of using stairs instead of lift for coming down or going up to the multi storey buildings.

(iv) They should be helped in deciding the amount of time being devoted for watching TV or using laptops / smart phones for social exposure and entertainment.

(v) They should be made to learn the art of proper time management for enabling them to find the time for the physical activities, games and sports, etc.

(vi) They should be helped in taking interest for the participation in physical activities, games and sports organized in the school by the school authorities and community centres on the part of community people.

4. In case even if by observing precautions like above for the prevention of obesity among children, there arises an appropriate increase in the weight of growing children, then no time should be wasted taking appropriate remedial steps. The medical experts should be properly consulted now for the treatment of child's obesity. The proper diagnosis about the seriousness of the state of obesity may be properly made through the needed clinical testing and medical examination along with its probable causes and future outcomes. The child should now be subjected to special dietary measures, instructions for getting engaged in physical activities, counselling at the hands of good counsellors / therapist. He or she may also be given some medicines or ultimately advised to go for surgical treatment in case all other measures fail for the treatment of his / her obesity.

C. Prevention and Treatment of obesity through sports activities and Yoga

Participation in sports activities and engaging in Yoga Sadhna may prove quite beneficial in the prevention as well as treatment of obesity among children. Let us try to think over it.

Prevention and Treatment of Obesity through Sports Activities

In schools, children are provided valuable opportunity for taking part in various types of games and sports activities organized on the regular basis under the supervision of games and sports teachers and instructors. While the indoor games like chess, carom, adds to mental exercise and entertainment, the games and sports in the form of inviting vigorous physical activities on the part of players help much in burning extra calories and reduction of the amounts of extra fat in the bodies of obese. We can name some of the games and sports activities, quite helpful in controlling obesity among children, as below.

(i) Hockey, Football, Volleyball, Cricket, Basketball, etc.

(ii) Indigenous games like Kabaddi and Kho Kho.

(iii) Badminton, Table Tennis, Lawn Tennis, Squash, etc.

(iv) Short and long distances races, swimming, cycling, etc.

All the above mentioned and sports activities are quite capable of exercising control over child obesity on account of the reasons given below.

1. The participation of the children in the sports and games activities

increases their total energy expenditure (burning of the calories) for helping them to lose weight and get rid of the accumulated extra fats on the body.

2. Many of the sports and games with their distinctive physical efforts made by the children in their execution, help much in reducing fat around the waist and total body fat helpful in getting rid of the abdominal obesity.

3. Weight lifting, wrestling, boxing, cycling, swimming, and other muscle strengthening sports activities helps the children in building muscle mass, increasing the energy that the body burns throughout the day (even when it's at rest) and making it easier for them to exercise control over their weight.

4. Physical exercise and efforts involved in engaging games and sports activities on the part of children may help the children in getting rid of the waves of depression, anxiety and stress effecting their mental health in the negative way at present. The benefits so derived then may prove quite helpful in doing away with the psychological reasons responsible for the development of their obesity.

In the way, it can be properly concluded that participation in games and sports activities may prove a big boon to the developing children in exercising proper control on their obesity.

Prevention and treatment of obesity through Yoga Sadhana

Apart from their participation in sports and games activities, the engagement in Yoga related activities may considerably help the children in the prevention as well cure of their obesity. Many of the yogic practices involved in yoga sadhana proves quite helpful or say boon to the children affected with the chronic problems of obesity in the manner given below:

1. The pranayama practices involved in Yoga Sadhna, particularly bhastrika, kapalbhati and suryabheda pranayams may help children in their efforts of controlling weight and say good bye to obesity.

2. The hath yoga practices referred to as shatkarmas or internal clearing techniques such as shank prakshalana (helpful in cleaning the entire alimentary canal), kunjal (helpful in cleaning stomach) and neti (helpful in cleaning the nasal passage) when performed regularly make the practitioner children to feel that their body / mind has got rid of any extra weight, physically as well as mentally. Moreover these practices always prove helpful in treating fat related problems in children.

3. Yoga sadhna requires from their practitioners to consume yogic diet, satyavik in nature. It helps the children to adopt such food habits that may prove a great boon in the prevention and treatment of obesity.

4. The other most effective yoga practice consists of performing a variety of those yogasans that have a striking effect on the prevention and treatment of the children obesity as detailed below:

(i) The practice of yogasans like pawan muktasan (wind releasing pose), utthanpadasana (raised leg position) chakrapadasana (leg rotation), etc. may prove quite effective in removing extra fat from the abdomen, hips and thighs.

(ii) The practice of dhanurasana (bow pose) is found helping the children in burning excessive fat in the body.

(iii) The practice of sarvangasana (shoulders stand pose) help in normalizing body weight by improving the efficiency of thyroid glands.

(iv) The practice of padahastasana (forward bending asana) helps in controlling obesity among children by improving the metabolic process of their body.

(v) The practice of paschimottanasana (back stretching pose) helps the children in removing excess fat in their abdominal region.

(vi) The practices bhujangasane (cobra pose) proves quite helpful for the obese children on account of its capability of massaging abdominal organs, increasing the flexibility of backbone and regulating the thyroid glands.

(vii) Practice of vipariti karni is helpful to the obese children on account of its capability of providing relief in the disorders related with thyroid and para thyroid glands.

(viii) The practice of yogasan like vajrasana (thunder bolt pose), singhasana (lion pose), shashankasana (pose of the moon), ushtrasana (camel pose), help children in controlling their obesity by strengthening their digestive and endocrine system.

(ix) The practice of yogasanas like gatyatmak meru vakrasana (dynmaic spinal twist) and chakrasana help the children in controlling obesity by massaging the abdominal organs and mobilizing extra fat tissues stored around them.

(x) Regular practice of halasana, matryasana along with surya namaskar help the children for getting rid of a number of problems related with obesity.

5. Apart from doing yogasanas narrated above, the yoga practice known as Surya Namaskar (Salutation to the Sun) proves most effective in getting rid of the obesity and its related problems. In fact Surya Namaskar is a complete yoga practice or Sadhna itself because it includes asana, pranayama, mantra and meditation. The daily practice of Surya Namaskar helps the children in controlling their obesity and treating obesity problems by regulating their endocrine and nervous system and helping to improve metabolic imbalances.

In the way, yoga practices in their various forms prove quite helpful in the prevention of treatment of obesity among the developing children.

12

Equity Issues and Inclusion

The Concept of Equity and Equality in Education

Our constitution talks about following the principlė of equity and equality in dealing with all its citizen irrespective of their differing in so many ways. The inclusive class room practices adopted for the education of children also lay due emphasis over equity and equality. Let us know about the meaning and concept of these two terms along with the inherent distinction/difference lying between them.

What is Equity?

Equity can be defined as the quality of treating individuals fairly based on their needs and requirements. This does not denote that an equal amount should be distributed to each and every individual. On the contrary, it highlights that things should be distributed based on the needs. Let us comprehend this through an example.

In our schools we have teachers, clerks and peons. All of them have their salaries on the basis of the nature of their work. Similarly, among the teachers also all do not get equal salary; PGT, TGT and diploma holders teachers get their salaries according to their nature of work, qualifications and experience. This explains the concept of equity. Equity thus stands for a concept that is governed by principal of justice and fairness in distributing and doing things for the people and not by dividing the things or works equally among them. Thus, while distributing refreshments to the unit of NCC or NSS, the teacher is supposed to distribute bananas or apples equally among them but when it comes to giving marks to them, he has to assess the ability of every child and give him or her numbers accordingly. This is known as the concept of equity.

What is Equality?

Equality can be defined as treating each and every individual in the same manner irrespective of their needs and requirements. This is to say that whatever the necessity of the individual is, it is ignored to promote the ideals of fairness and equal treatment.

Let us see by an example. If you are the teacher of a class and have been given the task of distributing chocolates to all the kids equally, what you will do is to divide the total number of chocolates you have by the total number of students in your class and arrive at the number to be given to each child. This is what is denoted by the concept of equality. But if you ask all your students to take off their shoes, mix them up and then throw two shoes at each student, though you have done no injustice and given two shoes to each child thereby following the concept of equality, you find every child complaining. Why, because no shoe is now fitting the feet to the children. Some have large feet and have got smaller shoes while those having small feet have got bigger shoes causing discontent among them.

Thus, it is clear that though equality is a good thing and needs to be followed across genders and religions, there is a concept called equity which states that everyone has different needs and requirements and should be treated accordingly. As a result while teaching in an inclusive class, the teacher has to follow the principle of equity and not equality while planning for the instructional work and methods of teaching to the students of different abilities such as students of low intelligence, average and gifted.

What is the Difference between Equity and Equality?

1. While equity is known as the quality of treating individuals fairly based on their needs and requirements, the equality on the other hand, stands for treating each and every individual in the same manner irrespective of needs and requirements.
2. While in principle, equity is based upon justness and fairness, the equality on the other hand, demands everyone be treated at the same level.
3. While in maintaining equity attention is paid to individual needs and requirements, in equality the individual needs and requirements are ignored.

Equity and Inclusion of Diverse Children (Differently abled, Street children and Other Marginalized Groups)

Inclusion has been accepted as basic policy for including the diverse children like differently abled, street children and other marginalized groups of our society (getting marginalized on the basis of gender, caste, socio-economic status, religion, locale and language) in the mainstream of our school education. It has been necessitated on account of providing equal opportunity to the future citizens of our country for their education, development and progress with no discrimination of any kind. In the inclusive setup, these has been made a provision that all children irrespective of their status of ability, or disability, marginalized or non-marginalized should get admission in the neighbourhood school. The provision like fee and compulsory education to the children through a Parliamentary Act Right to Education has made possible for the street children, children belonging to marginalized groups and children with disabilities to get equal and same opportunities as available to their normal and priviledged peers. As a result we may find in an inclusive class or inclusive learning and working setup the children of all abilities and kinds getting equal opportunity for actualizing their potential to the maximum extent possible. Thus the children identified as learning and visually impaired locomotor or orthopedically impaired, hearing disabled, mentally challenged, emotionally disturbed, socially deviant slow learners, backward, gifted and creative, all get their education in the same learning environment on equal footing in an inclusive education setting.

In this way the principle of equality is well followed in the inclusive setup of our schools. Here the same curriculum is followed for the teaching, learning of all students, equal opportunities are provided for acquiring learning experiences (curricular and co-curricular) to all the learners. They all get equal opportunity for the interaction with the staff, instructors and other resource personnel. Whatever thus exists in the school in the form of material and human resources, infrastructure and facilities, ideals and goals is equally shared by all the learners with no discrimination of any kind. With a sole aim of helping all the learners in the maximum development of their potentialities.

But now here some issues are involved and questions may be raised. Are all learners including the diverse ones can be benefited equally by providing them the same learning experiences or teaching a particular topic of the curriculum? Do they have the same or equal potential, previous experiences background, economical or family support, capacity of learning and acquiring, style and pace of learning and even the need of such learning and acquiring? Certainly not.. Therefore, there now arises an urgent need of making use the principle of equity in planning for the education and welfare of the diverse children along with the average or above average children of the inclusive setup.

Here, while following the principle of equity, the children belonging to the inclusive class will be treated quite fairly by planning to provide them what is needed for their adjustment, quality education and wholesome development in view of their potentialities, needs and requirements. For this purpose, teachers and school authorities may be required to bring a lot of accommodation, differentiation and adaptation in the learning environment, curricular and co-curricular experiences, teaching learning methods and approaches, use of teaching aids and learning material, interaction in the classroom or work environment, mode of evaluation and assessment, etc. well in tune with the learning needs, abilities and capacities and expectation or learning outcomes set for them in view of their individualities and exceptionalities. Let us illustrate it further.

(i) We will have to bring modification in the infrastructural facilities such as provision of ramps, railings, obstruction free pathways for providing fair and just treatment to a number of differently abled children such as orthopedically impaired, visually impaired, hearing impaired, etc.

(ii) Similarly, instead of providing equal treatment to the students of the class, the differently abled like orthopedically, visually or hearing impaired will be provided with some special preferred seating arrangement as nearness to the teacher and conditions helpful in their proper learning. The street children and marginalized, having poor exposure and previous knowledge, deficiency in conversation and use of language, social interaction and communication, will be provided extra attention, and coaching for removing their learning difficulties and deficiencies.

(iii) The educational and developmental goals for the diverse children — differently abled, street and marginalized — should be set well in accordance with their potential and capacities as well as limitations. For example, how can we follow the principle of equality by setting same learning goals and expectations from the mentally retarded or sensory impaired as set usually for children having average IQ and satisfactory sensority abilities. Here we essentially need to follow the principle of equity in setting learning objectives and providing learning experiences within the reach of their capacities.

(iv) Diverse learners present in an inclusive class besides possessing different abilities, different socio-economic background, prior knowledge and experience also differs in terms of their learning styles and capacity of being benefited from the use of one or the other teaching-learning strategies, use of teaching-learning aid and material. Hence, there is a great need of going for the needed adaptation, adoption and differentiation in the use of methods and strategies, aids and equipments, devices and approaches for the teaching-learning of the differently abled, (such as hearing, visual, locomotor and learning disabled) street and marginalized children.

(v) The same precaution is also to be practised for going with the evaluation of the learning outcomes of the diverse learners of an inclusive setting. Since we can't expect same type of progress and outcomes in the similar ways from the children with disability and disadvantaged children at par with their normal, non-disabled and priviledged peers. We have to go for the necessary modification and differentiation in the evaluation or assessment techniques used for the differently abled and marginalized children.

In this way while caring for the differently abled, street and marginalized children present in inclusive set up of the school we need to follow the principle of equity in its variety of shape besides providing equal opportunities for their wholesome development and quality education.

Equality and Strategies to achieve EFA

A democratic country like India wedded to the principle of equity and equality can't afford illiteracy and ignorance for its citizens. Besides arranging educational opportunities to the elderly people (who have been the victim of illiteracy on one or the other accounts) in the name of adult education program, Government of our Independent India has determined not to leave any child (the future citizen) illiterate and without education by calling for the mass campaigns like the Sarva Shiksha Abhayan (SSA) and

Rashtriya Madhyamik Shiksha Abhiyan (RMSA). Let us know about these campaigns and programmes designed for the education of children, the future citizen of our country in detail.

Sarva Shiksha Abhiyan (SSA)

"Sarva Shiksha Abhiyan", known as "Education for All Movement" in English, is a mass campaign and programme launched by the government of India for providing elementary level educational opportunities to all its future citizens in an universal way. It was launched in the year 2000-2001 by the then Prime Minister Atal Bihari Vajpayee to carry out the directive laid down in the 86th Amendment to the Constitution of India making free and compulsory education to children between the ages of 6 to 14 a fundamental right. The scheme is bound to be implemented at the hands of Government of India in partnership with state and local governments.

Main Features of SSA

1. Programme with a clear time frame for universal elementary education.
2. A response to the demand for quality basic education all over the country.
3. An opportunity for promoting social justice through basic education.
4. An expression of political will for universal elementary education across the country.
5. A partnership between the central, state and the local government.
6. An opportunity for states to develop their own vision of elementary education.
7. An effort at effective involving the Panchyati Raj Institutions, school management Committees, village and urban slum level Education Committees, Parent's Teachers' Associations, Mother-Teacher Associations. Tribal Autonomous councils and other grassroots level structures in the management of elementary schools.

Aims and Objective of SSA

SSA aims to achieve universal enrolment of all children in the age group 6-14 years in elementary education ensuring all children to learn at appropriate level grade. In its operation it has been aimed to provide for a variety of intervention for universal access and retention, bridging of gender and social category gaps in elementary education and improving the quality of learning.

Intervention under SSA for attaining its Objective

- Opening of new schools and alternate schooling facilities
- Construction of schools and additional classrooms and providing toilets and drinking water facilities.
- Provision for appointing teachers — regular and part time.
- In service training and academic resources support for teachers.
- Free text books and uniform to the students.

- Support for improving learning achievement levels / outcome of the students

However, with the passage of time SSA scheme has undergone into a number of significant changes specially on account of the enforcement of Right to Education Act (RTE) on 1 April 2010. In fact now it has been armed with the necessary legal force for ensuring education for all. Before the enforcement of RTE, it was a quite uphill task for seeking admission in the schools for number of children belonging to disadvantaged and marginalized groups of society, children with special needs, street children, orphanage, etc. Now under the provision of RTE Act, all children irrespective of any deviation, disadvantage, disability or deficiency of any kind have the right to get quality elementary education in their neighbourhood school. It has also called a halt for any type of discrimination, differentiation, biases and prejudices against the children on account of their belonging to disadvantaged and otherwise neglected section of the society. With the widening of the area of coverage of all types of children now it has been made more feasible to achieve the target 'education for all' as enshrined in the basic policy of SSA.

The Rashtriya Madhyamik Shiksha Abhiyana (RMSA)

The Rashtriya Madhyamik Shiksha Abhiyan (RMSA) is another flagship scheme of Government of India that aims to enhance universal access to education for its future citizen. Parallel to its scheme of Sarva Shiksha Abhiyan that aims to provide access to elementary education for all its future citizen in the age six to fourteen, RMSA while extending the span of this period aims to enhance the new access to secondary education and improve the quality of education provided at present at the secondary stage. Launched in March 2009, scheme thus aimed to universalize and boost the educational output at the secondary education system by laying down the following objectives:

Objectives of RMSA

- To achieve gross enrolment ratio of 75% from 52.26% in 2005-06 for classes IX-X with in five years of its implementation by providing a secondary school within reasonable distance of any habitation.
- To improve the quality of education imparted at secondary level by making all secondary schools conform to prescribed norms.
- To remove gender, socio-economic and disability barriers.
- To provide universal access to secondary level education by 2017, i.e. by the end of the 12th Five Years Plan.
- To enhance and universalize retention by 2020.

Caring for Equity and Inclusion in RMSA

RMSA takes care of the principles of equity and policy of inclusion by concentrating on the things like below:

(i) Giving priority to the educational development of children belonging to educationally backward and marginalized sections of the society such as SCs, STs, minorities, street children, etc.

(ii) Providing various measures including intensive micro planning to provide flexibility to develop context specific interventions for the reduction of educational inequalities by:

- (a) Giving priority to SC / ST / minority / educationally backward areas and population for opening of schools.
- (b) Launching special enrolment drive for the weaker sections
- (c) Appointing more female teachers in schools
- (d) Providing separate toilet blocks for girls.
- (e) Providing special camp and bridge courses, open and distance learning for the needy, disadvantaged and disabled children.
- (f) Providing hostel facilities to the children belonging to disadvantaged and marginalized groups especially for girls and children losing their parents.
- (g) Arranging coaching / remedial classes especially for educationally minority girls and children who are not doing academically well.
- (h) Extending resource support like providing text book, work book, stationary, uniform, footwear, bicycles, boarding and lodging for each child and stipend to day scholars and children belonging to SCs / STs including differently abled children at the secondary and higher secondary stage.

Ensuring Quality Education to all the Learners

RMSA scheme with a clear cut motive of providing quality education to all the learners of the secondary school stage with no discrimination has a provision of the needed interventions in the manner described ahead.

1. Provision of providing essential physical facilities

RMSA scheme has a provision of equipping the secondary schools with the essential physical facilities like below:

- (a) Additional classrooms.
- (b) Laboratories and libraries
- (c) Art and crafts room
- (d) Toilet blocks and drinking water provisions
- (e) Residential Hostels for Teachers in remote areas.

2. Provision of providing quality interventions

With an eye to bring qualitative improvement in the nature of education provided to the learners, RMSA scheme has a provision for the following:

- (i) Appointment of additional teachers to reduce pupil-teacher ratio to 30:1
- (ii) Focus on Science, Mathematics and English education

(iii) In service training of teachers and principals
(iv) Establishment and equipping of Science and Mathematics laboratories
(v) Providing ICT enabled education to the learners.
(vi) Bringing necessary curriculum and teaching learning reforms.
(vii) Subsuming other centrally sponsored schemes of Secondary Education — ICT at school, Girl's Hostel, Inclusive Education for Disabled at secondary stage and Vocational Education in their existing form under the umbrella of RMSA, for sparing more fund for bringing infrastructure and institutional improvement in secondary education.

Implementation Mechanism of the Scheme

Since, RMSA scheme is the flagship program of Government of India, the responsibility of its implementation largely stands in the hands of central government. It is the major fund providing agency for the implementation of RMSA scheme. The guidance, program of action and evaluation of the scheme is largely carried out under the direction of the central government. However, due efforts are also made for seeking active partnership and cooperation of state governments and local self government for the funding as well as implementing the tasks enshrined in the scheme. Apart from this, attempts are also made to seek support from a wide range of state holders including multilateral organization, NGOs, advisors and consultants, research agencies and institutions for funding, research, guidance and implementation purposes.

In this way RMSA scheme may be seen to fulfilling its responsibility of providing access to secondary education of good quality to all its future citizens in the age group 15-16 years while ensuring equality of opportunities and equity of the provisions for their development according of their capacities.

Schemes and Program of GOI for Gender Equity and Equality in Education

Gender bias and Gender discrimination has been much prevalent in the fabrics of our society as well as system of education. Government of India has launched a number of schemes and programs for doing away with such injustice to the girl child by promoting equity and equality of opportunities and services aimed for their adequate adjustment, education and progress. The few important one's of these schemes and programs are being discussed here for taking note of the work done in this field by Government of India.

A. Integrated Child Development Services (ICDS) Scheme

It is a welfare program launched by Government of India on October 2, 1975 which provides food, pre-school education and primary health care to children under six years of age and their mothers. These services are provided from Anganwadi centres established mainly in rural areas and staffed with frontline workers. In addition to fighting malnutrition and ill health, the program is also intended to combat gender inequality by providing girls the same resources as boys.

Objectives: The predefined objectives of 1CDS are

1. To raise the health and nutritional level of poor Indian children below six years of age.
2. To create a base for proper mental, physical and social development of children in India.
3. To reduce instances of mortality, malnutrition and school dropouts among Indian children.
4. To coordinate activities of policy formulation and implementation among all departments of various ministries involved in the different government programs and schemes aimed at child development across India.
5. To provide health and nutritional information and education to mothers of young children to enhance child caring capabilities of mothers in the country of India.
6. To provide nutritional food to the mothers of young children and also at the time of pregnancy period.

Services provided under ICDS

The ICDS scheme offers a package of six services mentioned below.

- Supplementary nutrition
- Pre-school non-formal education
- Nutrition and Health Education
- Immunization
- Health check-up and
- Referral services

B. The Kasturba Gandhi Balika Vidyalaya School

It was introduced by the Government of India as an independent program in August, 2004, but later on in 2008, it was integrated in the national program 'Sarva Shiksha Abhiyan'. It aims to provide educational facilities for girls belonging to Scheduled Castes, Scheduled Tribes, Other Backward Classes, minority communities and families below the poverty line and by opening residential schools in the educationally backward areas.

Objectives

1. To remove gender disparities especially in rural areas and among disadvantaged communities in the matter of the availability of educational opportunities at the school level.

2. To ensure the availability and accessibility of quality education to the girls of disadvantaged group of society by setting up residential schools with boarding facilities at elementary level.

Eligibility: The scheme was applicable since inception in 2004 in Educationally Backward Blocks (EBBs) where the rural female literacy is below the national average (46.13%: Census 2001) and gender gap in literacy is more than the national average (21.59%: Census 2001). Among these blocks, schools may be set up in areas with:

1. concentration of tribal population, with low female literacy and / or a large number of girls out of school:
2. concentration of SC, OBC and minority populations, with low female literacy and / or a large number of girls out of school;
3. areas with low female literacy; or
4. areas with a large number of small, scattered habitations that do not qualify for a school

The criteria of eligible blocks has been revised with effect from 1 April 2008 to include the following:

An additional 316 Educationally backward blocks with rural female literacy below 30%, and 94 Towns / cities having minority concentration (as per the list, identified by Ministry of Minority Affairs) with female literacy rate below the national average (53.67%: Census 2001).

C. Beti Bachao, Beti Padhao (Save girl child, educate girl child)

Beti Bachao, Beti Padhao scheme represents a social campaign launched by Government of India for generating awareness and improve the efficiency of welfare services meant for the girl child. As a scheme and campaign it was introduced in October, 2014 to address mainly the issue of declining child sex ratio. As a national social campaign, it represents a joint initiative of the Ministry of women and Child Development, the Ministry of Health and Family Welfare and the Ministry of Human Resource Development. This scheme has been given more weightage and priority in the states like Haryana, where girl child sex ratio has been declining to the extent of proving a matter of great concern. It is in this perspective that Government of Haryana invited Prime Minister Narendra Modi to launch the program on 22 January 2015 from Panipat (Haryana) and subsequently appointed Olympic 2016 bronze medallist Sakshi Malik as the brand ambassador of the 'Beti Bachao, Beti Padhao' initiative in Haryana.

Objectives of Beti Bachao, Beti Padhao Scheme

The objectives of the scheme are:

1. Preventing sex selective abortion
2. Ensuring survival and protection of a girl child
3. Ensuring education of the girl child

Strategies Recommended

For the success in carrying out the scheme, the strategies like below have been recommended:

- Implement a sustained Social Mobilization and Communication Campaign to create equal value for the girl child and promote her education.

- Place the issue of decline in CSR / SRB in public discourse, improvement of which would be an indicator for good governance.
- Focus on Gender Critical Districts and Cities low on CSR for intensive and integrated action.
- Mobilize and train Panchayati Raj Institutions / Urban local bodies / Grassroot workers as catalysts for social change, in partnership with local community / women's / youth groups.
- Ensure service delivery structures / schemes and programmes are sufficiently responsive to issues of gender and children's rights.
- Enable inter-sectoral and inter-institutional convergence at District / Block / Grassroot levels.

D. The Mid-day Meal Scheme

This scheme was launched on 15 August 1995 to give a boost to Universal Elementary Education (UEE) in terms of enrolment retention and attendance of the students. It supplies free lunches on working days for children in primary and upper primary classes in government, government aided, local body. Education Guarantee scheme and alternate innovative education centres, Madarsa and Maqtabs supported under Sarva Shikshsa Abhiyan and National Child Labour project School run by the Ministry of Labour.

Objective

- To boost universalization of Elementary education by improving enrolment, attendance, retention and learning levels of children especially those belonging to disadvantaged section (thus holding the principle of equality and equity in providing educational opportunity to all)
- To improve nutritional status of students of elementary classes and to provide nutritional support to students of elementary stage of affected areas during summer vacation also.

Entitlement

The nutritional guidelines for the minimum amount of food and calorie content per child per day supplied at the lunch time to the student of primary and upper primary classes are as under:

Entitlement norm per child per day under MDM

Items	*Primary (class one to five)*	*Upper primary (class six to eight)*
Calories	450	700
Protein (in grams)	12	20
Rice / wheat (in grams)	100	150
Dal (in grams)	20	30
Vegetables (in grams)	50	75
Oil and fat (in grams)	5	7.5

Finances

The central and state governments share the cost of the Mid-day Meal Scheme, with the Centre providing 60 per cent and the states 40 per cent. The central government provides grains and financing for other food. Costs for facilities, transportation, and labour is shared by the federal and state governments.

E. Rajiv Gandhi Scheme for Empowerment of Adolescent Girls (RGSEAG) — SABLA

Rajiv Gandhi Scheme for Empowerment of Adolescent Girls, designated also as "SABLA" came into existence by merging the erstwhile two schemes, namely. "Kishori Shakti Yozna" and "Nutrition Program for Adolescent Girls".

Kishori Shakti Yozna (KSY) was started by the Ministry of Women and Child Development Government of India in the year 2000. It used the infrastructure of Integrated Child Development Services (ICDS) with a clear cut aim of improving the nutritional and health status of girls in the age group of 11-18 years as well as to equip them to improve and upgrade their home-based and vocational skills; and to promote their overall development including awareness about their health, personal hygiene nutrition, family welfare and management.

The other scheme meant for the welfare of the adolescent girls named as "Nutrition Program for Adolescent Girls" (NPAG) was initiated in the year 2002-03 with the objective of addressing the program of under-nutrition among adolescent girls. But it was realized at the later stage that both these scheme meant for the welfare of adolescent girl were not showing the desired impact and consequently needed to be replaced by a more comprehensive and effective scheme and it was how a new scheme named Rajiv Gandhi Scheme for Empowerment of Adolescent Girl (RGSEAG) came into existence in the year 2009.

Objective of RGSEAG

- To enable the adolescent girls for self development and empowerment.
- To improve their nutrition and health status
- To promote awareness about health, hygiene, nutrition, Adolescent Reproductive and Sexual Health (ARSH) and family and child care.
- To upgrade their home-based skills, life skills and tie up with National Skill Development Program for vocational skills.
- To mainstream out of school adolescent girls into formal / non-formal education.
- To provide information / guidance about existing public services such as PHC, CHC, Post Office, Bank, Police Station, etc.

Target Group

Rajiv Gandhi Scheme for Empowerment of Adolescent Girls is aimed to cover adolescent girls in the age group of 11-18 years under all ICD projects in all the states / UTs in the country. It asks the all-out-of school adolescent girls for assembling at the Anganwadi centre as per the time table and frequency decided by the states / UTs. The others i.e. the school going girls would also meet at the Anganwadi centres at least twice a month and more frequently during vacation / holidays, where they will receive life skill education, nutritional health education, awareness about other socio-legal issues, etc. This will give an opportunity for mixed group interaction between in school and out-of-school girls, motivating the latter to join school.

Services provided under the Scheme

The services provided to adolescent girls in this scheme are as under:

- Nutrition provision
- Iron and Folic Acid (IFA) supplementation
- Health check up and referral services
- Nutrition and Health Education (NHE)
- Counselling / guidance on family welfare, ARSH, child care practices and home management
- Life skill education and accessing public services
- Vocational training for girls aged 16 and above under National Skill Development Program (NSDP)

All the schemes and programs discussed above may be found to work in full consonance of the principles of gender equity and equality being observed in the attempts of seeking welfare of the girl children especially belonging to weaker and disadvantageous section of the society. The schemes like Sarva Shiksha Abhiyan (SSA) and Rashtriya Madhyamik Shiksha Abhiyana (RMSA) discussed earlier in this chapter also stand for the welfare of girl children as they are aimed to provide them equal opportunity of getting education along with boys with no discrimination of any kind.

References and Suggested Readings

Baumrind, D. (1967), 'Child care practices anteceding three patterns of pre-school behaviour,' *Genetic Psychology*, Monographs, 75 (1), 43-88.

Bayley, Nancy (1993), Bayley Scales of Infant Development (2nd ed.), *Psychology Corporation*, USA.

Biggie, M.L. and Hunt, M.P., (1968), *Psychological Foundations of Education,* New York: Harper and Row.

Brine, J. (1919), *Under educating women: Globalization in equality,* Bunkingham, U.K.: Open University Press.

Crow, L.D. and Crow, A.; (1969), *Child Psychology*, New York: Barney and Noble.

Crow, L.D. and Crow, A. (1973) *Educational Psychology*, 3rd Indian Print, New Delhi: Eurasia Publishing House.

Dictionary.com. (2002), retrieved from dictionary, reference. Com / browse / permissive on 15.9.2015.

Erickson, E., (1950) *Childhood and Society,* New York: Norton.

Erickson, E., (1969) *Identity Youth and Crises,* New York: Norton,

Eysenck, H.J. et. al (1972), *Encyclopaedia of Psychology*, New York: Phil. Lib.

Freeman and Showel quoted by Hurlock, E.B. (1959) *Child Psychology*. (Asian student 3rd ed.), Tokyo: McGraw-Hill.

Garell, A., (1929) *Maturation and Infant Behaviour Pattern* Psycho. Rev. 36.

Garrett. H.E. (1968), *General Psychology* (Indian ed.), New Delhi: Eurasic Publishing House.

Gibson-Graham, J.K. (1996), *The end of capitalism (as we knew it): A feminist critique of political economy,* Cambridge, M.A. Blackwell.

Giddens, Antony (1990), *The Consequences of Modernity,* Cambridge, U.K.: Polity Press.

Gupta, G.R. (2000), 'Gender, sexuality and HIV / AIDS: The What, the Why and How, HIV / AIDS,' *Policy Law Rev*. 5(4) p. 86-93.

Harriman, P.L. (Ed.) (1946) *Encyclopaedia of Psychology,* New York: Phil. Lib.

Hurlock, E.B. and Schewartz (1964) quoted by Kuppuswamy B., *Advanced Educational Psychology*, Delhi University Publication, 1964.

Hurlock, E.B. (1956), *Child Psychology* (Asian Student ed.), Tokyo: Kogakusha Co. Ltd.

Hurlock, E.B. (1959), *Adolescent Development,* New York: Mc GrawHill.

Inheldev, B. and Piaget, J. (1958), *The Growth of Logical Thinking from Children and Adolescence* (Translated by Anne Parson and Stanley Milgram), New York: Basic Books.

Jersild; A.T., *et al.*, (1975) *Child Psychology,* New York: Macmillan,

Judd, Charles M. and Park, Bernadette (1993), "Definition and Assessment of Accuracy in social stereotypes" *Psychological Review*, 100(1): 109-128.

Kagan, J. (1964), "Acquisition and significance of sex typing and sex role identity", In M.L. Hoffman and L.W. Hoffman (Eds.), *Review of Child Development Research,* New York: Sage.

Kohlberg. L. (1963), *The Development of Children's Orientation Toward Moral Order: Sequence in the development of moral thought,* Vita Humana, 6, 11-33, 1963.

Kohlberg, L. (1964), The Development of Moral Character and Moral Ideology, in M. Hoffman and L. Hoffman (Eds.), *Review of Child Development Research,* Vol. I, New York: Russel Sage Foundations.

Kohlberg, L. (1968), The Child as a Moral Philosopher, *Psychology Today*, Vol. 2, pp. 25-30.

Kohlberg. L. (1975), *The Cognitive Development Approach to Moral Education,* Phi. Delta Kappan, 56. p. 671.

Kohlberg. L. (1976), "Moral Stages and Moralization: The Cognitive Development Approach" in T. Lickona (Ed.) *Moral Development and Behaviour*, New York: Holt, Rinehart and Winston.

Kohlberg. L. (1984), *Essays on Moral Development,* San Francisco; Harper and Row.

Kuppuswamy, B. (1964); *Advanced Educational Psychology,* Delhi, University Publication.

Kuppuswamy, B. (1971); *An introduction to Social Psychology,* Bombay: Publishing House.

Larseen Thomas. (2001), *The Race of the Top: The Real Story of Globalization* Washington D.C.: Cato Institute.

Lechner, F.J. and Boli, John (Eds.), (2011), *The Globalization Reader*, New Jersey: Willey Blackwell Publishers.

Maccoby, EE and Martin, J A. (1983). "Socialization in the context of the family: Parent-child interaction". In P. Mussen and E.M. Hetherington, editors, *Handbook of Child Psychology,* Volume IV: Socialization, personality and social development, chapter 1, pages 1-101. New York: Wiley, 4th edition.

Marten Albrew and Elizabeth King (1990), *Globalization, Knowledge and Society* London: Sage.

Mc Doughall, William (1949), An outline of Psychology (13th ed.), London:

McGarty, Craig; Yzerbyt, Vincent Y.; Spears, Russel (2002:7). *Stereotypes as explanations: The formation of meaningful beliefs about social groups.* Cambridge: Cambridge University Press, pp. 1-15.

McGeoch, J.A., *The Psychology of Human Learning,* New York: Longmans, 1942.

McGrow, M.B., Growth: *A Study of Johnny and Jimmy*, New Youk: Appleton-Century-Crofts, 1935.

Piaget, J., (1932), *The Moral Judgement of the Child,* New York: Harcourt and Brace, (and New York: Free Press, 1965).

Piaget, J., (1952), *The Origins of Intelligence in Children,* New York: International University Press, (and New York: Norton, 1963).

Piaget, J., (1966), *Psychology of Intelligence,* Totowa, N.J.: Little Field Adams.

Piaget J., (1977), *Equilibration of Cognitive Structures,* New York: Viking Press.

Random House Dictionary (2017), *Random House Dictionary*, Random House Inc.

Ross J.S. (1951), *Ground Work of Educational Psychology*, London: George G. Harrap & Co.

Sorenson, Herbert, (1948), *Psychology in Education,* New York: McGraw-Hill.

Sorenson, Herbert, (1977), *Psychology in Education,* New York: McGraw-Hill.

The American Heritage New Dictionary of Cultural Literacy (Third Edition), (2005), New York: Houghton Mifflin Company.

Watson, J.B. (1930), *Behaviourism,* London: Kegan Paul.

Webster's Seventh New Collegiate Dictionary (1970), Spring field, Massachusetts, G.C. Merriam Company, Publisher.

Woolfolk, Anita, (2004), *Educational Psychology (9th ed.)* First Indian Reprint, New York: Pearson.